SECOND EDITION

INFORMATION SYSTEMS

Technology, Economics, Applications, Management

SECOND EDITION

INFORMATION SYSTEMS

Technology, Economics, Applications, Management

Chris Mader

The Mader Group, Inc.
and
The Wharton School of the University of Pennsylvania

SCIENCE RESEARCH ASSOCIATES, INC.
Chicago, Palo Alto, Toronto, Henley-on-Thames, Sydney, Paris
A Subsidiary of IBM

Acquisition Editor	Stephen D. Mitchell
Project Editor	James C. Budd
Compositor	Dharma Press
Illustrator	Carol Schwartzback
Text Designer	Joe di Chiarro
Cover and Part Illustrations	Steve Rogowski,
	Creative Publications, Inc.

Printed in the United States of America.

Library of Congress Cataloging in Publication Data

Mader, Chris.
   Information systems.

   Includes index.
   1. Electronic data processing.   2. Electronic
digital computers.   I. Title.
QA76.M234 1979   001.6′4′044   78-13048
ISBN 0-574-21150-0

10   9   8   7   6   5   4   3   2   1

To our children,
Scott Erik
and
Paige Marie,
unique humans,
not
second editions

Contents

Preface

For over three decades the computer field has grown with unparallelled swiftness. By now, computers have become both essential and commonplace—reason enough to learn about today's opportunities for computer use. This second edition of *Information Systems* is designed to build a broad understanding of this field, for its own sake or as a base for further specialization.

The five-part flow of this book answers five questions:

1. What are information systems?
2. How do they work?
3. How can we use them?
4. How are they developed?
5. How should they be managed?

Part 1, **Information Systems**, introduces the uses of computers and information, including their impact on individuals, management, business, and society. Then Chapter 2 traces the development of computer-based information systems.

Part 2, **Hardware and Software**, explains computer concepts and devices. Hardware components and the processor in particular are reviewed and illustrated in Chapter 3. Chapter 4 deals with data storage and retrieval. Methods and devices for input/output are covered in Chapter 5. Chapter 6 surveys and compares six high-level computer languages: FORTRAN, COBOL, PL/1, RPG, BASIC, and APL. (Readers with minor interest in computer technology can omit or skim Part 2.)

Part 3, **Methods of Processing**, discusses information processing methods and their advantages and limitations. It covers alternate ways of organizing and accessing data, including sequential processing (Chapter 7) and direct access processing (Chapter 8). Chapter 9 reviews concepts and systems for managing and processing databases. Chapter 10 discusses combining and connecting large and small computer systems.

Part 4, **Applications and the Development Cycle**, presents a top-down view of information systems and the application development cycle. First, the concept of a MIS is described and illustrated in Chapter 11. Then Chapter 12 discusses systems analysis. This is followed by systems design, programming, and implementation in Chapter 13. Application development methods, costs, and management procedures are emphasized from requirements analysis through documentation, installation, and maintenance. Then Chapter 14 presents representative applications drawn from five different organizations.

Part 5, **Management Issues**, is concerned with managing information systems. In Chapter 15 managerial guidelines, organization and staffing, measuring effectiveness, and system selection are discussed. Important sectors of the computer industry are then analyzed in Chapter 16, including future technology and applications and their possible impact on society.

The need for this book and its approach have been verified during the past 12 years of the author's teaching responsibilities in undergraduate, graduate, and continuing education. The text serves introductory courses or those following a programming course. It is intended for present or future managers, users, and computer specialists. Previous or concomitant exposure to computer programming is helpful but not necessary.

This second edition of *Information Systems* explains computer hardware/software more succinctly and discusses input/output in Part 2. Part 3, on methods of processing, assumes the user's perspective. The discussions of database and distributed processing in particular have been expanded. Part 4 now emphasizes applications, their effectiveness, and how to develop them. It includes much new material on the applications development cycle. Parts 1 and 5 have added emphasis on the nonbusiness uses and societal impacts of computers. Each chapter again has a standard format with frequent headings and graphics to promote understanding and interest. Each has been updated and edited to be clear and concise.

Many associates have made valuable contributions to the two editions of this book. In particular, I gratefully acknowledge my previous coauthor, Dr. Robert Hagin, and Professors James Emery and John Lubin, who shaped the courses and curriculum from which this text evolved. Helpful critiques were supplied by Professors Alan Akman, E. M. Danziger, George Diehr, V. Thomas Dock, Henry Lucas, Ephraim McLean, Ed Rategan, and Donald H. Sanders, by author Marilyn Bohl, and by former students Jim Lenz, Mary Ann Morse, and Erich Weissenberger. Ultimately, I thank the tens of thousands of students, users, computer specialists, and managers who have participated in courses or self-study using this text.

C.M.

ACKNOWLEDGMENTS

Photos courtesy of the following:
Bunker Ramo—14-6, 14-7, 14-8.
Burroughs—1-9, 1-10, 1-11.
Computer Sciences Corporation—10-5, 10-6.
Credit Research Foundation, Inc.—13-2.
Digital Equipment Coproration—1-6.
Eastman Kodak Company—5-16.
Four-Phase Systems, Inc.—2-7, 5-4.
Hewlett-Packard—5-3, 10-8.
IBM—1-1, 1-8, 2-1, 2-2, 2-3, 2-4, 2-5, 2-6, 2-8, 3-13, 4-2,
    4-4, 4-5, 4-6, 4-8, 5-1, 5-8, 5-12,
    5-15, 14-1, 14-2, 14-4, 14-9, 16-1.
Inforex, Inc.—5-2.
Informatics, Inc.—9-5, 9-6.
The Mader Group, Inc.—5-14, 11-9.
McDonnell Douglas Automation Company—7-2.
National Cash Register Company—5-5, 5-11.
Shared Medical Systems—13-1.
Sperry Univac—1-7, 3-1, 5-10.
Tektronics, Inc.—5-13.
Texas Instruments, Incorporated—10-3.

Table data courtesy of the following:
Datamation magazine—16.2.
The Diebold Research Program—15.1.

Part One

**Information
Systems**

Chapter 1   **Information Systems**

Organizations draw on the resources of hardware,
software, and people in meeting their information
processing needs. Technical, economic, and
organizational factors affect the applications of
information systems.

Chapter 2   **Computer Development**

Computer technology and usage have grown rapidly.
Current capabilities and current problems are rooted
in the recent history of computer evolution.

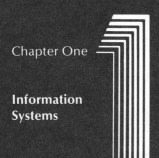

Chapter One

**Information
Systems**

Human behavior continually involves processing data to produce information. Optimally, the end result is wise decision making, leading to increased well-being and enjoyment of life. Or the result might be something less than this ideal. Your skills and judgment as a user of information may cause this crucial difference.

WHAT ARE INFORMATION SYSTEMS?

This book concerns **information systems**, that is, computer-assisted ways of dealing with information. **Information** is extracted from facts, symbols, or data—from observations drawn from the environment around us. Information is the meaning or content of what we observe and is essentially intangible. For convenience and permanent storage, the information is often recorded in a tangible form such as this printed page.

A **system** is a set of interrelated parts. It is organized or defined for some purpose, such as to produce a product or provide transportation. Thus, General Motors, as a company, is a system and the cars it produces are themselves systems. We will be concerned with computer-based systems. These collect, store, process, communicate, and display data as electronic, magnetic, or physical patterns. To the user, this data becomes information.

WHO USES INFORMATION SYSTEMS?

Information is the basis of civilization; it is widely sought and widely used. People and organizations in government, education, media, and entertainment need systems for processing information, because information is their primary product. Service activities such as health care, banking, insurance, and brokerage also generate "knowledge" or "paperwork" in great amounts.

Manufacturing firms also spend substantial amounts for information. Information is needed from the first step of material purchase throughout the manufacture, assembly, inventory, marketing, and distribution of the finished goods. The accompanying paperwork, beginning with the issuance of purchase orders and ending with the final collection of payments and disbursal of salaries and dividends, is a record of the organization's activities.

Transportation firms—from airlines to car renters—also use information systems for functions such as updating reservation lists and scheduling crews and equipment. And retailers can capture their basic operating data immediately with point-of-sale computer terminals. It is accurate to say that modern organizations now use computer-based systems, such as that shown in Figure 1-1, in most areas of their operations.

Yet, in spite of the many effective systems and the computer's enormous potential, many organizations have had only limited success in using computers. Fascination with "gee whiz" technology for its own sake has ebbed. In its place has evolved a growing sensitivity to processing methods, the cost and benefits of different applications, and impact on their users. Computer applications need to be economically and organizationally feasible—and implemented—if we are to benefit from the technology.

Figure 1-1. A typical computer-based information system

WHY USE INFORMATION SYSTEMS?

Individuals and organizations use information systems for two broad purposes of concern here:

1 To process transactions.
2 To aid decision making.

A third, and rapidly emerging purpose, is for personal entertainment. Equipment, retail stores, hobby clubs, and publications have mushroomed to meet this demand. This book primarily discusses the two economic reasons for computer usage. However, people's economic objectives exist to get the means to meet personal objectives—from survival on through entertainment. Thus we can expect the personal use of computers to grow and strengthen.

Processing Transactions

A **transaction** is an event of interest. For example, receiving a shipment of goods from a supplier is a business event of interest—a transaction. Figure 1–2 illustrates the processing of such a transaction, showing the steps from sensing the data describing the event through the production and display of information. The term **data** usually refers to pre-processed fact items. In contrast to data, information is the result of appropriate processing.

Some types of transactions occur frequently. The data describing

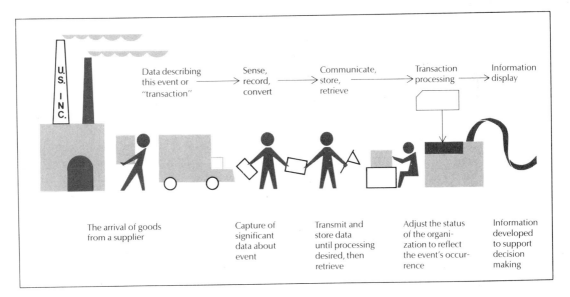

Figure 1–2. Processing a transaction

each event must be converted into meaningful information. Such repeated activities are usually well suited to computerized processing. In fact, the term **data processing** is often used to refer to all computer-related activities.

On the other hand, manual processing systems are often more economical for handling nonroutine transactions. This book will help you understand when automated processing is justified, how to specify the right system, and how to develop, implement, and manage it.

Aiding Decision Making

Knowledgeable decision making depends on information. Through their decisions, individuals and organizations try to achieve selected results. Examples of such decisions are choosing a college, setting company pricing policies, or simply deciding how many meals should be on board an airplane. If these decisions are ill conceived or are based on inaccurate or incomplete data, the actual results can be quite different from the desired ones. Thus, the quality of information produced depends on the quality of its components—hence the computer cliché "garbage in, garbage out."

But good information, produced by correctly processing accurate data, is not enough in itself. Even good information must be coupled with a rational way of producing decisions from the information. This information-generating and decision-making process guides and controls an organization's activities. For example, information about an airplane's average load factor and knowledge of seasonal variations and regional preferences can aid in deciding how many and what type of meals should be on board. Better still would be up-to-the-minute data about the number of passengers on this flight and their meal preferences.

To aid decision making, an information system should provide:

- the right information
- to the right person
- at the right time
- in a cost-effective way

Decision makers at all levels, in both large and small organizations, can benefit from the appropriate application of computers.

THE PRODUCTION OF INFORMATION

The production of information concept views information as if it were the result of some manufacturing operation. For example, the raw material would be data about some event that has been sensed, recorded, and converted to a suitable format. Then processing—whether computer-based or not—would modify the data. When the finished product is useful to some individual, it is called information. This process is shown in Figure 1–3.

Manual information production is usually inexpensive at first. By contrast, developing a computer-based system usually involves a large initial cost. But the improved quality and quantity of the information produced may more than repay this investment.

Computers are excellent tools for processing transactions. But using them to aid decision making is often more difficult. They are downright retarded in such human skills as creativity, pattern recognition, intuitive reasoning, associative recall, and physical dexterity. And they can neither see, hear, feel, smell, or taste (although some experimental machines can, to a limited extent). Their real advantage is an almost insatiable capacity for storing and processing data quickly and accurately.

But before we can use that capacity, a suitable **program**, or detailed set of instructions, must be prepared to direct the computer's internal operations. This initial cost—for systems analysis, design, programming, and implementation—is usually high. Therefore, a large volume of similar transactions or a few extremely complex tasks are usually necessary to justify computerization. Benefits result when either high-volume or high-complexity processing can be done for lower cost than manual methods. (Computerization costs, including initial cost and ongoing processing cost, are compared with manual methods in Figure 1–4.) In some cases, the required information cannot be produced quickly enough by any other technique, regardless of cost. Examples include spacecraft guidance and emergency medical information.

Two trends have spurred computer use:

1. improved methods of program development, and the availability of standardized programs, have lowered the initial cost;

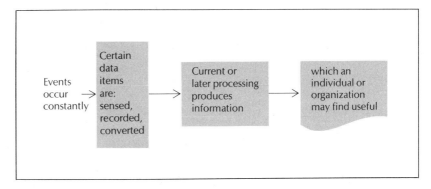

Figure 1-3.   The production of information

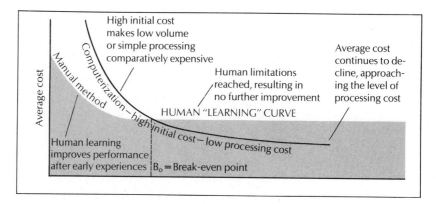

Figure 1-4. Average cost versus volume or complexity of processing

2. improved and less expensive computers have lowered ongoing processing cost.

Each factor—reduced initial cost and reduced ongoing cost—reduces the processing volume or complexity needed to break even, as shown in Figure 1-5.

Factor 1 produces the lower break-even point B_1 because reducing the initial cost makes it easier to recoup this investment. Alternately, factor 2 lowers the processing cost, especially for high volume or complex processing. This lowers the break-even point to B_2.

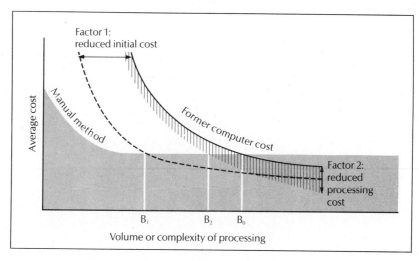

Figure 1-5. Average cost with lowered break-even points

Continuing progress in the manufacturing and use of computers has also dramatically expanded their market. For example, in the United States alone about $40 billion annually is spent for computer-based information systems—more than for all advertising or for all government and corporate research. Someday, but not soon, we may even approach Nobel prize winner Herbert A. Simon's 1960 prediction that "the automated factory of the future will operate on the basis of programmed decisions produced in the automated office beside it."

Of course, people and organizations have to process transactions and make decisions in some way, with or without computer-based information systems. However, computers are incredibly fast, accurate, reliable, and compact tools. They are of significant help in making people more productive. For certain information handling tasks, such as routine processing of bank checks, far fewer clerks are required when computers are used than when manual processing is used. In addition, the computer's speed, data storage capability, and accuracy can be used to return customer checks faster and to provide more informative statements of account activity. This doesn't always happen, of course. And the displaced clerks, even if employed elsewhere, can easily resent such computerization. Also, people's financial affairs and personal privacy are more subject to scrutiny by others. So computers get blame as well as credit for contributing to the modern state of affairs. In any case, computers themselves are only a portion of the total resources needed in information systems.

INFORMATION SYSTEMS RESOURCES

An information system requires three major resources:

- hardware
- software
- people

Ultimately, the skill of the people who build and combine hardware and software is singularly responsible for creating information systems. As a starting point, however, it is useful to look at these three resources separately.

Hardware

The physical equipment used for processing data into information is called **hardware**. Hardware includes the computer itself and related components for data entry, storage, communication, and display. In general, any physical equipment in the information system is called hardware. (Examples of mini-, small, medium, and large computer systems are shown in Figures 1-6 through 1-9.)

Figure 1-6. A minicomputer system: the Digital Equipment Corporation PDP 11/34

A **computer**, as the term is used here, refers to hardware that has the following major characteristics:

- electronic
- digital

Figure 1-7. A small business computer: the Sperry Univac BC/7

Figure 1-8. A medium-sized computer: the IBM System/370 Model 138

Figure 1-9. A large-scale computer: the Burroughs B6700

- internal storage capacity
- stored-program execution
- program modification

Electronic.   The circuits that store and manipulate data are electronic, thus permitting the computer to function at the speed of light. Electrically induced magnetic fields and electric current patterns guide operations. Devices such as miniaturized semiconductors and integrated circuits (shown in Figures 1-10 and 1-11) offer advantages of greater speed, accuracy, reliability, and compactness, and require less power and cost outlay than comparable mechanical devices.

Digital.   Almost all modern computers are **digital**. By using counting-based systems of expressing numbers, any desired degree of accuracy is possible—for example, to 10, 20, or more significant decimal digits. **Analog** computers, by contrast, measure rather than count. One common analog device is a slide rule, which multiplies by adding lengths that are proportional to logarithms. The digital calculator is much more popular than the slide rule because, among other reasons, it has greater

Figure 1-10. View of an integrated circuit

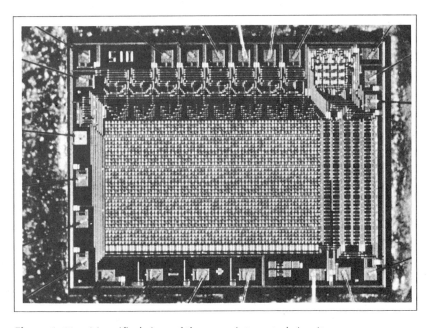

Figure 1-11. Magnified view of the same integrated circuit

accuracy. Digital computers are also easily reprogrammed—analog computers may need rewiring to change what is being measured.

Internal Storage Capacity.   The capacity for **internal storage**, or **memory**, permits the computer to store two things:

- instructions that dictate its operations
- data it processes to produce information

Thus, when a different set of instructions is read into the computer's memory, it changes the processing that will be done. Similarly, when different data is read in, the same set of instructions can produce different results. (This and the following computer characteristics are explained in detail in Chapter 3.)

Stored-Program Execution.   Once a program is stored in memory, it can be executed without human intervention. Automatic circuitry interprets the instructions of the stored program and then carries out the requested operations.

Program Modification.   A computer can modify its stored instructions automatically. This means that a computer can generate its own instructions in preprogrammed ways. Thus relatively few user-supplied instructions can cause it to execute many detailed tasks under its own control.

The compelling attribute of computers, unlike other machines, is that they emulate *mental* rather than physical functions. For example, computers perform computational operations such as adding, subtracting, and multltiplying. They also manipulate data logically, or illogically if told to. They do mundane things like reading people's names and sorting, comparing, or printing them. Actually, the number of such symbol-manipulating instructions usually exceeds the number of compute-oriented instructions. Thus the word *computer* is something of a misnomer. A computer is mainly an unequalled machine for data storage, retrieval, manipulation, and display—besides computation.

In summary, a computer is a device that uses electronic techniques to store, execute, and modify instructions that manipulate data in predefined ways, and it does more than merely compute. For reference, the major models of computers are listed in Table 1.1.

Software   A computer program is a sequence of detailed instructions designed to direct the computer to perform certain functions. Programs are frequently referred to as **software**. Software is thus the nonphysical por-

TABLE 1.1 REPRESENTATIVE COMPUTERS BY MANUFACTURER, BRAND NAME, AND RENTAL RATE

Hardware rental rates are shown in a ratio scale of dollars per month. Each computer includes typical related equipment. When sold, sale price approximates 40 times monthly rental.

Computer Model	$1000/month	$3000	$10,000	$30,000	$100,000
IBM—System/370		/115 /125	/138 /148	/158	/168
Post-/370		4331	4341	3031 3032	3033
Univac—90 Series	BC7	/25 /30	/40 /60	/80	
1100 Series			/10 /20	/40 /80	
Honeywell—Series 60		62 64	66	68	
Burroughs—B700	700	1700 2700	3700 4700	6700	
B800	800	1800 2800	3800 4800	6800	7800
Control Data—Cyber			171 172	173 174	175 176
Omega			480-I 480-II	480-III	
NCR—Century	50	101	200 201	251	
Criterion	8150	8200 8400	8500 8600	8650 8670	
Small or Minicomputers					
IBM	5100	Series 1 System 32 System 34	System 38		
Digital Equipment Corp.		PDP8 PDP 11 PDP 15	System 20 System 10		
Data General		Nova Super Nova Eclipse			
Hewlett Packard		HP250 HP300 HP300 HP3000			
Honeywell—Level 6	/23	/33 /43 /47 /53 /57			
Univac—V77		1200 1400 1600 1800			

tion of the information system. For example, a deck of punched cards may contain a program to produce paychecks and labor reports. The physical deck of cards (or magnetic tape, disk, or other storage device) is merely the storage medium. The data to be manipulated are not software either. Software refers only to the sets of instructions that cause the computer to function.

The instructions that direct the computer must be submitted to the machine in an acceptable form. Writing programs at the machine level requires detailed knowledge of the hardware's internal architechture. This is very tedious. Fortunately, programming languages such as FORTRAN, COBOL, and BASIC have been developed for specifying instructions to most computers, regardless of their internal design. These and other high-level languages are discussed in Chapter 6. Software already developed, and how to develop other software, are discussed in Part 4.

People   The third resource in an information system is people. Several representative titles, salaries, job functions, and backgrounds of information systems personnel are shown in Table 1.2. The most important person in an information system—the user—is not shown. Helping the user solve his or her problem is the purpose of an information system. The degree to which this is achieved is the measure of the system's value.

The role these people play can be illustrated by describing the process of developing an information system. This begins when the user (often with suggestions from the computer department) develops an awareness that information, and a system to provide it, might help solve some problem. Figure 1–12 diagrams the resulting interactions between the user and the various people in the information systems group.

A **systems analyst** helps the user to bring the problem into focus. Usually the problem definition and its information requirements are not clear enough at first to begin programming immediately. Therefore the systems analyst and the user must work together to develop an understanding of *what* the user needs to know, *when* it is needed, *why* it is needed, and *how* it will be used when it is received.

The systems analyst's role is crucial for success. Most analysts have programming skills. Some have computer operating skills as well. This kind of background provides familiarity with computer methods and costs for program development and operation.

Familiarity with user needs is also essential. Systems analysts must be capable of understanding the user's problem. They must help the user select the specific system that maximizes benefits relative to costs. The user and systems analyst can then work toward the successful completion and implementation of the chosen system.

TABLE 1.2 INFORMATION SYSTEMS POSITION GUIDE—1978

Representative Title	Approximate Annual Salary (in thousands)	Number in U.S.	Typical Functions	Typical Training and Experience
V.P. or director of information systems (large organization)	$40–60	3,000	Manage 50–200 persons and a one- to several million-dollar budget, allocating resources to projects, motivating and controlling progress	College degree, possible graduate degree, technical and analytical skills, knowledge of business problems and management ability, 10–20 years experience, mostly in information processing
V.P. or director of information systems (small organization)	$20–40	20,000	Manage 10–50 persons and a $200,000 to $2,000,000 budget	Essentially same as above
Project manager/section leader	$20–30	40,000	Manage information systems development	Usually college degree, five or more years of computer experience; and working knowledge of the organization's problems
Systems analyst	$15–30	200,000	Analyze and design information systems to solve user needs	Former programmer or business analyst with college likely
Senior programmer	$15–25	150,000	Design and develop advanced programs	Three to ten years programming experience after college or programming school
Programmer	$12–20	150,000	Design, write, and debug programs	Programming training and one to five years experience
Coder	$ 8–15	100,000	Write or modify programs designed and/or written by others	Programming language courses without college degree and less than two years experience
Operations manager	$15–30	25,000	Manage staff operating computer	Operator school and three years experience
Maintenance engineer	$12–25	20,000	Maintain equipment	Engineering or technical training and experience
Computer operator	$ 8–15	120,000	Load and run computer	Operator school and some experience
Data preparation operator	$ 6–10	400,000	Key, verify, edit data	Typing or keyboard training

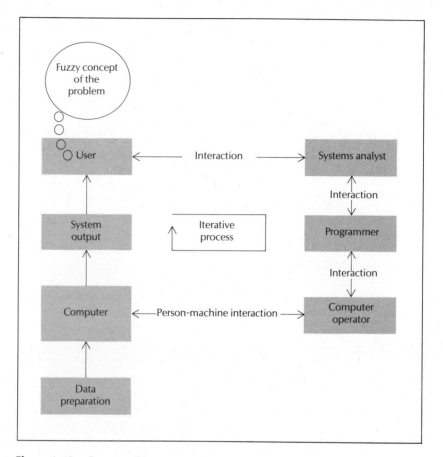

Figure 1–12. Personnel interactions

Many systems analysts start out as users. In such cases, they usually have an intimate awareness of user problems, but they may not fully understand computer techniques and costs. A second route to becoming a systems analyst is being promoted from programmer. This, too, can give a one-sided view of the skills really required. A third entry route to the systems analyst's position is by training, including classroom and "hands-on" or project work. This might mean a computer science and mathematics background for scientific applications. In business, it might mean combining information systems and a functional major in management, operations, finance, accounting, or marketing. In any case, by experience or training or both, the systems analyst must understand both the user and the computer viewpoints.

During and after specification of the system, the systems analyst (and sometimes the user) must interact with the **programmer** to design and develop the software for the proposed system. (In some cases, the

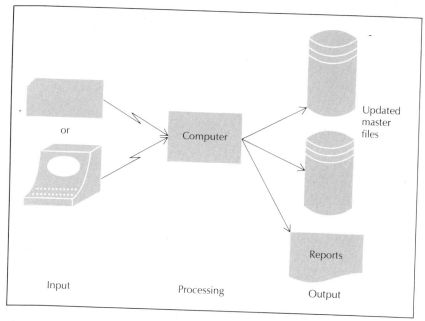

Figure 1-14.   Schematic diagram of online (direct-access) processing

complex processing of almost any available data. A year's worth of tedious arithmetic can be done in literally 1 second—with perfect accuracy.

However, the development or ongoing costs of some applications are too large a burden to be justified. And many development projects do not turn out as well as planned. Improvements in ie productivity or quality of information production may never materialize. On the other hand, competitive or legal factors may push the implementation of information systems; for example, offering quick reservations service or reporting on equal employment opportunity. A survey of representative applications in several different organizations, presented in Chapter 14, provides a useful benchmark.

Management Issues   The organizational constraint on technically possible and economically feasible systems is perhaps the most complex and frustrating constraint. The variables of human relations, leadership, motivation, resistance to change, authority, and responsibility all influence the system's effectiveness. Yet management, users, and computer specialists must judge whether the organization can and will use the information system to sufficient advantage.

Of all the computer-based applications that are technically, eco-

systems analyst may also be the programmer.) Programs should be written, tested, and **debugged**, or made error-free according to exacting standards. The programmer needs access to hardware during this testing and modification and hence interacts with a **computer operator**.

The computer operator's role is to manage and run the computer. Many computer installations allow only suitably trained operators to have access to the computer. At smaller, or less vital operations, systems analysts, programmers, and even users can execute programs and supply data themselves, without a trained operator. Direct access to computers is becoming widespread as more computer terminals and minicomputers are used at locations remote from the main operation itself.

Once a program (or set of programs) satisfies the user, it can be placed in a system library for routine use. New data can be used with the program but it must be made machine readable. Data entry personnel must keypunch or otherwise transcribe the data into some form acceptable to the computer. (Such data entry methods and devices are discussed in Chapter 5.)

Continuing use of an information system involves gathering, preparing, and processing data according to methods and programs specified by systems analysts and programmers. Thus, computer operators and data entry personnel are also involved in this ongoing cycle. Output information is delivered or transmitted to the user for solving problems. Frequently, systems must be modified after they are implemented. Thus, the overall process of creating and maintaining an information system is an iterative or repetitive process.

OVERVIEW OF INFORMATION SYSTEMS   A computer-based information system can be described by its cycle of activities, namely: *input-process-output*. Of course, this simplified cycle prompts more questions than it answers. First, we might wish to know how the hardware and software accomplish these input, processing, and output tasks. Second, what alternate methods of processing are possible and useful? .Third, what applications should information systems be developed for and how can they be created? Last, we might be curious about information systems and their impact on our lives. If these interests match yours, read on. The overview below and the chapters beyond cover this sequence of concerns.

Hardware and Software   Computer hardware executes the input of data, the logical steps required in processing, and the output of the resultant information. The software is a sequence of instructions, stored in the computer, which details the steps for these processes. The main computer component for this storage and processing function consists of the **main memory** and **central processing unit (CPU)**.

Input is often via a keyboard terminal or punched card reader, but it may also be from a magnetic tape, disk, or other device that stores data. Terminals, tapes, and disks are used for both **input and output (I/O)**. However, the most common input and output devices—the card reader for input and the printer for output—are single purpose. (The details of hardware and software, and how they accomplish the input-process-output cycle are presented in Part 2.)

Methods of Processing

Computer-based processing typically involves accessing data and producing reports. For example, a payroll program not only processes recent employment facts, it also accesses a file containing more permanent data such as addresses, wage rates, year-to-date earnings, number of dependents, and so forth. There are two basic modes of processing such data and updating files: batch processing and online processing. Each, or a combination, is more suitable for various applications.

The common method of processing data in a business environment is **batch processing**, which usually involves **sequential processing**. In batch processing, data from many similar transactions are grouped into a "batch." Each batch is usually sorted into the same sequence as some **master file**, which contains data that requires updating to reflect these particular transactions. Next, the batch of (sorted) data is **run**, or processed together with the master file. For example, payroll data for exployees 1, 2, 3, and so on, in turn, is processed during a batch run. This procedure is shown in Figure 1-13.

Or, for another example, several product orders might arrive every hour. Under batch processing, data from these transactions would not be processed immediately. Rather, the data would be grouped and sorted for a single, economical run against the appropriate master file, perhaps on a daily basis. Of course, batch processed results can get somewhat out of date, especially if the run frequency is only weekly or monthly. However, this negative effect is acceptably small for many applications.

Online processing, sometimes referred to as **direct access processing** or **real-time processing**, involves different strategies. Online means that a communication line connects the user's site to the computer. Online processing requires data that can be accessed "directly"—that is, without the delay of reading unwanted data. Real time implies that a transaction is processed as soon as it is received so that the user gets a response quickly enough to take appropriate action. Supporting such quick response often involves **database processing**, which seeks to

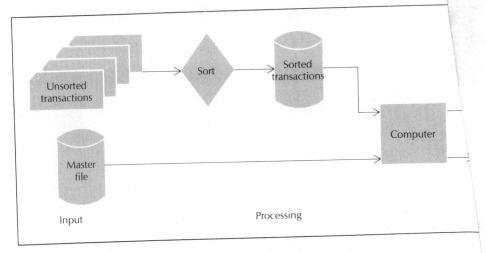

Figure 1-13. Schematic diagram of batch (sequential) processing

retrieve data selectively based on user needs. Also, this that users, data, programs, and hardware are located separ are connected—a scheme called **distributed processing**. cepts are discussed further in Part 3.)

Online processing requires more sophisticated har software than batch processing. But any extra costs are oft the added benefits of fast access to current data—that is, the availability of up-to-date information.

Online processing is illustrated in Figure 1-14. Example a of both batch and online modes of processing are shown 1-15.

Applications and the Development Cycle

The applications shown in Figure 1-15 are typical of those business and other organizations. Both the clerical activity cessing transactions and the managerial domain of decision have been improved by computers. The purpose of Part 4 is t such applications and discuss how they should be developed.

A top-down approach is followed. First, the ideal of a **mana information system (MIS)** is presented and illustrated. Th phases of systems analysis, design, programming, and impleme of an information system—called its **development cycle**—are exa Before embarking on these costly phases, the user should consic costs and benefits of the system. There are three basic tests of s feasibility: technical, economic, and organizational.

Thanks to the unprecedented growth of computer capabilit technical constraint is least likely to thwart the development of a formation system. Technology permits practically instantaneou

Purpose	Mode of Processing	
	Batch	Online
Transactions processing	• Weekly payroll • Daily checking account processing	• Point-of-sale data entry • Airline seat reservations
Decision aiding	• Inventory-on-hand listing • Exception report of overdue accounts receivable	• Credit limit inquiry • "What if" planning model

Figure 1-15. Example applications, classified by purpose and mode of processing

nomically, and organizationally feasible, only a fraction have been implemented. Despite three decades of growing usage, computers are still in their adolescence. And the management of computer resources can itself stand much improvement. Part 5 presents and discusses this almost boundless challenge and opportunity.

SUMMARY   People and organizations guide their behavior by processing data about relevant events and making decisions. Computer technology can assist these essentially mental functions. A computerized information system draws on three major resources—hardware, software, and people. Solving some user's problems is the ultimate goal. The main techniques are batch and online processing, sometimes involving database and distributed processing. Computer technology is declining in price, thereby making more and more applications economically feasible. But this leaves the formidable hurdles of development and implementation as potential barriers to success in the application and management of information systems. This book is designed to help managers, computer users, computer specialists, and students in these fields to understand and work effectively with information systems.

CONCEPTS

information system
information
system
transaction
data
data processing
program
hardware
computer
electronic
digital
analog
internal storage

memory
stored-program
    execution
program modification
software
systems analyst
programmer
debug
computer operator
main memory
central processing
    unit (CPU)
input and output
    (I/O)

batch processing
sequential processing
master file
run
online processing
direct access
    processing
real-time processing
database processing
distributed processing
management
    information
    system (MIS)
development cycle

QUESTIONS
1. Why are service firms such as banking, insurance, and brokerage comparatively more dependent on computers than manufacturing firms?
2. What are the main reasons for using an information system?
3. Why is it increasingly economical for organizations to develop automated systems for fulfilling their information needs?
4. What are the main characteristics that distinguish computer hardware from other machines?
5. Define an effective information system and state why the systems analyst is said to be crucial to its development.
6. Cite an example for which online processing should be used despite the fact that it will require more computer resources than batch processing.
7. What do you imagine to be the biggest barrier to the successful implementation of information systems within organizations?

Chapter Two

**Computer
Development**

Computer development since the mid-1940s has been phenomenal and has greatly affected modern organizations. Such a rate of change in computers—and in organizations—can be brought more into focus if we consider the pace of accomplishments prior to 1946.

Over two thousand years ago the Greek scholar Archimedes correctly defined the principles of leverage and specific gravity. Yet it was not until A.D. 1600 that the Italian scholar Galileo disproved another of Archimedes' "principles"—that objects fall with a speed proportional to their weight. Galileo's simple experiment was to drop two dense objects of different size and weight and note that they fell together.

The comparison of what people knew during the Renaissance and what they know today is startling. In fact, some modern scholars speculate that all scientific knowledge in 1600 could have been held in one person's brain. If this were true, we could accurately say that the problem of modern organizational management started in 1601—the year one person could no longer know everything.

THE INFORMATION AGE Apparently people learned to work together and share information. By the 1800s, the Industrial Revolution had begun. Machinery and energy began to replace human toil (although sometimes at the expense of human individuality or the environment). Many technical and scientific advances followed. This compounding of information is estimated to have doubled human knowledge between 1850 and 1900. Thereafter, the pace quickened.

For example, think of the major technologies developed between 1900 and the end of World War II. The Wright brothers flew at Kitty Hawk in 1903. A television picture was transmitted in 1927. Robert Goddard and Wernher Von Braun conducted experiments with liquid-fuel rockets in 1930. The first jet engine planes were flown in 1942. The holocaust of the first atomic bomb was wrought in 1945. And now it is estimated that the quantity of human knowledge is doubling every decade.

It is startling that the first electronic digital computer was completed in 1946. This is *after* the "modern" technological events cited above. Our current times have been called the Air Age, the Mass Media Age, the Rocket Age, the Jet Age, or the Atomic Age. Yet each of these technologies preceded computers. However, since 1946, computer-based information systems have aided in the continued development of each of these technologies and have made research in many new areas possible. In fact, largely because of computers, today's era is truly the Information Age.

DEVELOPMENT OF COMPUTER HARDWARE

The computer has contributed rapidly to progress—in part because of its own rapid development, as depicted in Figures 2–1 through 2–7.

1946—Zero Generation

The computer's development can be traced from the early calculating machines such as Charles Babbage's 1812 "difference engine" through early treatises on symbolic logic such as George Boole's 1854 *The Laws of Thought*. However, aside from such items of historical interest, significant developments did not occur until 1945. In that year, the gap between calculating machines such as Harvard's Mark I and modern computers was partially closed by the completion of **ENIAC** (*Electronic Numerical Integrator and Calculator*).

ENIAC was designed by J. Presper Eckert and John W. Mauchly at the Moore School of Electrical Engineering at the University of Pennsylvania. It was developed under a $460,000 research contract from the Ballistics Research Laboratory at the Aberdeen Proving Ground and MIT's Radiation Laboratory project on military radar. After 2½ years of design and construction, the 30-ton, 1500-square-foot ENIAC became operational in December 1945, and was accepted by the United States government on February 15, 1946.

By today's standards, ENIAC would not qualify as an electronic digital computer. Although it had many features of a modern computer, it lacked one necessary ingredient—a memory capable of holding stored-program instructions. Instead, ENIAC was programmed by moving switches and plug-in wire connections. Since it was more than an electronic calculator but something less than an electronic digital computer, it is best characterized as a "zero generation" machine.

Computer professionals do not always agree on what constitutes a generation of computers.

Figure 2-1. Babbage's difference engine, 1812

A **generation** means a single stage in a succession of natural descendants. Computer professionals do not always agree on what constitutes a generation of computers. Delineating one stage from another is usually the point of contention. Some hardware manufacturers quickly label their latest component as the next generation, but perhaps a better measure of a new generation is dramatically improved cost/performance, not merely the introduction of new equipment.

1954—First Generation The blueprint for a true stored-program computer (the first generation) was provided in a 1946 paper by John von Neumann, entitled

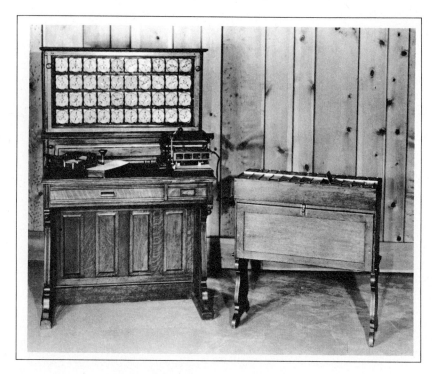

Figure 2-2. Hollerith tabulating machine, 1890

Figure 2-3. IBM automatic sequence controlled calculator, 1950

Figure 2-4. IBM 1401, 1960

"Preliminary Discussion of the Logical Design of an Electronic Computing Instrument." Though it took a while to build such computer hardware, and it has been improved greatly since then, the logical design outlined by von Neumann remains important.

The developers of ENIAC formed their own computer company and, in 1949, sold it to Remington Rand (now Sperry Rand). Two years later the first commercially built computer, Remington Rand's UNIVAC I, went into operation at the U.S. Bureau of the Census. But it was early 1954 before the first computer was installed in a private enterprise—a UNIVAC, at General Electric's Appliance Park in Louisville, Kentucky.

Today, this eight-year incubation period is hard to understand. We should remember, however, that these early machines used **vacuum tube** memories and circuits. Thus, the machines were expensive, tedious to use, and typically lacked the kind of reliability necessary for day-to-day business applications. The combined problems of cost and reliability led to slow commercial acceptance. This caused Remington Rand to make the now famous forecast that the potential market for computers was approximately 50 machines.

About this time, IBM decided to enter the computer market. It began with a rental policy for its products. The rental fee covered educational services, certain prewritten programs, and on-site analysis and support as well as the hardware itself. This decision helped forge IBM's persistent major share of the computer market, and it became the fastest growing company in history. Currently, the research and development budget of this one firm alone exceeds $1 billion—which is equal to the annual sales volume of all computer makers as recently as 1960.

Figure 2-5. IBM System/360 Model 40, 1965

1959—Second Generation In second-generation computers, the vacuum tube was replaced by the **transistor**. Computers made with transistors offered several advantages. They were less expensive to build. They were also significantly faster, more reliable, and smaller, and required less power and produced less heat. This meant that in addition to being more cost-effective they were easier to install and maintain. As such, they were recognized as a new generation of computers. These second-generation computers, produced between 1959 and 1965, represented roughly a tenfold improvement when compared to first-generation equipment.

1965—Third Generation The third generation of computers entered the marketplace in 1965. They provided roughly another tenfold increase in cost/performance over the original second-generation equipment.This improvement was gained by various forms of miniaturization and certain advances in making computer components. For example, IBM's System/360 series of computers—representative of third-generation hardware—used **solid-state** technology consisting of standardized transistors and **integrated circuits**. These could be mounted on mass-produced printed circuits. In addition to new internal electronics (illustrated in Figure

Figure 2-6.   IBM System/370 Model 135, 1971

2-8), third-generation hardware offered many features not previously available or economical in a single computer. These included:

- enlarged main memory
- fast-response secondary memory for bulk data storage
- programs that automated many tasks formerly done by computer operators

Figure 2–7. Modern computer-on-a-chip and related circuits, 1978

- improved data communications
- remote input/output
- standardized means of attaching related devices

These comprehensive capabilities are discussed in detail in Part 2.

1971—Third-and-a-Half Generation In 1971, computer manufacturers began delivering new product lines, of which the IBM System/370 is the most widely used. This computer series has **semiconductors** and integrated circuits that further miniaturize many circuit components onto a single "chip." Such circuits perform functions similar to their predecessors but are smaller, faster, and less costly.

The introduction of this new hardware was not hailed as a new generation. For one thing, it did not offer a full order of magnitude improvement over the prior generation's cost/performance. Furthermore, computer users wanted to avoid the massive conversion prob-

Figure 2-8. Size comparison of circuit chips and a transistor

lems faced in the earlier switch from second- to third-generation equipment. Hence these new computer series were designed to be largely
compatible with their predecessors. Also, different-sized models were
compatible and, to some extent, so were models from different manufacturers. As a result, the delineation of computer generations in the
1970s became less clear-cut and less important.

1977—Computer Evolution   In the mid- and later 1970s, new computer announcements took on an
evolutionary, rather than revolutionary, nature. That is, steady ad-
vances were made in components rather than in overall systems. Circuitry costs fell with volume and higher manufacturing yield. For example, the widespread switch from **cores** to semiconductors for main
memory helped make the latter not only smaller and faster, but also
cheaper. A second trend was toward increased use of scaled-down
computers—**minicomputers** and even single-chip **microprocessors**.
Sometimes these small computers serve as a component of a larger
system. Other components also gained popularity, such as mass data
storage systems; remote input/output terminals; and smaller, less
costly printers.

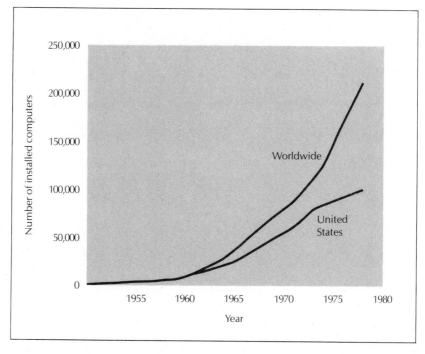

Figure 2-9. Time profile of installed computers (excludes minicomputers)

INDUSTRY GROWTH The computer industry has been one of the fastest-growing major industries ever. The world's capacity for producing information continues to expand rapidly. Ongoing improvements in hardware manufacturing, an increasing supply of available software, and a growing understanding of computers and their applications are increasing the breadth of computer use. This is shown by the time profile of the number of installed computers. As seen from Figure 2-9, by 1978, over 200,000 computers were in use worldwide. Their aggregate value amounted to nearly $70 billion. And this amount *excludes* an approximately equal number of installed minicomputers, each of which sells for up to $25,000, and of personal computers selling for about $1000 each.

Cost/Performance Improvement In an era of enlightened consumers, most people refuse to be persuaded by testimonials of product quality until they know what it costs. Most would agree that automakers have improved on Henry Ford's Model T. But such improvement has also produced increased prices, pollution, and pavement. In contrast, the computing industry has increased computer speed and reliability at *declining* costs. Hardware costs (excluding people, supplies, and so forth) have, on the

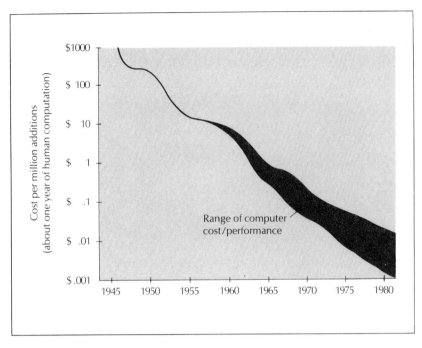

Figure 2-10.   Time profile of computer cost per unit of performance

average, been halved approximately every 3 years. The magnitude of this cost reduction (shown in Figure 2-10) can be dramatized by applying it to Ford's 1920 Model T. If automobile prices had experienced the same cost reduction rate as computing, you could drive to work and throw your car away like a paper cup!

Current Hardware Capabilities   We can appreciate modern computers more by stating four of their basic capabilities in understandable, familiar terms. We will use the following terms to describe the first capability, computer **processing speed**:

- **millisecond** = one-thousandth of a second
- **microsecond** = one-millionth of a second
- **nanosecond** = one-billionth of a second

For example, the time required for one basic computer operation (such as *add two numbers*) ranges from under 0.1 to over 10 microseconds, depending on the type of computer. To understand such computer speed better, let us consider a high-speed computer that can perform an elemental operation in 0.1 microsecond. This means it can execute 10 million instructions per second (called 10 **MIPS**). The blink of a human eye takes approximately 1/10 of a second. Thus, while a person blinks his eye, a fast computer can execute *one million instructions!*

The computer's **data storage capacity** is a second important dimension of its capability. Main memory is comparatively expensive. Therefore it is deliberately kept relatively small. Secondary storage devices are used to add capacity for storing data not in immediate demand. (In Chapter 4 we discuss the range and functions of these data storage devices, the most common of which are punched cards, magnetic tapes, and magnetic disks.)

Another analogy helps us understand the vast storage capacity of various devices. For instance, a double-spaced typed page contains about 200 words composed of about 1000 individual symbols called **characters**. A typical filing cabinet can store about 100 pages per file-drawer inch. Allowing for 20-inch drawers and five drawers per cabinet, then:

1 typed page	=	1000 characters
1 file-drawer inch	=	100,000 characters
1 file drawer	=	2,000,000 characters
1 file cabinet	=	10,000,000 characters
160 file cabinets	=	1600 million characters

The startling fact is that one single data storage device (composed of a set of eight double-density disk drives under common control) can store 1600 million characters of data. This is equivalent to a room full of file cabinets jammed with typed pages. Furthermore, a single large computer may have several of these storage devices attached to it, permitting it to control data on literally millions of separate accounts—customers, employees, products, and so forth.

An important aspect of data storage is the time required to retrieve the data. Thus, a third dimension of computer capability is the **average access time** required to obtain any data item from a storage device. The set of disks cited above can store massive quantities of data. Furthermore, any segment of those 1.6 billion characters can, if properly organized, be accessed in an average time of less than 50 milliseconds. In half the time of an eye blink, in effect, any word on any page in hundreds of file drawers can be retrieved. Even more startling is the access time of the computer's main memory—typically, 1 microsecond.

A fourth important dimension of computer capability is the rate at which it transfers data, once accessed. **Data transfer rates** are also awesome. For example, consider a textbook that contains approximately 500 words per page, or about 2500 characters per page. A few hundred pages of such a book could be read from punched cards in under half an hour. That data transfer time would be reduced to about 10 seconds using magnetic tape for storage. Using the fastest available disks, the book could be read into main storage in only a few seconds. Once in main memory, reading speeds are such that the entire book could be processed in less than 1 second. The historical trends of these four dimensions of performance are shown in Table 2.1.

Unfortunately the relatively slow speeds of input/output devices limit the practical speed at which we can effectively use a computer system. For example, a card reader allows input of about 100 to 1000 punched cards per minute. Terminals are limited even further by the speed of a human operator. The printer is faster: a high-speed printer can output about 2000 lines per minute, and even a medium-speed printer can print one line in the blink of an eye. (Chapter 5 discusses input/output methods, including several techniques developed to help relieve the input/output constraint.)

SOFTWARE DEVELOPMENT

Users need some way to tell the computer what instructions to execute. This user-computer interaction has been made easier by the development of **programming languages**. A language designed for written communication is a collection of arbitrary symbols that have generally understood meanings. Languages have been created for specifying instructions to computers. A chronology of change has taken place in this realm of software much like that of the hardware generations.

TABLE 2.1 TRENDS IN COMPUTER CAPABILITY FOR A TYPICAL LARGE SYSTEM

Performance Criteria	1945	50	55	60	65	70	75	80
Processing speed (MIPS)	<.001	.01	.05	.2	.5	1.0	3	10
Data storage capacity (thousand characters of main memory)	<1	4	16	100	250	1000	2000	4000
Average access time (seconds for fast secondary storage access)	—	100	10	1	.1	.03	.02	.01
Data transfer rate (thousand characters per second to secondary storage)	—	10	30	100	200	300	800	1000

Programming Languages   Initially, computers had to be programmed in **machine language**. This consists of a difficult-to-remember code for setting the desired electrical or magnetic states of the computer's circuit and memory components. Digital computers are **binary**, or two-state, machines because the most economical electronic and magnetic components have only two distinct stable states. An electronic switch, for instance, is either "on" or "off." Magnetizable elements are polarized in either one particular direction or its opposite. For convenience and brevity these on-or-off states are coded as "zero" for one state (usually "off") and "1" for the other state. Instructions in machine language, therefore, are meaningful combinations of these 0s and 1s. These instructions, once transmitted to the computer's circuitry and memory, cause it to react in desired ways.

Communicating with computers in machine language is cumbersome. The internal characteristics of various machines differ, so programmers at this level must learn excruciating details of the hardware's logical structure. More important, they must pay arduous attention to each data item's location in storage and to each minute step of the programming logic. In general, machine-language programming is too time consuming for the development and maintenance of the many diverse computer applications needed for an effective information system.

Higher Level Programming Languages   After early experiences with machine languages, techniques were sought to release programmers from the details of hardware design and its restrictive two-state vocabulary. One technique is to represent instructions by symbolic names rather than binary codes. In this approach, instead of writing binary notation such as "101101" to cause the computer circuitry to add two numbers, a symbolic, easy-to-remember code such as "ADD" can be substituted. However, before this can be done, the computer must be programmed to translate the symbol "ADD" into the binary codes it can recognize (in this example, "101101"). An easily remembered code may be described as **mnemonic**, a word meaning "aiding the memory."

The computer itself is used to convert this set of mnemonic symbols into the equivalent binary notation. **Language translators** are programs to do this conversion. They separate the programmer from hardware details. For example, **FLOWMATIC**, developed in 1956 by Dr. Grace Hopper at the University of Pennsylvania, consisted of symbolic codes for the various hardware functions and storage locations. This let programmers communicate with the language translator program that, in turn, generated equivalent instructions in machine language.

Thus, a **higher level language** provides mnemonic names for the various machine instructions, and users can also select names for designating storage locations. Most higher level languages also let the user combine many machine-level instructions into a single programming statement. The symbols used in such languages include the full gamut of commonly used English letters, numerals, and symbols.

After FLOWMATIC, many other higher level languages were developed. Several were oriented toward the special problem-solving needs of particular disciplines such as mathematics or civil engineering. Each language required that a translator program be written to link the new language back to the machine-language code of the particular computer. Thus the language translator program was **machine dependent**. On the other hand, the higher level language could be standardized and made **machine independent**—that is, independent of the architectural details of any particular computer.

High-Level Languages

There are now hundreds of **high-level languages** (that is, machine-independent languages designed to be user- or problem-oriented). The development of six common high-level languages is cited below. Their features are discussed in more detail in Chapter 6.

The first widely adopted, standardized, high-level language was **FORTRAN** (*FOR*mula *TRAN*slator). A version of this algebralike language, called FORTRAN II, was standardized in 1959. By 1963, FORTRAN IV, an expanded version, was developed, and it has remained widely used, particularly for computational problems. Major computer manufacturers have found it competitively desirable to create language translator programs that allow programs written in FORTRAN to run on their particular computers. Such support for a language means that programs written in it can be run at almost any installation.

By 1961, a group of computer users who found FORTRAN unsuitable to their needs met and defined another language called **COBOL** (*CO*mmon *B*usiness *O*riented *L*anguage). This language has convenient data handling, editing, and self-documenting features that are important in business and data processing applications.

However, lack of computer manufacturer support prevented widespread use of COBOL until 1966. Then the federal government required that manufacturers who wished to bid on a proposed Air Force contract for over 100 computer systems include software support for COBOL. As a result, COBOL became a supported language. By 1970, a majority of installations with problems suited to COBOL chose it as their primary language.

Another high-level language worth noting at this point is **PL/1** (*Pro*gramming *L*anguage *1*), introduced by IBM in the mid-1960s. It is designed to be comprehensive in capability, and yet it can be learned in steps. It was intended to coincide with widespread adoption of IBM's System/360 hardware. By introducing PL/1 programming, IBM hoped to increase the demand for hardware, particularly that featuring System/360 computer architecture. However, only IBM has strongly supported PL/1, and users have been relatively slow to implement the language.

The language **RPG** (Report Program Generator) is widely used with small business-oriented computers such as the IBM System/3 (introduced in 1969) and the more recent IBM System/32. RPG enables users to produce easily specified reports from existing records and files. This allows organizations with small, nonspecialist staffs to gain the advantages of in-house computer processing.

Two other languages in growing usage are **BASIC** (Beginners All-purpose Symbolic Instruction Code) and **APL** (A Programming Language). These are primarily oriented toward interactive use—that is, toward a user or programmer accessing the computer via a terminal and getting immediate feedback. This short turnaround cycle allows a dialogue or conversational format between person and machine. This interchange often improves the speed and quality of problem solving or programming. Although both languages can be traced back to the early 1960s, the growth of interactive processing, minicomputers, and terminals has led to their continually increasing usage.

Systems and Applications Software

Certain programs called **systems software** are designed to help run the system better, rather than to solve a particular user's problem. Programs for the latter purpose are referred to as **applications software**. A language translator, for instance, is categorized as systems software. In contrast, a program for payroll processing is considered applications software. Other systems programs manage computer operations, sort records, copy results automatically onto a backup file, determine the resources needed and costs for each job, and so on.

The term **utility program** refers to systems software for certain common tasks such as sorting or card-to-tape transfer. Because of their hardware orientation or general-purpose capabilities, systems programs are generally developed by the hardware manufacturer or by specialist software firms. **Application programs**, on the other hand, are usually developed within the user's organization. However, a sizable market exists for **proprietary packages**, which are tested and documented programs developed elsewhere.

As noted earlier, the phases of software development can be correlated somewhat with the generations of hardware. The first generation of computers generally used machine language, and then elementary higher level languages were developed. The second generation marked the availability of high-level languages and the rudiments of **operating systems**, which are programs to help manage computer operations. The third generation stressed high-level languages and was characterized by a dependence on operating systems. More recently, software for communications, database management, storage management, and interactive processing has become important.

In applications software, the philosophy has progressed from one of "code a current manual procedure and put it on the computer," to a more enlightened view of an information system's potential. Today, separately located offices may share a database or require interrelated processing. New methods, new jobs, and even new organizations have emerged due to computers. For example, software for standard applications is often purchased or leased from such outside organizations. And the availability of modern systems often engenders new approaches to existing problems.

To date, computers have been applied to an extremely broad range of problems. For instance, many banks offer 24-hour automated credit checking and cash issuance. Manufacturers routinely control inventories of thousands of items, producing reorder notices whenever a stock level reaches a reorder point. Retailers log transactions using point-of-sale terminals to capture more data accurately. Architects use computers to mathematically simulate earthquake stresses to test various building designs. It is not unusual for a single organization to use hundreds or even thousands of computer programs.

The supply of available software, for both systems and applications, has continued to grow. Standardized high-level languages and compatible families of hardware models have facilitated this expanding cache of developed software. It has become advantageous to seek out already prepared programs, often called **canned software**, before needlessly "reinventing the wheel."

COMPUTERS AND SOCIETY

The history of computers is relatively short, yet they have affected many facets of our daily activities. Given the projected growth in the number of computers and their expanding performance per dollar, it is reasonable to predict that the world's computer processing capacity will double within *2 years from today*. This has indeed been the trend for the past 25 years. Few organizations and few functions within them will be unaffected by computers in the years ahead.

Unfortunately, some people believe that computers have depersonalized modern commerce. Yet personalization is synonymous with variety and choice—two dimensions seldom available in the pioneer's general store—but dimensions that computer systems can facilitate.

For instance, roughly 6000 new products enter drug and grocery store marketing channels each year. These products are partially the results of computer-based analyses of consumer preferences. They are probably manufactured, distributed, and purchased according to computer-assisted plans. When they are received, they become part of the retailer's computer-controlled inventory, and so forth. The myriad alternatives, styles, options, and colors now available are economically feasible largely because computers aid in the massive planning, coordination, and control tasks that such product variety spawns.

Decision makers similarly face an increased variety of potential information. Choosing sound techniques for producing the most worthwhile information is an increasingly complex task. For some, this is stressful, while others label it "progress."

While computers can improve productivity and aid decision making, some people fear a loss of human control over computers or their applications. Indeed, intrusions on privacy and computer-concealed frauds have occurred. But fear of computers on these grounds is not supported by general experience, and neither are rosy forecasts of our early retirement. Computers are simply very helpful tools. Those who understand hardware and software, methods of processing, applications and the development cycle, and management issues are better prepared for tomorrow's decisions.

SUMMARY   It took several years of development after the first electronic computer in 1946 to produce the first generation of commercial computers. A second generation of machines followed, based on transistorized electronics. Third-generation computers, introduced in the mid-1960s, were of larger capacity, and were faster, more automatic, and more cost-effective than their predecessors. With their widespread adoption, the computer industry grew rapidly. Currently, over 200,000 computers (excluding minicomputers) are installed worldwide. Computers continue to provide more performance per dollar. Hardware capability is typically measured in terms of processing speed, data storage capacity, average access time, and data transfer rate.

Software development has paralleled that of hardware. At first, computers had to be programmed in machine language, a tedious specification of each electronic step to be executed. The subsequent development of high-level languages—such as FORTRAN, COBOL, PL/1, RPG, BASIC, and APL—allows easier programming. The computer then performs the necessary translation or interpretation of such programs into executable instructions. Programs now include those helping computerization, called systems software, and those providing results directly for users, called applications software. The supply of both hardware and software is expanding, and society will be increasingly affected by the computer and its applications.

CONCEPTS

ENIAC	MIPS	high-level language
generation	data storage capacity	FORTRAN
vacuum tube	character	COBOL
transistor	average access time	PL/1
solid state	data transfer rate	RPG
integrated circuit	programming language	BASIC
semiconductor	machine language	APL
core	binary	systems software
minicomputer	mnemonic	applications software
microprocessor	language translator	utility program
processing speed	FLOWMATIC	application program
millisecond	higher level language	proprietary package
microsecond	machine dependent	operating system
nanosecond	machine independent	canned software

QUESTIONS

1. What factors have contributed to the acceleration of human knowledge during the last few centuries? The last few decades?
2. What do you believe is the most important development in computer hardware? In computer software?
3. Compare the growth rate of the computer industry with industries in different phases of maturity.
4. What are four key measures of computer processing capability?
5. Why is it expensive yet necessary for computer manufacturers to write translator programs for common high-level languages?
6. Interview the management of a local company that uses computers and trace the evolution of the firm's hardware, systems software, and major applications.
7. Examine and describe your own attitude toward increasing computerization.

Part Two

**Hardware
and Software**

Chapter 3   **Computer Concepts and Components**

The logical functions of computers are discussed.
Then the specifics of computer architecture, data
representation, instructions, and operations are
considered.

Chapter 4   **Data Storage and Retrieval**

The several types of data storage devices and access
mechanisms permit users to match their information
retrieval demands to the available alternatives.

Chapter 5   **Input/Output Methods and Devices**

Data must be sensed, recorded, and converted to
machine-compatible format—hopefully without
great costs, errors, and delays—before processed
results can be made available and displayed to users.

Chapter 6   **Survey of High-Level Languages**

Six high-level languages are reviewed, compared,
and illustrated. A sample application programmed in
each language is included.

Chapter Three

**Computer
Concepts and
Components**

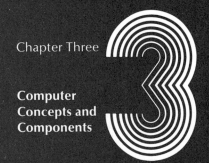

Part 1 provided a preview of information systems—what they are; who uses them and why; what resources are involved; and the historical development of hardware, software, and applications. Part 2 focuses on the technology of information systems, particularly how computer hardware works and how various high-level languages help in specifying software. In this chapter we examine the concepts and components of a modern computer system. Then the next three chapters cover data storage and retrieval, I/O methods and devices, and high-level languages.

FUNCTIONS OF A COMPUTER SYSTEM

To understand the functions of a computer system, think first of a **calculator**. The functions they share are:

- **input**
- **storage**
- **processing**
- **output**

The fifth computer function—**communication**—is not needed or available with calculators since they are small enough to be in one place, and cheap enough to be nearly every place! The keyboard of the small computer in Figure 3-1 has a keyboard for inputting both data and instructions. Data items are entered into storage by pressing the appropriate buttons. Calculators are usually limited to processing numeric data (computers deal also with alphabetic and other symbols). Data is held in storage until an instruction button is pressed. This triggers processing and the display of results.

Both the data storage capacity and the available processing instructions of a calculator are limited. It may store only two numbers—the number being input from the keyboard and the current result, which is displayed until new input begins. Similarly, it may be limited to only a few different instructions. An example

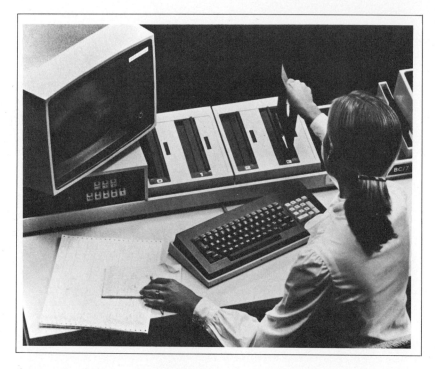

Figure 3-1. Computer keyboard for prekeying data or for online processing

of one such instruction is pressing the button labeled "+," which adds the input data just entered to the current result and clears the keyboard for subsequent data entry. More advanced calculators have dozens of instructions. Some are **programmable**; that is, the user can specify and store a sequence of instructions.

Processor Performance A calculator's **throughput**, the amount of completed processing, is limited by how fast an operator can manually input the desired data and instructions. A computer system automates these manual activities. For example, the data is often stored on machine-readable punched cards (or on tape or disk storage) and read by a mechanized card reader (or other appropriate reader). This occurs at hundreds or thousands of times the speed of direct human input. Also, the data keying and instruction preparation can be done **offline**. This means the computer's memory-processor unit is not tied up. It can be used for other jobs in the meanwhile. Offline data entry and computer functions are compared with calculator functions in Figure 3-2.

Similarly, system throughput can be increased by prekeying in-

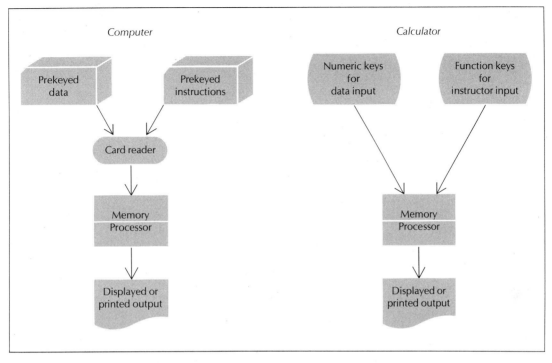

Figure 3-2.   Comparison of prekeyed data and instructions, used with a computer, and the dedicated key entry functions of a calculator.

structions. These instructions can be written, put into machine-readable format, tested, and stored for future processing. Storing the instruction sequence, or program, keeps it easily available for whenever it is useful. That is, this same set of instructions can be applied to many data items. This represents an important operational breakthrough relative to calculators. Entering—and reentering—a complex, lengthy set of instructions manually provides great opportunities for error.

Naturally, the computer must have a memory large enough to store both the instructions and the data to be processed. Also, its processor must be able to access, interpret, and execute the stored instructions. This approach is a direct application of the **stored-program concept**. It is a capability of the computer's **central processing unit**, or **CPU**, as shown in Figure 3-3.

The ability to store instructions, coupled with processor-controlled input and output, forms the essence of a stored-program computer.

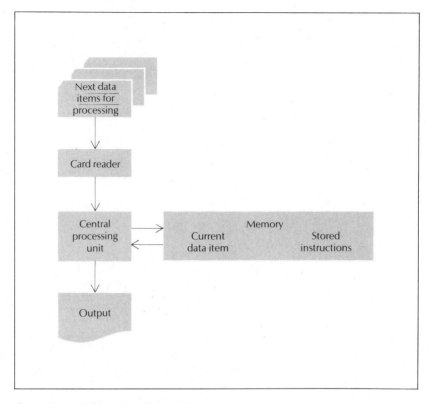

Figure 3-3. Schematic of internally stored instructions

Once a program has been read into memory, the computer can repeat the sequence of

- *read*
- *process* via instructions
- *write* information output

according to its stored program.

The total time required to carry out a *read-process-write* sequence is the sum of these three separate steps. Consequently, the next step in improving system throughput is to try to keep each component—input device, memory-processor, and output device—busy more of the time. This is usually done by a technique called **overlapped processing**, illustrated in Figure 3–4. By having the reader, processor, and printer working simultaneously as much as possible, more throughput can be achieved, even though each data item takes as long (or longer) to get through the system.

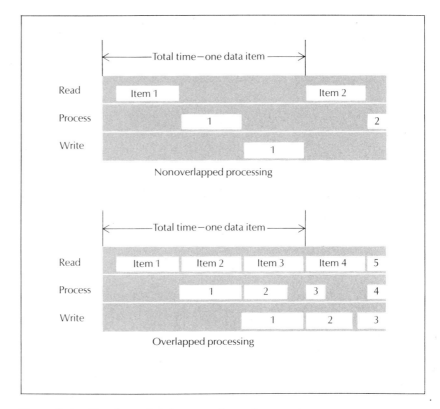

Figure 3-4. Overlapped and nonoverlapped processing

I/O Performance   To ease coordination between processing and the I/O functions, **standard interfaces** are used. The term **interface** refers to a boundary between systems or components. Having a standard or generally accepted interface between I/O devices and the processor permits connecting a range of devices to each other. This is possible because signals entering or leaving the processor then have the same kind of electronic form. Thus, the processor can easily be connected to any standard input or output device that is **plug compatible**; that is, the connecting devices match at their interface—the plug connecting them.

Hardware external to the memory-processor is often described as **peripheral equipment**. The peripheral equipment must be able to interpret standard signals from the CPU. This means that each type of I/O device must have a control unit, usually called its **controller**. The controller is a signal-modifying device that connects the peripheral device to the CPU via a channel. A **channel** is a unit that allows standardized signals to enter and leave the processor. Thus, channels direct and control I/O activity for the processor. Actually, channels are limited-capacity computers in themselves. They can store and execute instructions to control the flow of data. They operate on command from the CPU. These components of a modern computer system are depicted in Figure 3-5.

Another component useful in improving I/O performance is called a **buffer**. This is a small capacity storage area, usually a designated por-

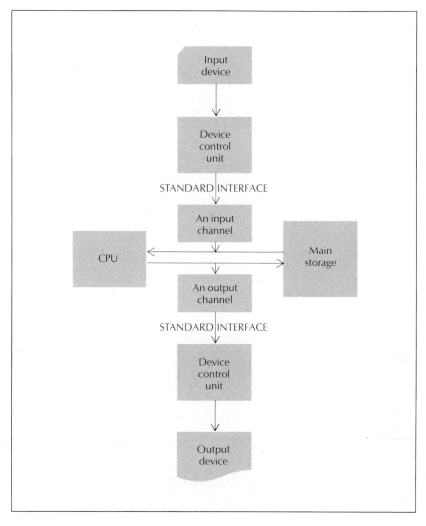

Figure 3-5.   Computer components and configuration

tion of main memory, which acts like a warehouse for data. Thus, input being received from a channel need not command the CPU's immediate attention. It can be dumped into a buffer and stored (much like raw materials inventories are stored for manufacturing firms). Then, when the CPU can effectively deal with this input, it is processed and returned to the same or another buffer. When output is convenient, a channel can communicate the results to the appropriate display device. This is like meeting sales demand from a supply of finished goods inventory. Thus, buffers enhance the efficiency and independence of the input-process-output stages, without sacrificing their overall interrelationship.

A wide variety of I/O components can be connected to the processor via controllers and suitable channels. (The reasons for selecting certain I/O devices and their capabilities are discussed in Chapter 5.) The common I/O devices are:

- keyboard terminals
- card readers
- printers
- card punches
- magnetic tape units
- magnetic disk units   } primarily storage devices, but also capable of inputting data or receiving output
- magnetic ink character readers
- optical mark readers
- optical character readers
- paper tape readers
- paper tape punches
- audio response units
- visual display units

In summary, the three capabilities of these components, and the configuration shown in Figure 3–5, are:

1. Store instructions and data
2. Electronically process instructions and access stored data
3. Coordinate independent I/O devices, under CPU control

Storage Components

While the input-processing-output cycle describes computer usage, we often wish to *delay* the processing and output steps or to *save* some results for later reprocessing. This requires *storage* capability. The computer's **main memory** is a storage component, but it is expensive. **Secondary storage** units have been devised that are cheaper per unit of data stored. Consequently, it is feasible and economical to retain rather large amounts of data in computer-readable form. Disks, tapes, and mass storage systems are the principal devices used. (Their characteristics and economics are discussed in detail in Chapter 4.)

Communication Links Not all computer systems involve communications links, but most do. Communication permits one or more components of the overall system to be remotely located. Most frequently, an off-site, keyboard-driven computer **terminal** will be used for low volume, quick response interaction with a distant computer. (The techniques, costs, and benefits of data communication are covered in Chapter 10.)

CPU CONCEPTS The central processing unit is the heart, or "brains," of the computer system. The term refers to both the **processor**, in which the instructions are executed, and the main memory, where both instructions and data are stored.

We can think of the functioning of the computer's main memory in terms of the mailboxes of a post office. Such a systematic array of storage capacity is illustrated in Figure 3–6. Only 16 separate storage locations are shown, but the main memories of modern computers have from several thousand to a few million separately addressable storage locations.

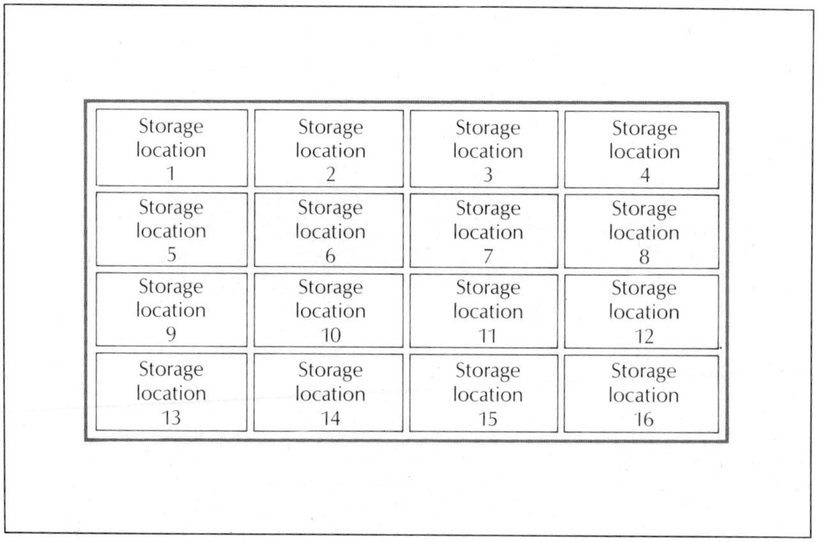

Storage location 1	Storage location 2	Storage location 3	Storage location 4
Storage location 5	Storage location 6	Storage location 7	Storage location 8
Storage location 9	Storage location 10	Storage location 11	Storage location 12
Storage location 13	Storage location 14	Storage location 15	Storage location 16

Figure 3–6. A systematic grouping of storage locations

Address versus Contents

Each storage compartment in a computer's main memory has a unique, numeric **address**. This is the label assigned to identify that particular **storage location**. The **contents** of a storage location are the symbols currently stored in that location. For example, in a multiplication problem we might need to multiply the hours worked by the hourly rate to determine pay. A programmer would designate certain storage locations to hold these three numbers. The instructions to manipulate, or multiply, these data items would use their addresses. The result would then be stored as the contents of the storage location known as "pay" to the programmer. However, within the computer this storage location would also be referenced by its unique numeric address.

Computer Architecture

A trio of hardware terms is used to describe the memory organization of most third-generation and later computers.[1] This internal architecture was introduced with IBM's System/360 in the mid-1960s and is also used by several other computer manufacturers. The hardware terms are, from the smallest to the largest unit of storage:

- **bit**
- **byte**
- **word**

A bit is a physical component capable of storing exactly one of two possible conditions. Usually these two states are referred to as 0 and 1 or as off and on. The word bit derives from a contraction of the term *bi*nary dig*it*.

A byte refers to a group of bits treated as a unit. In most current computers, a byte is an addressable eight-bit unit. A byte of this size can store eight separate 0 or 1 states using its individual bits. The various patterns of 0s and 1s can represent the alphabetical symbols, the dollar sign, and so forth. In this way, meaningful data can be stored.

A word of storage, in turn, is a group of bytes treated as a unit. Four is the common number of bytes per word. This is often used for storing fixed-length data requiring only this amount of storage capacity. However, a variable number of bytes may be used for storing a data

---

[1]Because of varying computer architecture among different manufacturers (and sometimes among the various models of the same manufacturer), care must be taken in comparing memory sizes. The number of addressable storage locations is usually cited with K, or 1024, as the unit. Thus, 256K bytes of memory is 262,144 groups of 8-bit storage capacity. However, storage capacities of early computers and those that are not byte-addressable are quoted in different units. For example, the Control Data 7600 uses a 60-bit word; some minicomputer memory sizes are quoted in terms of 18-bit or 36-bit words. When the units quoted are different, a comparison should be made either of the number of bits in each memory or of each memory's character capacity.

item, especially if it might not fit in a single four-byte word. Therefore, half-words and double-words are also used, as seen in Figure 3–7.

The number of bits per byte and bytes per word have differed from computer to computer over the years, depending on the intended use and manufacturing costs. Currently, two technologies are used for main memory: the older **core** and the newer **semiconductor** circuit.

A core is a tiny iron-alloy, doughnut-shaped device. It can store exactly one bit of data because it can be magnetically polarized in exactly one of two directions. Electrical currents can be applied to read it or to set it to either magnetic polarity. It will then maintain this state until reset. Figure 3–8 illustrates a magnetizable core with four wires through its center. The wires are used for setting, reading, and resetting the core's polarity.

Fabricating cores, each about the size of a pinhead, is mostly automated but still expensive. Consequently, an alternate technology for main memory has largely replaced core for cost/performance reasons. Using semiconductors, this newer technique basically relies on a switchable on-off circuit to store and maintain either of two bit states. The circuit can be first set to either state. It can then be read by testing its ability to carry a current. If it can carry one, it is "on"; if not, it is "off." A size comparison of core and semiconductor memories is shown in Figure 3–9.

It is important to note that any storage device should have four properties:

1. Its state can be set according to user desires.
2. Its condition, once set, will remain intact. (One problem with semiconductor memory is that a power failure wipes out its contents.)
3. Its state can be read without changing it. (One problem with core memory is that a read operation can change its contents, so that a separate restoring cycle is needed.)
4. Its state can be reset at will.

Although a single bit has just two states—0 and 1—it has the four properties required of a storage device. However, when several bits are grouped, a more meaningful amount of data can be stored.

DATA REPRESENTATION Data items are unprocessed facts, either numeric or otherwise, which the computer is to act on. Data might be numbers to be added, names to be stored, report titles to be printed, or calculated results. Once in main memory, data is stored in some assigned or available storage

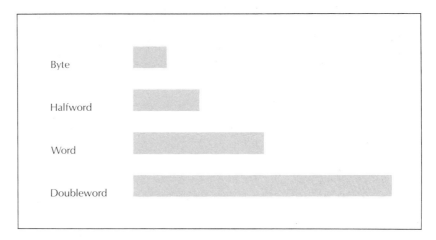

Figure 3-7. Hardware "word" hierarchy

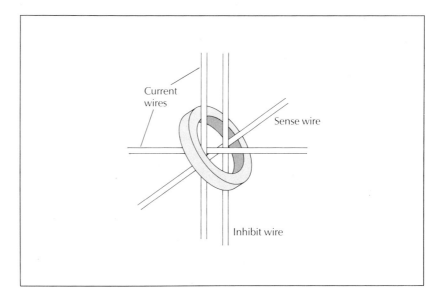

Figure 3-8. Core with four wires

location. References to the stored data item refer to it by the address at which it is stored. Using high-level languages, data can be referenced by a user-chosen name, and the system will automatically choose and monitor where it is stored.

The issue we will discuss next is how the user's data is represented

Figure 3-9. 8000 bits of core and semiconductor storage (actual size above and enlarged below)

using the bits, bytes, and words of some computer. Then we will explore how instructions are executed to process this stored data.

Data Hierarchy Data are often organized into a hierarchy of categories. However, the smallest element, a bit, is usually not a meaningful amount of data from the user's viewpoint. Users typically think of data in terms of:

- **character**
- **field**
- **group**
- **record**
- **file**
- **database**

Character.   This is a group of bits treated as a unit. The collective 0s and 1s making up each character indicate some particular symbol, such as the letter A.

Field.   This is one or more characters treated as a unit. A field has meaning as a data item beyond the meaning of its separate characters, as, for example, a last name does.

Group.   This is one or more fields treated as a unit; for example, a full name includes first name, middle name, and last name fields.

Record.   This is one or more fields or groups treated as a unit. A record consists of all fields related to some common entity, such as full name and full address.

File.   This is many records treated as a unit. A file usually contains records of similar type used for a common purpose, such as that depicted in Figure 3–10.

Database.   This is many files, records, groups, or fields treated as a unit. A database usually consists of data related in its use or users.

It is important to realize that, inside the computer, all data is represented as a series of 0s and 1s stored as individual bits. It is the *organization* and *codes used* that give meaning to these electronic and magnetic representations.

Data Storage Codes   A review of number systems is useful before discussing how data items are actually coded for storage. Counting systems can have bases other than the familiar base-10 of the decimal system. For example, the **binary number system** has a **radix** (number system base) of 2 rather than 10. Numbers of any system derive meaning from two conventions:

1. **Symbol value** is the meaning of individual numeric symbols, such as bit values 0 and 1 or digit values 0 through 9.

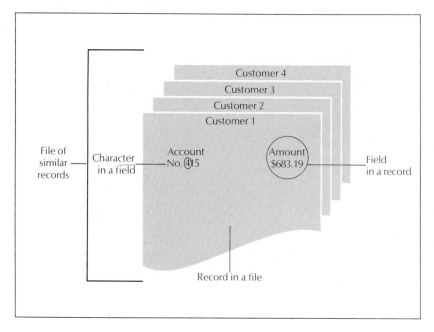

Figure 3-10. Relationships in the data hierarchy

2. **Positional value** is the order of magnitude of the units of symbol value. Increasing powers of the radix occupy successive positions moving to the left.

For example, the decimal number 943 represents symbol value and position value in the following way:

Decimal number	Symbol value	×	Positional value	=	Decimal equivalent
9 4 3	3	×	$10^0 = 3 \times 1$	=	3
	4	×	$10^1 = 4 \times 10$	=	40
	9	×	$10^2 = 9 \times 100$	=	900
					943

In the binary number system, we again use both symbol and positional values. However, the number of unique single-position symbols in any number system equals its radix. The binary number system accordingly has only two symbols, designated as 0 and 1. Thus, the binary number 10110 represents symbol value and positional value as follows:

Binary number	Symbol value	×	Positional value	=	Decimal equivalent
10110	0	×	$2^0 = 0 \times 1$	=	0
	1	×	$2^1 = 1 \times 2$	=	2
	1	×	$2^2 = 1 \times 4$	=	4
	0	×	$2^3 = 0 \times 8$	=	0
	1	×	$2^4 = 1 \times 16$	=	16
					22

Binary number schemes are important because they require only two storage states. They correspond perfectly to the most economical storage devices for computers, which are two-state, electronic, and/or magnetic devices. Arithmetic and other data manipulations are also simplified when data is expressed in binary. For example, the binary addition and multiplication tables shown in Figure 3-11 are much briefer than the corresponding 10-by-10 decimal tables.

Integer Storage. In many computers, an integer number is stored in a 32-bit word. The leftmost bit is used to indicate a + or – sign. The remaining 31 bits of storage express the number, with leading zeros filling the positional values that are not needed. For example, the decimal number 22 is converted into binary as 10110. The first bit of the word is used to indicate the integers's sign (that is, 0 for positive). Thus, 22 is stored as:

00000000000000000000000000010110

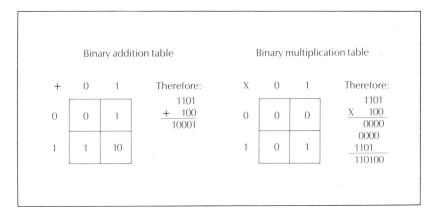

Figure 3-11. Binary arithmetic tables

Fractional Numbers. In contrast to integers, a *fractional number* has a decimal point. The term **floating point** is often applied to this type of data representation. Any fractional number, such as 123.45, can be transformed, unchanged in value, into two parts—a **normalized fraction**, which ranges from .1 to 1.0, and an **exponent**. Thus, 123.45 becomes $.12345 \times 10^3$. This form of expressing numbers is called **exponential form** or **scientific notation**. It has the advantage of always placing the decimal point in the same location—preceding the leftmost significant digit. With the number converted to this notation, the computer need store only:

1. The digits of the normalized fraction, including the sign.
2. The exponent, including the sign.

These two pieces of information define the original number. Now, however, the computer need only store two signed integers. In this case, a hardware word is allocated in two parts. The exponent and its sign are stored in one part. This leaves the remaining part for storing the digits and sign. However, the limited storage may produce a truncation, or round-off, error in the represented number.

Alphameric Codes. Other symbols, besides numbers, are also processed by computers. The word **alphameric** includes alphabetic, numeric, and other types of symbols, such as (/)*$&; and .. These symbols must be represented by some coding and storage scheme relying only on 0 and 1—the two possible states of a single bit. A byte, or other group of bits taken as a whole, can then store 0 and 1 patterns that have meaning for users.

Several codes exist for representing a complete **character set**, or list of defined symbols. Among the most widely used are **BCD** (*Binary Coded Decimal*); **ASCII** (*American Standard Code for Information Interchange*); and **EBCDIC** (*Extended Binary Coded Decimal Interchange Code*). Such codes use six, seven, or eight bits to represent a single character. If the characters are known to be digit symbols (for example, 0 through 9), then some economy of storage can be effected and only four bits need be used. This is called **packed decimal**.

In addition, to provide a means of self-checking, computers usually store and process an additional bit called a **parity bit**. Its value is based on whether the number of 1s in the character or bit group is either odd or even. After computation, I/O operation, or communications, the parity bit can be checked and will probably reveal whether any malfunction occurred.

Data representation can be summarized by noting that a unit of storage is merely some number of bits, each being either a 0 or a 1. The contents of any byte or word are separately addressable in most computers. Such contents are interpreted by decoding these 0s and 1s according to whether the contents are:

- integers
- fractional numbers
- an alphameric code

INSTRUCTIONS Computer instruction codes for internal storage vary among different computer designs. However, such instructions usually consist of an **operator** and an **operand**. In essence, the operator specifies what the computer is to do and the operand designates the data to be acted on.

The operand portion of an instruction usually designates the address of some storage location, which contains the data to be operated on. For instance, the exact quantity that is to be added next during a summation need not be known at the time the *add* instruction is written. Rather, the programmer need only indicate the storage location whose contents will be tallied. The actual data need not be available until the instruction is executed. Thus, programmers can write general programs independent of the specific data that will be acted on at execution time.

TABLE 3.1 SUMMARY OF MACHINE INSTRUCTION'S FUNCTION

Name	Synonym	Definition	Example
Operator	"Op Code"	"What to do"	Add . . . to the current sum . . .
Operand	"Address"	"What to do it to" (often designated by the address of some storage location, the contents of which are to be operated on)	The contents of the storage location with the address specified by the operand

Instruction Storage A hardware word might be used to store one computer instruction. The automatic execution of such a stored instruction begins by retrieving it from memory. It is then interpreted and executed via CPU circuitry. Instructions are retrieved and executed in their sequence of storage unless an instruction specifies otherwise.

Storing instructions requires various amounts of hardware, depending on the instruction format. An instruction often has one operator and only one operand, although it may have more. Such an instruction is frequently stored in exactly one hardware word with the first byte storing the operator (**op code**) and the three remaining bytes storing the operand. It is therefore possible to represent up to 2^8, or 256, different op codes in the eight bits allowed. Since computers usually have about 150 operators in their instruction set, eight bits are adequate for coding each instruction differently. The three bytes often used for the operand or address portion of the instruction imply a 24-bit addressing scheme. This is sufficient to represent 2^{24} or over 16 million separately addressable bytes of main memory!

Some instructions require two operands, and some use an abbreviated notation for the operand addresses. Consequently, there are instructions that use other than exactly one hardware word of storage.

The schemes for data representation and instruction storage depend on the particular computer's internal architecture. Such design changes made third-generation and later computers incompatible with most earlier machines.

Instruction Execution

How computers are able to execute instructions is a mystery to the uninitiated. Yet the concepts developed in this chapter now permit an explanation of this process. What will remain as an awesome, almost incomprehensible fact is the speed of instruction execution—now measured as so many million instructions per second (**MIPS**). Also, the accuracy is astonishing. Aided by error-checking and correcting circuitry, computers can execute billions or even trillions of instructions without a hardware logic error. There are, of course, still enough programmer and data errors to keep things from becoming dull.

Recall that the main memory contains thousands of storage locations. Each has an address—a unique binary number assigned as its identifier and by which circuitry can locate it. Also, each storage location can hold some contents—data in a 0s and 1s format representing coded integer, fractional, or alphameric data. Instructions, like data, are also represented and stored as a code of 0s and 1s.

In order to execute an instruction, let's assume that it has already been stored in main memory by a **loader**, which is a program for reading instructions and then turning control over to them. Control over instruction execution means having some way to tell the computer what to do next. The **instruction counter** performs this role. It is a special-purpose storage location in which the computer stores the address of the location containing the next instruction to be executed. Thus, to know what to do next at any split microsecond, the CPU reads the instruction counter's contents—a string of 0s and 1s. It interprets this as an address in main memory. It then fetches the contents stored at the location having this address. These contents are then interpreted as the next instruction, thereby telling the computer what to do next.

Now we are ready to execute this instruction. A certain portion of the 0s and 1s are the *op code*, or *operator*. This calls on circuitry for a certain function, such as "add a data item to the existing subtotal." Of course, a calculator's circuitry can do this. However, in a computer, the data item to be operated on need not be manually entered via a keyboard. The data has been previously read into main memory.

Each data item has been stored in some location the computer keeps track of. To add a data item to a subtotal, the proper machine instruction is coded, including the "add to subtotal" operator. The operand portion of the instruction specifies the address of the storage location holding the desired data item. Executing the instruction means fetching data from the location having the indicated address and running it through circuitry specified by the op code. Thus, in this case, the data item would be retrieved and added to the existing subtotal.

Program Execution

A program is a (usually lengthy) set of instructions. To execute an entire program, the computer simply executes individual instructions one after another. To execute instructions in sequence, all that is required is to store them in consecutive locations. Then the instruction counter's contents can be systematically augmented after each instruction is executed. Since the instruction counter is used to direct control, the next instruction executed will be the one stored next in the memory. To change this sequence of execution, an instruction must alter what is stored in the instruction counter. Then the next instruction, instead of being fetched from the next consecutive location, will be sought at the newly indicated location.

A special instruction notes the end of a program. This instruction causes the computer to redirect execution control over to another program. Usually, an **operating system** is the program called on next. The operating system is software designed to manage and run the computer hardware. We will discuss it below as a part of computer system operations.

COMPUTER SYSTEM OPERATIONS

Modern computer system design reflects years of widespread experience with post-third-generation hardware and software. As noted, the development of third-generation computers themselves provided roughly a tenfold increase in cost/performance over earlier machines.

Today's computers have enhanced efficiency by using improved circuitry, faster storage units, and other improved peripheral devices. But integrating such computer components into a logical, functioning system has been as important as technological invention. Throughout this evolutionary process, designers have sought to reduce distinctions between commercial and scientific computers; batch and online systems; and tape, disk, or card I/O. A general-purpose computer can now accommodate an increasing variety and volume of applications.

CPU Operations

Once data or an instruction has been retrieved from storage, the next steps take place in the CPU, or central processing unit. It has two parts—a **control unit** and an **arithmetic unit** (pronounced arithmet'ic). The control unit consists of circuitry and **registers**. Electrical signals arriving from storage consist of the presence or absence of an electrical pulse for each bit. The control unit accepts these signals by placing them temporarily in its registers. These are devices designed to accept, store, and release electrical pulses under the direction of the control unit's circuits.

The actual execution of instructions takes place in the arithmetic unit, also known as the **arithmetic and logic unit** or **ALU**. The computer operation called for might be comparison, addition, multiplication, or some other operation as stated by the instruction's op code. The ALU's logic and switching circuitry handles this. These operations may involve integer, fractional, or alphameric data, as discussed. The interactions of these CPU components and main storage are diagrammed in Figure 3–12, showing a representative logic flow in a CPU.

One method for speeding up the CPU's effective operating rate involves a storage device called a **high-speed buffer** or **cache memory**. This technique is used in certain computers, particularly those with large main memories. The high-speed buffer is a small, fast addition to main storage. It acts as a high-speed go-between by reading the contents of main memory locations into the high-speed buffer in anticipation of a CPU request. Figure 3–13 illustrates this access relationship.

Each time the CPU requests bytes from memory, the index of buffer contents depicted in Figure 3–13 is checked to determine if the bytes actually sought next are in the high-speed buffer. If they are not, they must be transferred from main storage to the CPU, after which the next 32 consecutive bytes in main memory are copied into the high-speed buffer storage. Since both programs and data tend to be read in sequence from memory, there is a high probability that the next access request can be satisfied by the high-speed buffer. This shortens the effective access time.

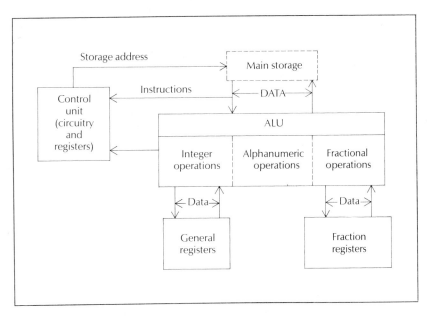

Figure 3-12. Representative CPU logic flow

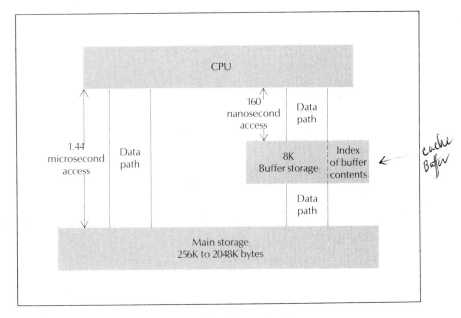

Figure 3-13. Example of high-speed buffer and main storage access

Another concept that improves utilization involves assigning contents to main memory locations. Computer operations refer to these locations by exact numeric addresses. Often these addresses can be stated relative to some other storage location, or **base address**. Should it then become desirable to relocate the program in memory, the new sequence of specific addresses can be generated merely by using the new base address. The specific address sought still has the same relative address compared to the revised starting point. This allows a block of data, often called a **page**, to be moved in the memory with less need for a tedious recomputation of all the specific addresses. Only the new base address and the old relative addresses need be known to identify the new specific storage locations.

Efficient computer operation requires a balancing of the speed of internal processing with the generally slower speed of I/O operations. High-speed I/O devices alone cannot solve this problem. Under typical conditions, high-speed tape or disk drives can transfer data perhaps only one-tenth as fast as a CPU can manipulate bytes of data. Considering the CPU's high cost and its capability, hardware and software designers and users attempt to keep the CPU busy by balancing its demands for processing and I/O. As discussed, this involves channels and buffers to relieve the CPU from controlling I/O directly and to allow for multiple I/O sources.

For example, executing channel commands governing input causes three things to happen:

1. Signals are sent to the input device's control unit, which in turn activates that part of the input operation.
2. Details of the input data are transmitted to main memory and stored there, perhaps in a designated buffer area.
3. The CPU is notified that the input operation is complete and that the results are available beginning at some specified address.

Three principal types of channels are widely used. A **selector channel** is one dedicated to "talking" to a single high-speed I/O device. In contrast, a **multiplexor channel** talks to many devices, usually of lower speeds. It appropriately intermixes, or multiplexes, their signals to get more channel and CPU throughput. A **block multiplexor channel** intermixes longer signals (blocks of data) from several high-speed devices. In any case, once the CPU tells the channel to handle I/O, it is free to do other processing. This allows overlapped operations for input, processing, and output.

However, even with overlapped processing, a perfect balance is seldom achieved. Very often, either channels or the processor are actually idle during a particular microsecond. CPU and channel utilization are therefore important measures of operating efficiency and indicators of system balance.

One common scheme for coordinating I/O and processing is called **flip-flop buffering**. In this approach two areas of main memory are set aside. Each is divided into an *input* buffer area and an *output* buffer area, as shown in Figure 3–14.

Suppose the CPU is processing data stored in input buffer 1 and storing processed results in output buffer 1. Then, the channels can concurrently be reading data into input buffer 2 and outputting data from output buffer 2. When the CPU completes its work with the first pair of buffers and the channel completes the I/O transfers with the second pair, the functions *flip-flop*. Then, the CPU works with buffer 2 while the channels load and unload the first pair of I/O buffers. This scheme improves each component's throughput and can be tailored to attempt to balance I/O and processing resources.

Notice that there is only one data path to and from main storage. All instruction fetching or data movement that is initiated either by the CPU or by a channel must use this single **shared data path**. This leads to

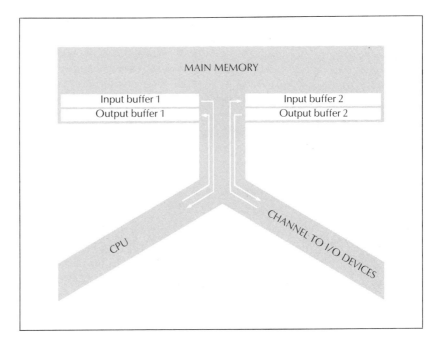

Figure 3–14. Flip-flop buffering

competition (often called **contention**) for this shared data path. Suppose, for example, that a channel and the CPU both want access to main storage. When this happens, I/O operations are given the higher priority. The CPU, in effect, is immobilized during such an I/O operation.

Operating Systems

Operating systems became widespread with third-generation hardware and are still evolving today. Because of their complexity and machine dependence, they are typically developed by the computer manufacturer. However, the user may have systems programmers tinker with the operating system to add features or to "fine tune" it for a particular configuration or job mix. Commercial users tend to do less of such sophisticated reprogramming than do software firms, universities, or research-oriented users.

Current operating systems have various features. IBM, for example, offers a few different operating systems depending on the processor model and the system configuration. Currently it features **VS2**, standing for *Virtual Storage*, to be discussed shortly. Burroughs Corporation features **MCP** for its *Master Control Program*. Generally, each manufacturer tries to ensure that its operating systems (and their periodically updated versions, or **releases**) improve the performance of the manufacturer's product line in running the user's programs.

The **supervisor**, also called the **executive** or **monitor** portion of the operating system, is a subset that controls the rest of the system's activities. It must be able to respond immediately to any of several types of **interrupts**—calls for supervision. Therefore, it is stored in main memory, where it is quickly accessible for execution. Lesser used portions of the overall operating system are stored on high-speed secondary storage and are called in by the supervisor only as needed. Nonetheless, operating systems occupy a significant portion of main memory and also consume some of the processor's execution time. The functions of an operating system are diagrammed in Figure 3–15.

Multiprogramming and Virtual Storage

In **multiprogramming**, several programs can be in the main memory at the same time. Assume that the main memory is divided into several **partitions**. Each is an arbitrary subdivision of main storage that might be used by a separate program. For example, the operating system might require one such memory area. In addition, several user programs with various priorities can be stored in other areas. These would be run in priority order, possibly subject to interrupts. Thus, each

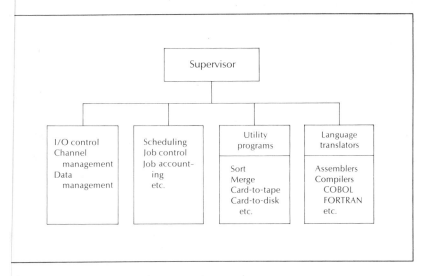

Figure 3-15.   Functions of an operating system

program is processed from time to time, depending on any pattern of interrupts.

It is important to note that although several programs are in main memory simultaneously, only one is being executed at any moment. The others provide backup work in case of an interrupt, such as when a high-priority program must wait for I/O and then when that I/O delay is over. Most large computers use multiprogramming to improve efficiency. Increasingly, systems also use **multiprocessing**—multiple processors accessing the same memory. Practically speaking, this is like applying multiple computers to the same processing task.

Different strategies are used for allocating memory in a multiprogramming environment. One such concept is called **virtual storage**. This technique allows the user to assume a large memory partition. Virtual storage cannot, of course, provide the user with a larger main memory than is really there. Rather, it divides the user's program into subsets, often called pages, and keeps the bulk of them in secondary storage when they are not in use. The remaining pages fit nicely into main memory along with various pages of many other programs. The penalty for this privilege of assuming a large memory is that if a program's execution requires a page not currently in main memory, there is a delay while it is read in. Of course, the processor need not remain idle waiting for this I/O. There are probably other programs in main memory ready for processing.

SUMMARY   This chapter has discussed computer concepts and components, including their evolution from calculators to modern CPUs. Throughput and utilization are improved by designing computer systems that overlap their input-processing-output activities. Channels and controllers link the CPU to the various I/O devices. And standard interfaces and buffers support their independent, yet coordinated operation.

The computer's main memory is organized as a set of separately addressable storage locations. Each location can hold some contents, representing either data or an instruction. These are stored as a group of bits, each either a 0 or a 1. Using such hardware capacity, characters, fields, groups, records, files, and databases can be coded and stored. Alphabetic, numeric, and other symbols are each assigned a unique bit pattern for this purpose. Integer and fractional numbers can be represented using the binary number system.

Instruction execution typically involves interpreting an op code and fetching requested data from memory by citing its address. Instructions are executed in sequence unless directed otherwise by the program. Cache memory, base addressing, channels, and buffers are techniques to increase CPU utilization and achieve balance with I/O. An operating system, which is the software supplied with the computer, manages overall operations. It schedules jobs, allocates storage, and manages programs simultaneously in modes including multiprogramming and virtual storage.

CONCEPTS

calculator	character	operating system
input	field	control unit
storage	group	arithmetic unit
processing	record	register
output	file	arithmetic and
communication	database	logical unit
programmable	binary number system	(ALU)
throughput	radix	high-speed buffer
off line	symbol value	cache memory
stored-program concept	positional value	base address
central processing unit	floating point	page
(CPU)	normalized fraction	selector channel
overlapped processing	exponent	multiplexor channel
standard interface	exponential form	block multiplexor
interface	scientific notation	channel
plug compatible	alphameric	flip-flop buffering
peripheral equipment	character set	shared data path

controller	core	contention
channel	semiconductor	VS2
buffer	BCD	MCP
main memory	ASCII	release
secondary storage	EBCDIC	supervisor
terminal	packed decimal	executive
processor	parity bit	monitor
address	operator	interrupt
storage location	operand	multiprogramming
contents	opcode	partition
bit	MIPS	multiprocessing
byte	loader	virtual storage
word	instruction counter	

QUESTIONS

1. What improvements can be made to a calculator to upgrade it to a stored-program computer's capability?
2. How does overlapped processing increase overall throughput?
3. What is meant by the standard interface concept?
4. Storage locations can be accessed either by their addresses or by their contents. State and discuss if this is true.
5. Discuss whether data can always be expressed as a series of bits.
6. List some different types of codes for representing data, including some precomputer coding schemes.
7. What is the parallel between the data hierarchy and the architecture of hardware storage?
8. Construct a conversion table relating the decimal numbers 20 through 30 to their binary equivalents.
9. State briefly how instructions are stored and executed.
10. What techniques have been devised to improve CPU throughput?
11. Why are operating systems typically developed and supplied by the computer system manufacturer?
12. Explain virtual storage and cite an example of how it could be disadvantageous.
13. Discuss whether a manager needs to know how computers work, or just how to use them.

Chapter Four

**Data
Storage
and
Retrieval**

In this chapter we extend our discussion of computer concepts and components by reviewing the various devices used for data storage and retrieval. We also discuss the relevant dimensions of performance for storage devices. This is meant to assist you in choosing the "best" storage device, given the use to be made of it.

Storage performance is often measured in **cost per byte** stored and **storage capacity**. In terms of such measures, main memory is both expensive and limited in capacity. It overcomes these relative disadvantages by two other factors—an extraordinarily fast **average access time** and a rapid **data transfer rate**. Other storage devices are available for economically storing massive data files. Such devices make computer systems more efficient by offering capabilities different from those of main memory. Thus, there is a **hierarchy of storage devices**. Each device has some respective advantage over other available equipment for at least one important measure of performance. The four major measures of performance are:

- cost per byte of storage
- storage capacity
- average access time
- data transfer rate

MAIN MEMORY   Main memory, often called **primary storage**, is usually housed with the computer's central processor. Primary storage typically ranges in capacity from 4000 characters of storage, or 4K, up to 4 million characters. A million bytes is sometimes called a **megabyte**. As discussed in Chapter 3, main memory is usually constructed of either core or semiconductor components.

Core memories are built up by organizing individual cores into appropriately wired rows and columns called planes. Several **core planes** are stacked to form a complete memory unit.

Semiconductor memory uses either **metal-oxide semiconductor (MOS)** or **bipolar semiconductor** technology. Each on-off circuit can store one bit of data. Technology is rapidly reducing the manufacturing costs of semiconductor memory. Thus, semiconductors are increasingly used for main memory.

In the past, some computers were designed with still different technologies for main memory, such as thin-film and plated-wire techniques. They have not been widely adopted. Newer memory techniques include **lasers** and **holograms**, **charged coupled devices**, and **bubble memories**. These promising techniques will likely be used more in the future. They can each potentially store data more compactly and cheaper than existing techniques.

SECONDARY STORAGE

Several storage media have been devised for storing large amounts of data at less cost than is possible with main memory. These devices are called **secondary storage**. Included among them are devices for the following storage media:

- magnetic tape
- drum
- disk
- mass storage
- microfilm
- punched cards, tapes, and tags

MAGNETIC TAPE

Magnetic tape for computers, like home stereo recording tape, consists of a magnetizable ferrous oxide coating on a flexible, tough base. A standard computer tape reel is a half inch wide and 2400 feet long; it costs about $10. Data is stored on tape by recording tiny magnetic fields polarized in one direction or the opposite along the tape's linear dimension. Several such rows of magnetic fields, called **recording channels** or **tracks**, can be spread across the width of the tape. Generally, data is recorded in enough rows to store exactly one data character in one "column" across the tape width. A standard tape format is illustrated in Figure 4–1.

Tapes that correspond to third-generation or later hardware typically use nine tracks, or rows of data, across the tape width. Eight tracks are needed to represent an eight-bit character and one is for a *parity bit*. This acts as a check on the accuracy of the group of bits in that byte.

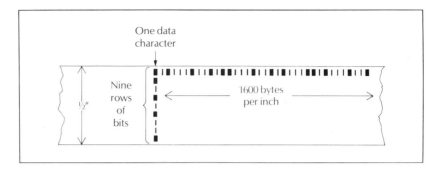

Figure 4-1. Magnetic tape data storage

Some computer components also use tapes of different sizes and recording formats. For example, small cassettes have become popular, especially for data entry or as secondary storage for minicomputers.

Magnetic fields are recorded so compactly along the tape's linear dimensions that 1600 characters or **bytes per inch (bpi)** are commonly stored. Other standard recording densities are 6250, 800, 556, and 200 bpi. The higher storage densities reflect more recent technology. High storage densities allow faster reading and writing and economize on tape needs.

To read or write on a tape's magnetizable surface, a **tape drive** is required. A tape drive costs from $8000 to $25,000—especially for high-performance ones such as that shown in Figure 4-2. Small cassette tape drives might cost only a few hundred dollars.

To be read, the tape's surface must move past a **read/write head**. This is a coil of wire in which electric currents are induced by moving the tape's stored magnetic fields past the coil. The electric currents generated in the wire of the read/write head correspond to the pattern of the tape's magnetic fields moving past it. The computer interprets these currents as 0s and 1s during a read of the tape. Similarly, to write on tape, the computer sends flip-flopping electric signals representing 0s and 1s into the read/write head. Such signals create corresponding patterns of magnetic fields on the tape as it moves past the read/write head. This is illustrated in Figure 4-3.

Notice that for reading or writing to occur, the magnetic fields on the tape and the wire coil of the read/write head must be in relative motion. For simplicity, the tape moves and the heads are fixed, one for each row of data across the tape width. The tape is moved on computer command and passes over the read/write heads at a precise speed. A representative tape transport speed is 100 to 200 inches per second (ips), which is considerably faster than audio tape speed.

Figure 4-2. A tape drive.

The *data transfer rate*—the speed of reading or writing data between a storage medium and the computer—is quite rapid for magnetic tape. Typically, 100,000 characters per second or more can be transferred. In comparison, a card reader for 80-column punched cards might have up to a 1000-card-per-minute reading capacity. Thus, magnetic tapes provide approximately one hundred times the card reader's rate of data transfer. Yet, in comparison to disk, tapes can be slow at retrieving specific data sought as an inquiry into a large file.

The **recording density**—the compaction of data—on magnetic tape is also advantageous compared to punched cards, but again not to disk. A box of 2000 punched cards with 80-character capacity costs about $4 and holds at most 160,000 characters. A similar amount of data would take only 100 or 200 inches of magnetic tape at 1600 or 800 bpi,

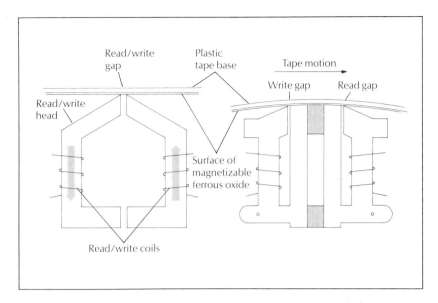

Figure 4–3. Operation of read/write heads

respectively. Yet, a modern disk device can store as much data as several conventional size magnetic tape reels.

Large amounts of data cannot be stored continuously on tape. Retrieval requires that some gaps be allowed for decelerating the tape to a stop and then reaccelerating it up to normal reading speed. Thus, half or more of a tape is usually blank. Still, data equivalent to 100 boxes of punched cards can be stored on a single 2400-foot tape. Yet tape costs only a few percent of the card cost and occupies perhaps 1/100 of the physical volume. In practice, 400-foot tapes are also popular, since small files or programs are often stored with each on a separate tape. Cassette tapes are also used for this purpose.

Magnetic tape is quite cheap per byte of storage capacity. Also, virtually unlimited storage is possible with multiple tapes. The data transfer rate can be rather high, especially when compared to card reading. The major limitation of magnetic tape is that it is inherently a **sequential access storage device**—that is, it can be read and written on only in physical sequence. Thus, average access time can be unacceptably long, depending on the physical locations of requested data. Shorter tapes, and drives with a rapid rewind or read-in-reverse capability, help mitigate this access delay problem somewhat. Still, another class of secondary storage device has gained prominence due to its quick response capability.

DIRECT ACCESS STORAGE DEVICES

To support quick retrieval, other types of storage devices are used. These devices are called **direct access storage devices (DASDs)**. They can perform "direct" retrieval without having to search sequentially through unwanted data. DASDs can retrieve data from anywhere in the file, if they are given the address of the location storing it.

The address dictates the proper positioning of a read/write head so that the desired data is read directly, with a minimum of intervening data. In essence, a DASD can directly retrieve any data stored on it from any random location on the file. Hence such devices are sometimes referred to as **random access storage devices**.

In addition to main memory, which also has direct access capability, three secondary DASDs are depicted in Figures 4-4 to 4-6. They are:

- drum
- disk
- mass storage

Many important data retrieval and processing applications are possible because of direct access storage devices. Airline reservation systems are an early large-scale (and still important) example of rapid-access file processing. Only by directly retrieving up-to-date records from massive seat-inventory files and passenger reservation records can the airlines provide quick, reliable, and convenient passenger booking. DASDs also facilitate instant stock price quotation

Figure 4-4. A drum—a fixed-head, direct access storage device

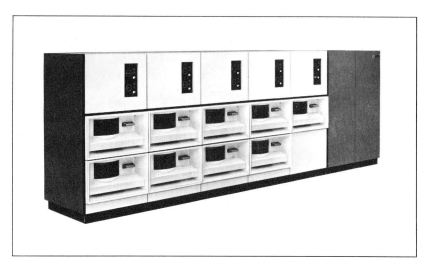

Figure 4–5. A set of disk drives for direct access

Figure 4–6. IBM 3850 Mass Storage System, showing tape cartridges

systems as well as many less glamorous applications. (The methods of organizing data for such processing are discussed in Part 3.)

One advantage of DASDs is their typically large storage capacity. DASD storage capacity is stated as the number of characters the device holds on its magnetic surface(s). This is often 100 million characters or more per device.

Access time—usually expressed as a maximum, minimum, or average—is the delay encountered in physically seeking out the desired data. In addition, the two other measures of storage performance also apply to drums, disks, and mass storage. These are the data transfer rate from the device into the computer and the device's cost per byte of storage capacity.

Drum A **drum** is a polished metal cylinder with a magnetizable surface coating. As the drum is rotated, bits representing data or programs can be read or written. This is done by a row of fixed read/write heads that hover close to the drum's surface. The drum's motion past a read/write head induces electrical currents in it corresponding to the data bits stored on the drum. Similarly, signals sent from the computer can be used to write magnetic fields on the drum's spinning surface.

As with magnetic tape, reading from a drum is nondestructive—that is, data can be read again and again. However, writing on the drum, as with tape, eliminates previously stored data. Thus, either storage medium can be used over and over for new contents, but protections against unintended erasing are advised.

The cylindrical surface of the drum is composed of a number of tracks. These are parallel circles of data stored around the drum's surface. The data bits on each track are stored **serially by bit**, or bit by bit in sequence around the circumference of each drum track. Each track is read or written on by the read/write head fixed in position adjacent to it. Thus, a single head is "on" at any time and it reads several bits in sequence on a single track to compose each separate byte of data. Figure 4-7 represents a drum schematically and cites a typical storage capacity.

The drum has a modest storage capacity because of its limited magnetizable surface area. In compensation, however, the fixed-head-per-track design allows rapid direct access to data. When the computer requests data from a certain drum address (and thus from a certain physical location on the drum), the appropriate read/write head begins to read the track revolving under it. Some **rotational delay**, or **latency**, is usually encountered. This period averages one-half of the drum's revolution time and is the time required to find a particular data item once the read operation begins.

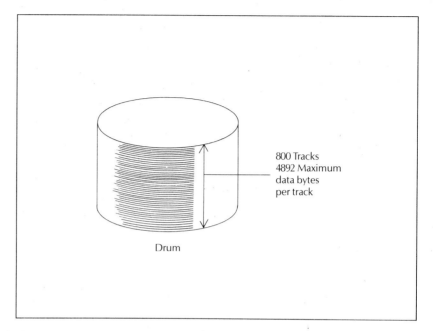

800 Tracks
4892 Maximum
data bytes
per track

Drum

Figure 4-7. Drum DASD schematic

Switching to the proper read/write head is an electronic, nearly instantaneous function. However, rotational delay is significant, even though the drum revolves rapidly (about 50+ revolutions per second). At this speed, latency averages nearly 1/100 of a second, or 10 milliseconds. The computer could process thousands of instructions during this delay. On the other hand, the drum's average access time is still quite fast compared to other DASDs.

If the next desired item happens to be stored in sequence on the same track of the drum, it can be read very quickly. Such data will be the next to rotate under the read/write head that is already switched on. In fact, the full sequential stream of data from a single track can be transferred into the computer in just one revolution.

For example, the IBM Model 2303 drum rotates at around 60 revolutions per second. Therefore, a complete track can be read in about one-sixtieth of a second. Nearly 5000 bytes are stored per track. Consequently, the maximum data transfer rate from the drum to main memory is about 300,000 bytes per second. The average access time, equal approximately to the time for a half rotation, is about 8.6 milliseconds. The storage capacity of the drum's 800 tracks (at about 5000 bytes each) is nearly 4 million bytes.

Read/write heads are fairly expensive. Since one head is adjacent to each track on the drum's surface, drum devices are also expensive. Furthermore, the drum cylinder may not be removed from its cabinet; it stays mounted on its drive unit and is not interchangeable as are tapes and most disks. Cost per byte of storage is lower than for main memory but high relative to other direct access storage devices. (The capabilities of each of these devices are summarized in Table 4.1 at the end of this chapter.)

Disk   **Disk packs**, or **disks**, are another direct access storage medium. They consist of several metal plates, or disks, which have magnetizable surfaces and are fixed onto a common spindle. Disk packs come in various standard sizes, with 11 plates per pack being most common. Both surfaces of each disk are magnetizable and provide storage capacity. To minimize the effects of dust particles that can cause storage or reading errors, disk packs are kept in plastic containers when stored. As further protection, the top and bottom surfaces of the pack are not used. A pack with 11 disk plates therefore has 20 inside recording surfaces.

A disk pack and its container are shown in Figure 4–8. The disk pack must be mounted on a **disk drive** for reading or writing under computer control. Some disk drives have nonremovable disk packs. Usually, however, any pack of the proper size can be mounted on a particular drive. The drive rotates the disk pack continuously, ready for accessing. It contains one read/write head for each recording surface. These heads are designed to hover on air cushions very close to their respective disk surfaces. They are fixed at the end of movable **access arms** that move back and forth in unison between the disks. Thus, the read/write heads can be positioned as a group over any desired portion of the rotating disks' surfaces. However, only one of these read/write heads is actually in use at any instant. Figure 4–9 illustrates a drive's read/write heads mounted on access arms.

Each disk surface is composed of concentric tracks on which data are recorded. Unlike the grooves on a long-playing record, disk tracks do not spiral continuously into each other. They are concentric. A single read/write head can access an entire track without moving—by having the disk rotate past it. To read a different track, the read/write head must be repositioned to the proper location. All the read/write heads move together as a group.

The same amount of data is stored on each track of a disk pack, even though the outside tracks have a longer circumference. Data are simply proportioned more sparsely on the outer tracks. Thus, the angular sweep of a particular data item is constant, regardless of whether it is

Figure 4-8. Changing a disk pack on one of four disk drives

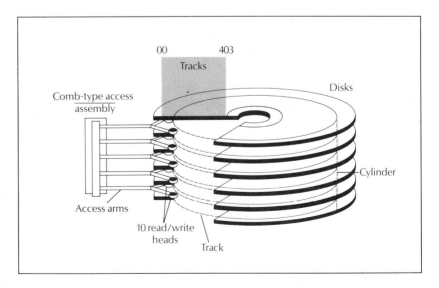

Figure 4-9. Diagram of disk pack showing retrieval concepts

stored on a longer outside track or on a track closer to the disk's center. This simplifies reading and writing since all the tracks have the same data transfer rate.

Some permanently mounted disks are called **fixed head per track**. That is, they have a separate read/write head for every track on each disk surface. This configuration eliminates the need for repositioning a head over the desired track. Thus, the average time required to access data is reduced in comparison to that of **moving-head disks**.

Alternately, some disk drives are designed with more than one movable read/write head per surface. These multiple-head-per-surface designs attempt to shorten rather than eliminate head movement delay. For example, different heads might traverse different sets of tracks, thereby reducing the average span an individual head travels. Another design sets multiple heads at angles around the disk's perimeter, thereby reducing the average rotational delay encountered when using the appropriate head. However, since read/write heads are expensive components, the most widely used disk drives have a single movable head per disk surface.

Data on a particular disk pack is accessed when a computer command addresses some track on one of its surfaces. The drive's read/write heads are positioned to the designated track and the right one is switched on. The desired data are thus accessed directly by reading that track until the desired data rotates around and is read. The time to access data stored on a disk is the sum of:

- disk drive selection time (nearly instantaneous)
- read/write head movement time to specified track
- read/write head switch time (nearly instantaneous)
- latency or rotational delay until the desired data is read

A moving-head disk encounters an extra delay in average access time compared with drum devices—read/write head movement time. The disk drive's read/write heads are generally mounted on a connected group of access arms. As these heads move in and out together, not only is the average access time longer than that for drum, but it is also highly variable. It depends significantly on the physical relationships of the storage locations being accessed. For example, if the next data item to be read resides on the same track, head movement delay is eliminated; if it does not, retrieval is delayed because the head must be moved. Therefore, the way data files are organized on disk storage can greatly affect the time and economics of retrieval.

For convenience in referencing, the tracks on each surface are numbered. The outside track is generally designated as 000; numbers increase for inner circles. For example, the disk drive can read the entire sequence of data stored on track 150 of some surface during one disk pack revolution. Then it can quickly switch to another read/write head and read another full track of data from track 150 on that other surface. It is therefore best to organize a sequence of data consecutively on one track of one surface and to continue it on the same track number of the remaining surfaces.

A **cylinder** is the set of all tracks with the same number. Thus, a cylinder consists of all similarly located tracks, one for each surface. These tracks form an imaginary cylinder passing vertically through the disk pack. The cylinder concept is important because, as we have seen, an entire cylinder can be read by successively switching to another head after each disk revolution without the delay of head movement. The disk has as many cylinders as it has tracks on each surface.

Access time is greatly affected by the physical relationship between the disk storage location just read and the next location to be read. The fastest access to the next item occurs if it lies on the same surface and same track, and is just behind the first data item as the disk rotates. Retrieval can then occur at the disk's maximum transfer rate. Transfer rates are determined by multiplying the number of bytes stored per track times the number of tracks read per second. The maximum number of tracks readable per second equals the number of disk revolutions per second. Thus, the data transfer rate from a disk depends on its storage density and rotational speed. Typical maximum data transfer rates range from 156,000 to 885,000 characters per second, depending on the disk drive.

In terms of computer processing speed, a significant time delay is encountered in jumping from cylinder to cylinder for data retrieval or writing. The disk drive's ability to reposition its access arms quickly varies among disk models.

Average disk access time—including some delay for this head movement time and some for rotational latency—usually ranges from 20 to 100 milliseconds. For most disk devices, however, there is a large contrast between their minimum and maximum access times. For example, a device might require only 1 millisecond to read a record in sequence on the same track. By contrast, 100 milliseconds might be required to read a record from some distant cylinder. Thus, proper organization of data on disks is crucial for efficiency.

The disk's capacity for data storage, of course, varies with the number of tracks per surface and surfaces per pack as well as the pack's recording density. For example, a standard pack with 11 disks has 20 inside recording surfaces. Data is recorded serially by bit on each individual track. Some tracks are reserved for automatically controlled backup to overcome dust particles, scratches, or other imperfections that might cause storage errors. There are some 10,000 usable tracks on the entire pack. It can store nearly 10,000 bytes per track. Thus, it has a capacity of about 100 million bytes in all.

A disk pack's cost per byte is about 10 times as much as for magnetic tape. This is an important difference while data is being stored on the shelf. However, both tapes and disks must be mounted on their respective drive units to be available for processing. Since these drive units are comparable in cost (typically, $20,000) and far exceed the cost of the pack or tape, on-line storage cost per byte is roughly comparable for disk and tape.

Average access time for disk is superior to tape. Maximum transfer rates from disk are usually also faster than from tape. However, a disk's access time is about 10 times longer than for a drum and very much longer than for main memory.

Disk packs often have multiple drive units (shown in Figure 4–8). A single control unit provides a standard interface to a high-speed channel. This in turn communicates with the CPU. Such an array of associated disk packs may have a storage capacity of hundreds of millions of bytes. Yet, access to any byte can still be had within about 1/10 of a second or less. Thus, disk packs have increasingly replaced magnetic tapes in many types of applications. And, like tape cassettes, the disk medium has also been made available in small capacity, easily handled sizes. Such **diskettes** are often used in data entry (discussed in the next chapter) as well as for data storage.

Mass Storage   A new hybrid of magnetic tape and magnetic disk has been developed in recent years. Typically called **mass storage**, it is designed to provide vast storage capacity and a relatively quick response time. It is a hybrid because tape and disk capabilities are combined to give the desired performance at acceptably low cost. The IBM 3850 Mass Storage System, a device using this storage concept, was first delivered to users in 1976. It can store up to 472 *billion* characters on line (see Figure 4–6).

In this device, data are stored on magnetic tape of a special cartridge size. These tape cartridges fill honeycomb-like pockets in an automatically accessed storage rack. Effectively, then, the data are stored on tape with low on-the-shelf costs. But relatively fast access is provided by the automatic cartridge accessing unit. Once fetched, the tape's content is read onto disk in only a matter of seconds. Once stored on disk, of course, the data can be retrieved directly by the user. Therefore, the overall access time includes the steps of:

- Determining the tape cartridge storing the requested data
- Physically selecting and fetching the correct tape cartridge
- Mounting the cartridge on the reader and copying it onto disk
- Directly accessing the sought data, now that it is stored on disk

For the IBM 3850, the average access time for these steps is about 7 seconds. This gives this device the capability of an **automated tape library**. That is, data are stored in large quantity, yet cheaply, on tape. Retrieval is automatic, direct, and relatively fast.

MICROFILM   Another technique for data storage involves using **microfilm**. This medium consists of miniaturized photographic images. Its advantage lies in the vast amount of data (including graphics) that can be stored compactly. Also, **computer output microfilm (COM)** devices can output computer results onto microfilm much faster than printers can output onto paper. Microfilm's disadvantage is that retrieval of microfilmed data is awkward. Mechanical devices and human readers usually have to retrieve any microfilmed output. Nonetheless, this technique is economical for storing lengthy and infrequently accessed outputs. This type of application is often called **archival storage**.

PUNCHED CARDS,   **Punched cards** of various sizes and **paper tapes** and **tags** are other
TAPES, AND TAGS   storage media. Their tangibility, easily read printing, and low cost per physical unit make them convenient for small volumes of data that require some human handling. Thus, programs in the process of being debugged, small sets of data, and retail inventory control records might rely on punched paper cards, tapes, and tags. When read by an appropriate reading device, such stored data is available for computer processing. The constraints of these media stem from their limited storage capacity; comparative bulk per unit of stored data; slow reading speeds; and their susceptibility to being folded, spindled, or mutilated.

SUMMARY   This chapter has discussed a hierarchy of devices for data storage. Primary storage or main memory is accessible to the CPU directly and nearly instantaneously. Secondary storage devices take longer to access but offer advantages of lower cost per byte and large capacities with acceptable access times and data transfer rates to main memory. In particular, magnetic tape is convenient for storing a sequence of data items. Direct access storage devices (DASDs), in contrast, can retrieve stored data rapidly and in any sequence. Drums, disks, and mass storage were explained and compared. Finally, microfilm and paper media for data storage were briefly discussed. A summary comparison of this hierarchy of storage devices and their retrieval performance is presented in Table 4.1 on the facing page.

TABLE 4.1 TYPICAL STORAGE HARDWARE AND ITS RETRIEVAL PERFORMANCE—1978

Storage Device	Storage Cost/ Kb-Year[a]	Average Access Time	Maximum Transfer Rate	Typical Storage Capacity	Cost/Kb Retrieved & Read	
					1st Kb[b]	Next Kb[c]
Semiconductor memory	$ 50	.5 μ sec	8000+ Kb/sec	500 Kb	.001¢	.001¢
Core memory	$100	1 μ sec	4000 Kb/sec	500 Kb	.001¢	.001¢
Drum	$ 1	8 ms	300 Kb/sec	4 Mb	.1¢	.03¢
Disk-3330 online	10¢	30 ms	806 Kb/sec	800 Mb	.2¢	.01¢
Disk Pack-3330 offline	.3¢	3 min	—	100 Mb/pack	—	—
Mass Storage-3850	.01¢	7 sec	806 Kb/sec	10,000 Mb	.3¢	.01¢
Tape online	10¢	1 min	320 Kb/sec	10 Mb	$1	.02¢
Tape offline	.01¢	3 min	—	10 Mb/tape	—	—
Microfilm off line	.01¢	3 min	—	open-ended	—	—
Punched cards	2¢	1 min	1 Kb/sec	80 char/card	3¢	3¢
Ordinary paper	2¢	1 min	—	1000 char/page	—	—

[a] Cost is the annual rental (including maintenance) of each storage device per Kb (Kilo-byte, or 1000 characters of data) or per Mb (megabyte, or 1,000,000 characters).
[b] Cost includes medium-sized processor and related hardware for the time to retrieve 1 Kb on *inquiry*.
[c] Cost includes hardware, as above, and illustrates the variable costs to retrieve the next 1 Kb.

CONCEPTS

cost per byte
storage capacity
average access time
data transfer rate
hierarchy of
   storage devices
primary storage
megabyte
core memory
core plane
semiconductor
   memory
metal-oxide
   semiconductor (MOS)
bipolar semiconductor
laser
hologram
charged coupled
   device

bubble memory
secondary storage
magnetic tape
recording channel
track
bytes per inch (bpi)
tape drive
read/write head
recording density
sequential access
   storage device
direct access storage
   device (DASD)
random access storage
   device
drum
serially by bit
rotational delay
latency

disk pack
disk
disk drive
access arm
fixed head
   per track
moving-head disk
cylinder
diskette
mass storage
automated tape
   library
microfilm
computer output
   microfilm (COM)
archival storage
punched card
paper tape
paper tag

QUESTIONS

1. What are four important measures of performance for a data storage device?
2. Why must computer users become aware of the several major types of devices for data storage and retrieval?
3. Compare the capabilities of a CPU interacting with main memory to those of a person handling data with a pencil and scratch pad.
4. Magnetic tape drives represent a declining proportion of computer hardware expenditures. Why?
5. When is drum storage preferable to moving-head disk storage?
6. A drum and fixed-head disk are logically similar. Explain.
7. What causes the wide variations in data access time when a moving-head disk device is used?

8. Discuss why disks currently are more broadly accepted than computer output microfilm techniques.

9. Calculate the number of characters of data about each person on earth that could be stored on an IBM 3850. What might it cost to gather and enter all this data? Is there risk to individual privacy due to such a capability? What will prevent this possibility from happening?

10. When are paper data storage media preferable?

11. Report on the performance of some newly announced storage device.

Chapter Five

**Input/Output
Methods and
Devices**

5

In any sizable organization, no one knows everything firsthand. Instead, the information system is relied on for data about significant events, such as a sales transaction or an inquiry about a scheduled delivery date. Chapters 3 and 4 discussed the processing and storage aspects of information systems. This chapter deals with computer input/output methods and devices.

Input/output deserves special attention for three reasons. I/O is a high-volume, repetitive, time-consuming, and costly task. All data in the system stems from some input operation and all results stored or displayed involve output. The number of input characters and displayed reports often surprises the average user. Yet, unfortunately, many systems specialists and managers have mentally categorized I/O tasks as ones to be endured rather than evaluated.

Second, it is impossible for a computer-based system to be better than its I/O procedures. The activities of data collection and conversion to machine-readable format are frequently the weak links in a computer system because they are widely dispersed and often taken for granted. Data entry is, in fact, the largest source of error in ongoing systems.

Third, in the past several years, new I/O methods and devices have become available. This increases user options—and complicates choice, as well.

This chapter surveys such I/O equipment. It also discusses techniques for improving three crucial measures of data entry performance: costs, errors, and delays. Then display methods are reviewed. Attention is paid to user needs and to techniques for helping the user understand the processed information.

OVERVIEW OF DATA COLLECTION AND ENTRY   When evaluating an existing system or designing a new one, it is useful to determine the volume of input data and to set a tolerable error rate. When this is done, a study of alternative schemes for data collection and entry can be made. These steps assure that the input portion of the system receives its proper due, even though it is less glamorous than the hardware or software aspects.

A very useful diagnostic technique for studying data collection and entry procedures is to classify each step in the process as being either

- **sensing**
- **recording**
- **converting**

Sensing here means the initial measurement of something to be computer processed. This is often a human function. *Recording* involves the capturing of the data in more or less permanent form, for example, filling out a sales receipt. *Converting* is any further transformation of this recorded data and is usually done to permit input to a computer.

In this classification scheme, data items are sensed and recorded only once. Subsequent procedures are conversions. Recording what has been sensed allows it to be used later. Conversion steps change the form of data but do not (hopefully) alter its content. One or more conversions often occur in getting data into machine-readable form. (Any step that intentionally alters data content is actually a data processing step and should not be classified as data conversion.)

Once the data collection and entry process has been dissected into a sequence of sensing, recording, and converting steps, the procedure's fixed and variable costs should be calculated. Some costs are constant regardless of the volume of data; others are incurred for each data entry transaction. As a general rule, each conversion step increases the total cost, introduces some probability of error, and causes delays.

This diagnostic approach can be illustrated by applying it to a hypothetical data entry system for a library. In this system, the spine of each library book has been carefully labeled with pertinent code numbers. To check out books, a librarian stamps each one with the appropriate due date and then stacks them on end next to the borrower's library card. The labeled ends of the books are then photographed with the user's card. With the books and the card in this position, the pertinent data are *sensed* by a camera and *recorded* on film. Subsequently, this data is *converted* by developing the film, projecting it on a screen, and then keypunching the appropriate data items onto cards. Table 5.1 applies the diagnostic technique to this system.

Notice that the system has three cascading conversions steps. Also, the costs of identifying the books and the checkout librarian's salary

TABLE 5.1   ANALYSIS OF FILM-BASED LIBRARY DATA ENTRY SYSTEM

Step	Activity	Fixed Cost	Variable Cost
Snap picture	Sense	Camera	
Record on film	Record		Film
Develop film	Convert		Developing
Project image	Convert	Projector	
Keypunch	Convert	Keypunch	Salary and cards

are omitted, since they would probably be required by any data entry procedure. This system has benefits over directly keypunching the data at the checkout desk: it reduces library noise and permits scheduling to eliminate keypunching lulls and queuing at peak demand periods. However, while this system appears to be highly automated, it is actually ill conceived. Its many data conversion steps generate needless costs, errors, and delays.

A better system might avoid the repetitive conversions and their high variable costs. Suppose, for example, that the library used a dual-badge (that is, like a credit card) reader that was capable of reading and recording data from the book's and the borrower's badges. This would allow immediate data capture at the source of the transaction. The diagnostic approach is applied to this system in Table 5.2.

Notice that the reader is the only fixed cost. It is assumed that the library user needs an identity card in any event. Also, creating the book badge is included in the book labeling procedure, in lieu of a book card. The only variable cost in the badge-reader system is the minimal expense for punched cards. In fact, a more suitable storage medium might be a reusable tape cassette or diskette, thus eliminating the punched cards, or direct entry to the computer processor.

In summary, data collection and entry activities should be classified as *sense*, *record*, or *convert*, and the costs associated with each step should be analyzed for fixed and variable components. This approach permits systems analysts to compare alternatives and avoid inappropriate designs. As a general rule, it is advisable to bring data entry as close to the original source of the data as possible and to minimize conversion steps.

TABLE 5.2   ANALYSIS OF BADGE-READER LIBRARY DATA ENTRY SYSTEM

Step	Activity	Fixed Cost	Variable Cost
Read badges	Sense	Reader	
Record data on punched cards	Record		Cards

KEYED DATA ENTRY   One anomaly of modern computer systems is that, despite instruction execution times measured in nanoseconds, most data preparation proceeds with the glacial slowness of a manual **keypunch** operation, shown in Figure 5–1. The problem of devising an efficient input system is often synonymous with the problem of finding an alternative to keypunching. The fact that some 500,000 card punch machines are currently in use stands as mute testimony to this technique's durability and to the high cost of data preparation.

In 1880, there were 54 million people in the United States. Not surprisingly, with manual procedures it took a veritable army of clerical personnel 7 years to tabulate that year's census data. Herman Hollerith had an idea that it would help the 1890 census tabulation if the data could be recorded on machine-readable punched cards. Using old mint equipment that moved paper over printing plates, Hollerith devised his first punched-card tabulating machine in 1888. This concept proved successful when Hollerith's machine helped tabulate the 1890 census in one-third the time (still years, however) that would have been required to do the job manually.

In 1896, Hollerith formed the Tabulating Machine Company to manufacture and sell his successful new machines. Fifteen years later, he joined forces with Thomas Watson, Sr., and formed the Computing, Tabulating, and Recording Company, which later became the International Business Machine Corporation (IBM). One of their major products introduced in 1914 was the keypunch. Since then, electromechanical operations have been improved. For example, the Model 129 keypunch shown in Figure 5–1 has buffer storage and card formatting features. And today's principal data entry device is still a keyboard, and cards are still a frequent storage media. They require a **card reader** for input of their content into the CPU.

Like typing, the speed and accuracy of a keyboard operator varies with the individual. Extremely fast operators can average 16,000 characters per hour. According to the National Bureau of Standards, a typical operator averages about 7500 characters per hour. Data conversion speeds also depend on the format of the source document; the number of alphabetic, numeric, and special symbols in the data; the number of characters per record; and so forth. However, the main constraint is the speed limit of the human operator. Also, the operator costs more: a typical salary is $700 per month; an average rental figure for a keyboard device is approximately $100 per month.

A **verify** operation consists of giving the keyed data, together with the underlying source documents, to another operator who rekeys the same data on a **verifier**. The verifier reads each previously entered character to determine whether the second operator struck the same key.

Figure 5–1. IBM Model 129 keypunch

(If the original operator made a keystroke error, it is unlikely that the verifying operator will make the identical error.) When the second operator's character does not match the existing one, a discrepancy is indicated by notching the card, locking the keyboard, or providing some other signal. The error, which could be in the verification or the original punching, is then resolved and corrected. Such key verification tends to ensure the accuracy of data entry but practically doubles cost. Furthermore, an error in sensing or recording data on the source document cannot be detected by verification.

KEY-TO-. . . DEVICES A host of data entry devices can now replace traditional keypunching. Many involve keying data onto a storage medium other than a punched card. These include:

- key to cassette
- key to tape

- key to diskette
- key to disk
- online data entry

The advantages claimed for these devices are:

1. *Elimination of punched cards.* Storing data on magnetic recording surfaces drastically reduces the need for card handling and storage space. For example, storing data on tape decreases storage volume up to a hundredfold. However, for small files or programs, storage space may be no problem and cards can also be read by people whereas magnetic media cannot. In terms of cost, a keypunch can consume 400,000 cards per year, or several hundred dollars in variable expense. Of course, tape or another storage medium will also cost, but magnetic media are reusable.

2. *Elimination of card-to-tape or card-to-disk conversions.* By recording data initially on tape for input to a tape-oriented system, a costly card-to-tape conversion step can be bypassed. However, this benefit is somewhat illusory. Consider, for example, a keytape operator who enters 8000 characters per hour. At a recording density of 800 characters per inch (exclusive of interrecord gaps), 10 inches of recorded tape per hour are produced. Putting this small amount of data on a high-speed tape drive capable of reading at 200 inches of tape *per second* is a mismatch. To overcome this problem, keytape output is *pooled* to accumulate meaningful amounts of computer input. This operation requires an additional special-purpose device, called a **data-pooler**.

3. *Faster data preparation.* A keyboard operator can transcribe data only as fast as his or her fingers can strike the keys. However, the key-to-. . . systems can skip or duplicate fields faster than card punches. Also, operator-detected errors can be corrected faster by backspacing, which erases, and rekeying. Punched cards can't be erased, and duplication takes time and is itself prone to error. However, recent keypunch designs also store and display keystroked results before punching. This allows easy error correction.

4. *Versatile equipment.* The conventional keypunch is constrained by its recording medium—the 80-column (or 96-column) card. Devices that use magnetic storage on tape or disk allow more versatile data formatting. Also, a separate machine for key verifying is not necessary as in the case with many card punches. Instead, these devices can be switched to a comparison mode, rather than encoding, and thus can be used for verification.

5. *Low noise.* Keypunches are noisy, whereas a magnetic device does not punch a hole and makes no noise. In fact, some early

machines were made absolutely silent, but it was soon discovered that some feedback noise helps an operator to type efficiently. After much work, some vendors now claim "optimal" noise and increased operator satisfaction.

The inherent shortcoming of the key-to- . . . devices is that they merely replace the storage medium, not the act of manual keying. Data entry speeds and error rates are still dictated by operator proficiency, although throughput may increase. In the final analysis, the efficiency of any data collection and entry procedure depends on its cost per unit, its error rate, and on the time lag it may cause.

Key to Tape   **Key-to-tape** devices began to grow in popularity during the mid-1960s. Several firms now make key-to-tape data recorders. Typically, each keyboard records directly on a magnetic tape reel. These stand-alone devices rent for about $200 per month per key station. A system of pooled key entry stations is shown in Figure 5–2. This configuration is

Figure 5–2. Eight-station Intelligent Key Entry System with CRTs for visual data verification

less expensive per station because it centralizes the recording hardware. Individual I/O terminals can also be equipped with cassette tape data recording, as shown in Figure 5–3.

Key to Disk   A multiple-station **key-to-disk** configuration typically shares a centralized disk storage device controlled by a minicomputer. Complex pooling, formatting, and entering fixed data fields are automatically possible with this degree of logic and direct-access storage. Each key station consists of a keyboard and a CRT (cathode-ray tube) display that the operator uses for visual verification. Eight key stations with related equipment rent for about $1000 per month.

Another data recording medium can be used for storing each key station's results. It is a small, flexible magnetic disk called a **diskette** or **floppy disk**. One example of this is the IBM 3740 data entry station. The operator inserts a diskette into a slot and enters data via a typewriter-like keyboard. Data items are visually displayed on a screen for verification and are then recorded on the diskette. Each 8 inch in

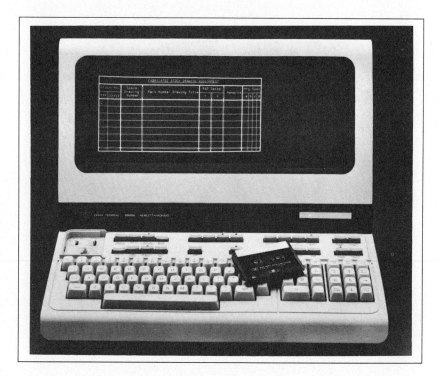

Figure 5–3.   I/O terminal with cassette tape for data recording

diameter diskette stores several hundred thousand characters. It is packaged in plastic with a cutout slot for read/write head access and is easily handled, filed, or mailed.

Key to Processor   **Online data entry** means input keyed directly to a computer processor, as shown in Figure 5–4. When a small, local processor is part of this input device, it is often called an **intelligent terminal**. Online entry makes substantial logic available to the data entry operator. Such instantaneous feedback can be used, for example, to guide a complex transaction or to spot likely errors.

Entering data directly from the source means that the terminal operator probably understands the data, which tends to reduce errors. Responsibility for errors may be pinpointed as well, a further incentive

Figure 5–4.   Online data entry

for producing quality input. And source data entry eliminates the costs, errors, and delays of conversion steps.

One example of an online data entry device is the **point-of-sale (POS) terminal**. Such a device captures sales transaction data at its source, as shown in Figure 5-5. For example, at each sale, a credit card can be verified on line and the inventory, cash-on-hand, receivables, and commissions lists can be updated instantly. Sometimes, this data may not be needed immediately and may instead be recorded on a self-contained tape cassette, which is automatically read and posted at the end of the day. In either case, such a system makes accurate and timely information available to store management.

OPTICAL SCANNING   Given the high labor content involved in keyed data entry, it is apparent that more automated techniques could be beneficial. **Optical scanning** is the automatic converting of data into a machine-usable form by visual pattern detection techniques. An optical scanning de-

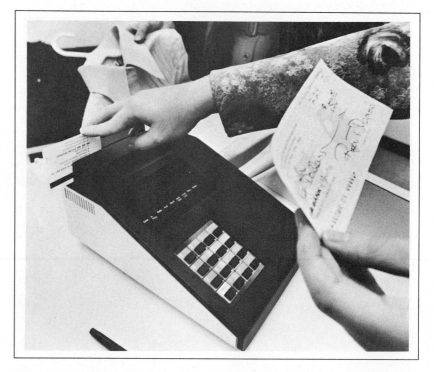

Figure 5-5. POS terminal, including check verification feature

vice can "read" certain types and shapes of marks, characters, and special symbols by using electric mark sensors and photocells to detect darkness or reflectance levels. It notes the pattern and compares it with a set of acceptable patterns. The appropriate character is then stored on a computer-readable medium such as tape or is entered directly to a processor. The rejection rate due to unidentified characters varies with the quality of the input forms and their marks, but is usually a few percent of the documents read.

Magnetic Ink Character Readers (MICR)

Widely used by the banking industry for processing more than 27 billion checks per year, **MICR** is one standard method for data entry via optical scanning. In this case, the character set is limited to 10 digit symbols and four banking-related special symbols, as shown in Figures 5-6 and 5-7. MICR equipment typically rejects only a few percent of the checks fed to it and enables banks to process checks economically. An MICR check reader and sorter is depicted in Figure 5-8.

Optical Mark Readers (OMR)

An **OMR** device optically senses and records data on forms and converts it to machine-readable format. Since the device also verifies itself, the OMR process can be compared to the combined process of keying and verifying, but it requires much less labor (except for the form filler's time). OMR forms are relatively expensive and must be printed within exacting tolerances so the marks will be located over

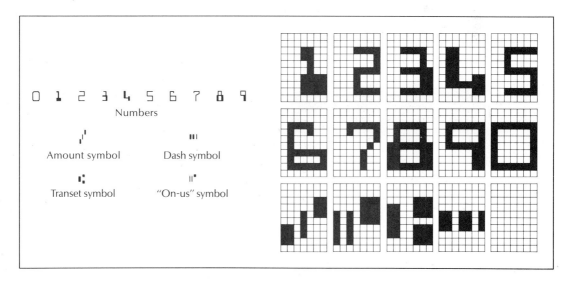

Figure 5-6.   Magnetic ink character set

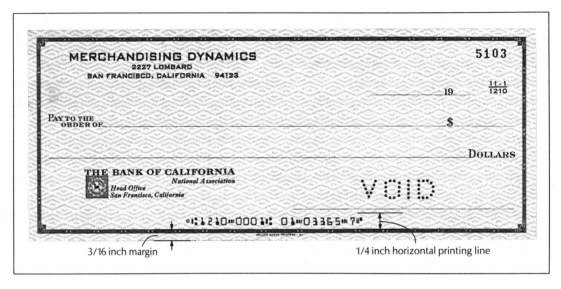

Figure 5-7. Typical check document with preprinted data

Figure 5-8. IBM Model 1419 magnetic ink character reader and sorter

the appropriate optical sensors when read. A typical 8½ × 11-inch OMR form has places for 1280 marks—each corresponding to an optical sensor position. The layout design of an OMR form is up to the user's ingenuity.

Optical Character Readers (OCR)

There are a variety of character readers that optically read special character sets. One application is in the credit-card industry. Here they convert specially printed characters into punches on the same card. Conventional devices can then read the punched holes.

OCR readers are very fast. These self-punch card readers can, for example, process up to 500 cards per minute. With 15 characters per card, the conversion speed is 15 times 500, or 7500 characters per minute. Thus, this OCR reader is equivalent to about 60 keypunch operators, yet it costs only about three times an operator's salary.

Special-font and multifont character readers similarly provide great reductions in the cost per unit of data entry versus keypunching. The break-even volume depends on the specific characteristics of the application but, in general, economic benefits can be attained if there are large volumes of standardized data. Some people feel the ultimate data entry breakthrough will be OCR using hand-printed symbols. These machines are also available, but the user must observe the handwriting rules shown in Figure 5–9. Furthermore, slow human printing speed may itself be the major cost constraint.

The function of an optical scanning device is to convert recorded data to a standard computer-readable format on a traditional storage medium. Such a device generally costs more than keying equipment, but it can handle large volumes and bypass manual keying operations. An OCR can typically convert several hundred characters per second, whereas the manual keying rate is about two characters per second. Its error rates and elapsed time delays are also usually favorable. Thus, optical scanning is a useful data entry technique for high-volume standardized operations.

DIRECT SENSING

Direct sensing of data means that the computer-based system itself perceives and records relevant facts about particular events. In effect, data collection and entry are automated. This tends to produce complete, accurate data with a minimum of variable costs, personnel, and data entry delays. However, such benefits should be compared to the fixed costs of implementing the direct sensing hardware and procedures.

Direct sensing is common in laboratory and scientific work. Satellites, for example, continually sense various environmental data and

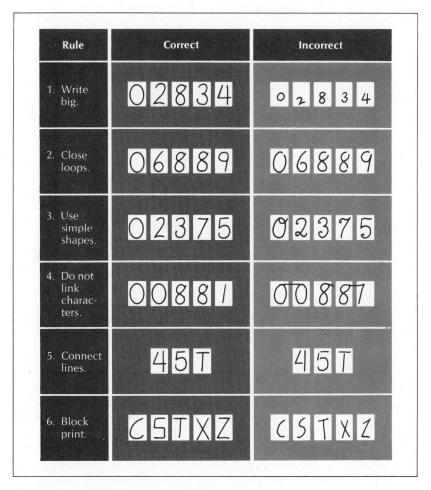

Figure 5–9. Handwriting rules for optical character reading

automatically telemeter it to earth for computer analysis. Figure 5–10 shows the Martian landscape as transmitted by such a satellite. The digital data describing this scene was computer processed to add contrast, thereby enabling scientists to observe otherwise invisible details.

Closer to home, direct sensing is now incorporated in many grocery store and retail checkout stations. One such product tag reader is shown in Figure 5–11. Direct sensing may also monitor and read utility meters or even replace them. Other direct sensing systems are used in process control, numerically controlled machining, badge-activated

Figure 5-10. Computer retouched photo of Mars, highlighting its surface terrain, developed by processing data transmitted across 140 million miles of space.

access to secured areas, and intensive-care patient monitoring. Specialized minicomputers or microprocessors are often at the heart of direct sensing systems. The computer-readable data they generate may be communicated to larger computers for further processing or storage.

COST AND ERROR CONTROL

Three ways to reduce the costs of data entry and error control are:

- increase personnel efficiency
- reduce volume
- add mechanization

Since data preparation involves well-defined activities, it is subject to classical industrial engineering techniques for increasing task efficiency. Specialization, balanced workloads, proper work layout and flow, streamlined procedures, and better forms can all contribute to greater personnel productivity.

Often, the volume of data entry can be reduced. Any data items with an expected value less than their cost should not be collected at all. Fixed data items may be generated automatically. Also, efficient sampling plans may be substituted for more comprehensive data collec-

Figure 5-11. Retail POS terminal with direct sensing capability

tion. Sampling can be used to test product quality and to determine consumer preferences. Data can often be collected at a single point and communicated to other parts of the system, thereby reducing duplicated data.

Classifying and coding data can also greatly reduce the number of characters needed to represent the same data content. Such **data classification** limits the future content of the recorded data, however. Retrieval is also limited by the classification categories. (Of course, all recording of data imposes some degree of classification on the underlying events.)

When justified by sufficient volume, automatic devices can significantly reduce data entry costs. It may even become economically feasible to collect more detailed data. A summary of data collection technologies and their representative costs and error rates is presented in Table 5.3.

There are two facets of error control—*prevention* and *detection*. The key to preventing errors is to design the system to report when they arise and to assign responsibility for them. The problem may be with personnel (such as lack of training or poor motivation), with equipment (such as malfunctions or poor human-factor design), or with procedures (such as complicated steps or a poor sequence). Mechanized systems typically have much lower error rates than manual systems. For example, users of optical scanners have reported accuracy improvements of a factor of 100 or more.

The second facet of error control is detecting errors. Some form of data **redundancy** is the typical method. Redundancy refers to the degree of extra information contained in a message or processing step. Although no amount of redundancy can guarantee detecting all errors, the probability of error can be made as small as desired—at a cost. Common forms of redundancy are *duplication*, such as verification of keypunched data or retransmission of a message; and *individual data field redundancy*, such as with a check digit.

TABLE 5.3 DATA COLLECTION AND CONVERSION COSTS AND ERROR RATES

Technology	Representative Cost per Thousand Characters	Typical Undetected Errors per Thousand Characters
Handwriting	$1	1
Key to paper/card/ tape/disk/processor	$ .50	2
Optical scanning	$ .05	.1
Direct sensing	$ .01	.01

A **check digit** is a redundant character appended to a data field to ensure against undetected errors. It is verified by a standard procedure each time the data item is processed. For example, a credit card number's last digit is often derived by some arithmetic involving the other account number digits. This final digit probably will not "check" if any digit of the number has been changed. Upon entry into the system, the proper check digit can be computed and compared to the actual one. Accuracy is assumed if these two digits check; otherwise, an error has been committed.

Predicting reasonable values for data items is also useful in determining whether the data items entered into the system are what they should be. Data outside certain limits are assumed to have a high probability of error. Thus, a reasonableness check might trigger a manual investigation of data accuracy. This technique can be used for inventory withdrawals, amounts on a payroll check, and so forth.

INPUT SYSTEMS Input systems improve if costs are lowered at constant quality, if error levels or consequences are reduced at constant cost, or if data preparation delays are curtailed when quick information has extra value. Thus, the goals of input systems are doing the job while reducing system costs, errors, and delays. The following design guidelines frequently help to achieve these objectives:

1. Collect and convert only those data items that have an expected value greater than their cost.
2. Diagnose alternative data collection and entry procedures according to their steps of *sense*, *record*, or *convert*, and according to each step's fixed and variable costs.
3. Reduce data entry volume via sampling, coding, or prerecording fixed data items. A computer-prepared punched card is frequently used as a **turnaround document**. This accompanies a transaction and contains most or all of the data pertinent to it. The punched card accompanying your telephone bill is an example of such prerecorded data that, when returned with your check, reduces subsequent manual data entry.
4. Avoid data conversions by capturing data in a machine-readable form near its source.
5. Validate data, when justified, by redundant entry, check digits and fields; data format validation, and/or reasonableness confirmations.

6. Control source documents with labels, routing slips, transmittal logs, or similar orderly procedures.
7. Analyze the likely types of errors and their consequences and design the system to report error types and rates.
8. Assign responsibility for errors and establish procedures for their detection and correction.
9. Design forms, procedures, and working conditions that foster speed and accuracy.
10. Consider a lower cost, higher speed technology when data volume and standardized inputs warrant one.

OVERVIEW OF DATA DISPLAY

Data display is the final link in the input-processing-output cycle. Traditionally, computer outputs have been provided by high-speed printers located at the computer installation. However, terminals can also provide visual, audio, or printed outputs. Such low-cost devices can justify direct delivery of computer output, even to low-volume users. Coupled to a computer via data communications, these display devices allow computer access from remote locations.

The usefulness of computers increases when human interaction with them is simplified. Accordingly, several output methods have been developed. Probably the most common is the **printout**. This form of output has been familiar to paper users for several centuries since printing began. Thus, it seems natural that most computer-processed information is recorded as printed matter on paper. The 11 × 14⅞ inch computer printout is now ubiquitous, although reports can also be printed on many different sizes of paper. (The various types and speeds of printers will be discussed later.)

A second family of devices for data display consists of terminals. Unlike printers, these often serve as both input and output devices, are typically of low capacity, and are located remotely from the computer. Terminals may provide paper (or **hard copy**) output and/or a visual display.

Two additional classes of output methods (also discussed later) are **audio response**, which gives the user an intelligible voicelike signal, and **computer output microfilm (COM)**, a compact photographic display technique.

The critical performance factor for output devices is their cost per character. In turn, this depends on three factors:

- display rate
- cost
- utilization rate

There is a wide range of device display rates and costs, and it is important to match capacity with need. Striving for high utilization must contend with the effects of peak loads of output. Thus, a low-volume user might do well with a Teletype terminal printing 10 characters per second even though it would be costly per character compared to a fully utilized high-speed printer. A relative comparison of this issue provides a useful overview. As Table 5.4 shows, the relative cost of output decreases by using higher speed devices, if the demand generates a high utilization rate.

The medium desired for data display is also a factor in selecting one device instead of another. Paper, as we noted, has historically been most popular. It can be preprinted with fixed information, such as company name, address, phone, and logo, plus data titles and column headings. Color can be used to highlight content. It provides a permanent copy, and may also provide carbon or carbonless extra copies. It is easily storable, but must be manually handled for printing setup, dispatching of output, filing, and subsequent retrieval.

A visual display medium (typically a cathode ray tube) is useful for transient outputs when no permanent copy is needed. Both visual and paper media allow tabular or graphic output, which very often helps the user to understand complex data.

Microfilm is rapidly improving as an output display medium and already boasts several advantages. Because it involves photographic rather than physical recording of data, it can be exposed automatically at high speed by computer electronics. Its relative costs are low for fully utilized equipment. The microfilm media is compact—typically only 1 or 2 percent of the size of the printed paper it supplants. Thus, its shelf storage cost is also low. Techniques for accessing, retrieving, and reading microfilm were clumsy in the past, but they are changing. Coded page numbers allow rapid random access and compact microfilm readers are now available. These make microfilm acceptable in

TABLE 5.4   DATA DISPLAY CHARACTERISTICS

Device Type	Data Rate (cps)	Device Cost/Month	Relative Cost at Full Usage
Audio response	2–10 (two digits or two words)	$20	1
Teletype terminal	10	$60	1
CRT terminal	30	$75	.4
Character printer	120	$150	.2
Line printer	2400	$1000	.07
COM (microfilm)	20,000	$1200	.01

more applications, in addition to its traditional role in **archival storage**—the long-term, low-access retention of records.

Audio response is a suitable form of output for limited-volume, highly formalized messages. It is used, for example, by banks for quoting checking account data to tellers from a central computer. Receiving oral answers from computers would seem to be, at first, an exotic technology. In fact, a voice answerback unit merely plays a series of half-second recordings, much as a jukebox can play any randomly selected record sequence. These messages form the machine's vocabulary. Played in a designated order, a multitude of different responses can be "spoken." This medium, used with telephones, is inexpensive although limited in data rate and flexibility.

Printers Printers are usually connected by a channel directly to the CPU. This is called **online printing**. Alternately, a card reader or magnetic tape unit might be used to accomplish **offline printing** without a CPU. Most high-speed devices operate as **line printers**, illustrated in Figure 5–12. These produce output in the same way a typewriter does, by having metal symbols impact against a carbon paper roll and the output page. Unlike a typewriter, however, a whole line is printed rapidly, not necessarily in character sequence. A print chain rotates and properly timed hammers strike the paper to impress character images against the page. Line spacing is determined by computer instructions and a carriage control paper tape in the printer. The result is a neatly printed report.

Various line printers operate at speeds ranging from 100 lines per minute (lpm) up to 3000 lpm. For a full character set and 132 print positions, a speed of 1000 to 1500 lpm is typical. A **print buffer** may hold a line of print data at a time, thereby intermittently freeing the CPU for processing. Continuous forms with perforated pages and pin-feed holes allow automatic operation, subject to occasional form breaks; improper refolding after printing; decollating copies; separating different jobs; and changing paper stock between certain jobs. Hardware prices increase with printing speed, but a typical 1100 lpm printer rents for about $1000 per month.

A **character printer**, in contrast to a line printer, produces its output in sequence symbol by symbol. Most print from left to right, but some print in both directions. They use various schemes of rotating balls and wheels, ink jets, and thermal sensitizers to create symbol images on the appropriate paper stock.

Another classification of paper output devices is between **impact printers** and **nonimpact printers**, which do not require a physical impression to get symbols on the page. Nonimpact printers use various

Figure 5–12. IBM Model 3211 high-speed line printer

electrostatic, thermal, and ink spray techniques. Such techniques usually allow fast printing speeds because mechanical motion is reduced, but they are often limited to printing one character at a time.

Terminals Various types of terminals also offer data display capabilities, as shown in Figure 5–13. Keyboard terminals for individuals rely on two principal media—*hard copy* and *CRT display*. Typewriter-like terminals generally operate at 10 to 30 characters per second. Note that this is only a few percent of the speed of most line printers. CRT terminals generate characters electronically, sometimes at higher speeds. Output stays on the screen until it is replaced by new data, either all at once or line by line.

Graphic output devices often help to display data that are not easily comprehended in other forms, such as scale drawings, isometric views, mathematical relationships, graphs or artwork. These graphics are often economically produced by ink-pen plotters guided by computer-generated data. Special CRT terminals can also display geometric shapes with clarity. Of course, any printer or CRT can be made to display patterns by properly positioning and repeating any output symbol. Viewed from a distance, the resolution is often acceptable.

Figure 5-13.   CRT display of graphic data

And since the author has been expressing his views on the computer, Figure 5–14 lets the computer express its view of the author.

Audio Response   One device that provides voice answerback capability is the IBM 7770 Audio Response Unit. It can be used with a portable keyboard, as shown in Figure 5–15, and Touch-tone telephones. The spoken output is computer selected from a stored vocabulary ranging from 32 to 128 words.

Figure 5–14.   Computer-produced view of the author

Figure 5-15. Audio output from a portable terminal

Microfilm Computer output microfilm devices are a means of displaying processed information rapidly and compactly. COM devices do not require mechanical printing; they photograph electronic images, which allows output speeds of 10,000 to 40,000 lines per minute—10 or more times faster than line printers. Such speed can help eliminate the bottleneck faced by an output-bound processor and free printers to produce reports for which microfilm is not appropriate. The medium itself also has advantages—compactness and increasing ease of access and readability.

Banks have traditionally been microfilm users since the 1920s, when the microfilming of cancelled checks began. Microfilm has been used for high-speed computer output for the past decade; its cost/effectiveness is still improving. Already, many banks keep computer-produced copies of their customers' monthly statements and other reports on microfilm rather than storing paper records for the number of years legally required. In addition to reducing output time and paper costs, microfilm storage and access may also cost less. In one application, look-up time averaged 3 minutes with a paper file and less than 1 minute using microfilmed output and a random access viewer (shown in Figure 5–16). Operator satisfaction and customer service were both improved.

SUMMARY   I/O methods and devices deserve scrutiny because data entry is costly, time-consuming, repetitive, and often inadequately evaluated; it is the largest source of errors. Data entry performance can be measured by its costs per unit, error rate, and elapsed time delay. Such an evaluation might include classifying each data preparation step as to whether it is *sensing, recording,* or *converting*. It is also useful to review the fixed and variable costs of each step.

There are three types of devices for data preparation: manual keying, optical scanning, and direct sensing. Keypunching of data onto cards is the most familiar of these methods. Other keying devices permit data recording and verification on storage media other than cards, such as key-to-tape, key-to-disk, and online devices.

Optical scanning senses visual patterns of recorded data and converts them to a machine-processable form. For example, the banking industry processes checks by using magnetic ink character readers (MICR) for the check amount, account, and routing data. Other devices include optical mark readers (OMR) and optical character readers (OCR). The latter can read typed or printed characters of one or more type fonts and can even read neatly hand-printed data.

Direct sensing is the automatic perception and recording of data in computer-compatible form. Where applicable, it can often reduce costs, errors, and delays. Other means of obtaining these objectives involve avoiding data conversion steps, collecting only worthwhile data, sampling or coding data to reduce its volume, using check digits

Figure 5-16. A microfilm viewer

and verification procedures, and using a lower cost technology when input volumes and standardization permit.

Several output methods are also available. In addition to traditional line printers, there are character printers, nonimpact printers, graphic plotters, computer output microfilm (COM) devices, and a family of terminals that provide hard copy or visual display.

CONCEPTS

sensing
recording
converting
keypunch
online data entry
intelligent terminal
point-of-sale (POS)
  terminal
optical scanning
MICR
OMR
OCR
direct sensing

card reader
verify
verifier
data-pooler
data classification
redundancy
check digit
turnaround document
printout
hard copy
audio response
computer output
  microfilm (COM)

key-to-tape
key-to-disk
diskette
floppy disk
archival storage
online printing
offline printing
line printer
print buffer
character printer
impact printer
nonimpact printer

QUESTIONS
1. "I/O techniques have not changed for years." Discuss this statement.
2. By what measures of performance should input be evaluated?
3. Describe a computer data entry scheme you are familiar with and diagnose its fixed and variable costs for each of its *sense, record,* and *convert* activities.
4. Compare keypunching's advantages and disadvantages to those of key-to-disk data entry.
5. What are the benefits of a system of premarked grocery items and point-of-sale (POS) checkout terminals in a supermarket?
6. What conditions and devices can permit optical scanning of data at one-tenth the cost of keyed data entry?
7. State three different methods for detecting data errors. For reducing the volume of data collected.
8. Evaluate any recently announced terminal as to its I/O costs and effectiveness.
9. What advantages does a centralized high-speed printer offer? What disadvantages?
10. Cite an application using COM.

Chapter Six

**Survey of
High-Level
Languages**

Intellectuals in foreign policy have quipped that "old-timers study the Russian language, but newcomers study Chinese," to which other pundits respond, "but realists learn computer languages." Actually, even a noncomputer professional is likely to benefit from surveying and perhaps using some alternative computer languages. However, we will not attempt language instruction in this chapter, since there are various programming manuals available for the details of each standard language.

Several hundred high-level languages have been created and documented by computer manufacturers, software firms, and even individuals. Yet, only a few of them are widely used for computer solutions to major classes of problems. In this chapter, we review six high-level languages: FORTRAN, COBOL, PL/1, RPG, BASIC, and APL. We examine their objectives; design features; types of acceptable statements, including an example program; and their applications. Lastly, their comparative advantages and disadvantages are summarized.

PROGRAMMING IN A HIGH-LEVEL LANGUAGE Skill and speed in programming in a particular language and one's ability to create efficient solutions to problems usually increase with experience. The first step involves envisioning and analyzing the problem. Next is creating a sequence of small steps leading to the problem's solution. Programmers already experienced in one language (for example, BASIC) can usually learn the specific features and **syntax**, or coding rules, of another language fairly quickly—within a few days. However, developing problem-solving facility and efficiency in the language may require several days to several months. Concentrated immersion and frequent or interactive access to a computer will speed the learning process.

But learning computer languages and writing programs are only parts of the overall task of solving problems with computers. The application development cycle (discussed in Part 4) can be described as 10 activities:

1. Problem realization and definition
2. Systems analysis
3. Systems design
4. Program design
5. Programming
6. Compilation (or assembly)
7. Testing
8. Debugging
9. Documentation
10. Implementation

Each step of this process, except the first and the last, is affected by the use of high-level languages. For example, the goal of the systems analysis and design stage is to specify the most beneficial information system. Such a decision depends in part on the costs of alternative programming methods. Similarly, the best programming design depends on the computer language chosen. The ease and efficiency of program design, programming, compilation, testing, debugging, and documentation also depend on the programming language.

No matter which programming language is used, the factors discussed below bear on the effectiveness of the completed program:

- correctness
- efficiency
- "good" I/O design
- modularity
- generality
- flexibility
- documentation
- structure

Correctness   Computer output may look imposing yet be incorrect. In addition to input data errors, operator errors, and programming logic errors, the computer itself can be a source of processing or I/O errors. Rounding errors, for example, can become significant after a long series of calculations. Also, if a large, slightly inaccurate number is subtracted from a nearly equal number, the answer is subject to a magnified degree of error. The body of knowledge concerned with the accuracy and efficiency of computational techniques is called **numerical analysis**.

Efficiency   Efficiency requires that all system resources—hardware, software, and people—be used effectively. The most efficient program for a one-shot problem is likely to be the one written fastest, even though it may run slowly on the hardware. But when a program is to be run frequently, the programmer should pay careful attention to machine execution speed. High-level languages tend to increase the programmer's efficiency. But they often incur the modest penalty of extra computer time. When a trade-off between personnel efficiency and computer efficiency is possible, it is increasingly wise to use people's time well since computing costs are declining while salaries are increasing.

"Good" I/O Design Special care in the design of data collection, conversion, and input methods can dramatically affect the costs, error rates, and delays of data preparation. (Chapter 5 details these considerations.) Likewise, an orderly, well-labeled output format makes a report more useful and reduces its chance of being misinterpreted.

Modularity A *modular* program is one designed as a collection of highly separable pieces. Thus, each piece is much smaller than the whole. This allows the work to be divided among programmers, if necessary. Each piece is also easier to develop, test, and maintain. Yet, all the pieces need to fit together. They should therefore have a standard interface with their environment. For example, each module might have only one entry point and one exit point. Thus, changes inside the module tend not to affect how it fits the whole. When completed, a modular program is also easier to understand and update over time than the equivalent code written as a single module.

Generality A *general* program is one that can be applied to many situations or that has broad capability. Options that can be adopted or disregarded easily are often introduced to increase a program's generality. Programs offered for sale are frequently very general to accommodate the problem differences of their many potential users.

Flexibility Flexibility is the ability to use and change a program easily. Programs seem inevitably to evolve beyond their original conception. If the programmer anticipates this, she or he can adopt programming techniques and documentation methods that allow future changes. Modularity—relying on modules or subroutines for specific functions—is one way to make a program more flexible. Selecting variable names that correspond to their actual definitions also simplifies modification or reprogramming if it is required.

Documentation Documentation assures that anyone can learn to use a program properly and that a specialist can understand the program itself. Thus, a programming investment becomes available to others besides the initial programmer. (This is especially important in organizations that reuse their programs but have a high rate of personnel turnover.) Adequate documentation usually includes:

- a user manual detailing usage instructions
- a program listing, including explanatory comments
- a dictionary defining the variables used
- a sample of input and output reports, including explanation
- a flowchart, detailed sufficiently to portray program logic

Documentation is usually prepared after a program is completed —although working flowcharts, listings, and so forth may be used during programming. As much as possible, documentation should rely on the machine's capability for producing listings; printing a dictionary and comments (often embedded in the program listing); running sample cases; and even flowcharting.

Structure   Structure means that an orderly flow exists through the program. This programming style helps achieve each of the foregoing factors. Errors, for example, are easier to prevent or trace through orderly logic. Programmer efficiency is often also improved. (Further discussion of the applications development cycle, beyond our present concern with programming in a high-level language, is presented in Part 4.)

LANGUAGE   As briefly recounted in Chapter 2, language translator programs al-
TRANSLATION   ready exist. They permit the computer itself to translate programs written in high-level languages into equivalent patterns of 0s and 1s of a machine language. There are many such user-oriented languages. Six of them—FORTRAN, COBOL, PL/1, RPG, BASIC, and APL—are surveyed in this chapter. Such high-level languages consist of a set of predefined symbols and rules for combining them into processing procedures. They greatly assist easy, efficient, and accurate interaction with computers.

A particular language translator program applies only to a single high-level language. As shown in Figure 6-1, instructions written in the high-level language are input to the translator program. Its output is the equivalent machine language. Also, if the high-level language program contains errors of format or certain logical errors, the language translator can usually detect them. In such cases, useful diagnostic messages are the output of the translation attempt.

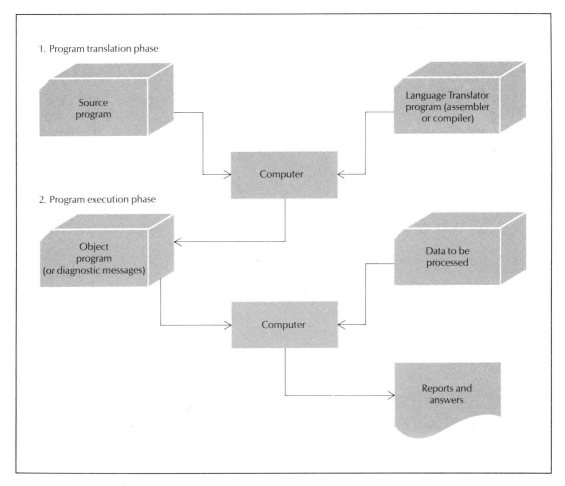

Figure 6-1. Translating a high-level computer program

The high-level language program is often called the **source program**. Its machine-language equivalent, as produced by the language translator, is called the **object program**. Once an object program has been produced, it can be run directly until the program must be changed. This saves the bother of translation again. When a change is required, the source program must be modified first. Then another translation is required before the new object program can be run on the computer.

One type of language is called an **assembly-level language**; it is one step above machine level. An assembly-level language substitutes a symbolic, easy-to-remember code for the numeric binary code needed at the machine level. The corresponding translator program is called an **assembler**.

Compiler-level languages are of a higher level. Their language translator programs are called **compilers**. Compiler-level languages, of which FORTRAN, COBOL, and PL/1 are examples, abstract one step further from machine-level than do assembly-level languages. They can incorporate several machine-level instructions into a single high-level instruction. Thus, in FORTRAN, the single programming statement

$$A = B + C * D/E + F$$

calls for several specific machine-level instructions. The computed result is referenced merely as A. As part of compilation, a storage location would be assigned for storing this result.

Making compilers and assemblers so that they use hardware efficiently is extremely important. Their performance has two dimensions:

1. Efficiency of the translation process
2. Efficiency of the machine-language object program produced by translating the source program

In designing compilers or assemblers, there is a trade-off between attaining these two types of efficiency. For example, **quick-and-dirty compilers** do quick translations, but produce object programs that are relatively slow when executed. Such a compiler is most useful when a program is being debugged. At this stage, the source program is being translated after each revision with little execution of object programs.

Conversely, other compilers or assemblers are designed to produce efficient object programs. Such **optimizing compilers** usually require a longer translation time than quick-and-dirty compilers. However, this fault can be ignored if the user's programs are compiled once and then used frequently thereafter. For such repeated use, an efficient object program is crucial. Compiler trade-off and other measures of language performance are shown in Table 6.1. Notice that high-level languages make the best use of human resources, but at the expense of some additional hardware resources.

Many high-level languages have been defined and standardized. Each must have, depending on its level, a translator that links it back ultimately to machine-level language. There are languages at many different levels of abstraction. For example, the language SIMSCRIPT has a translator program that produces standard FORTRAN as its out-

TABLE 6.1 LANGUAGE LEVEL AND LANGUAGE PERFORMANCE

	Human Time Factors			Machine Time Factors	
	Time to Write Program	Ease of Debugging	Documentation	Language Translation Time	Computer Time to Execute
Machine language	Worst	Worst	Worst	None	Least
Assembly language	Better	Better	Better	Very little	Close to least
Compiler language (with optimizing compiler)	Best	Best	Best	Most	More
Compiler language (with quick-and-dirty compiler)	Best	Best	Best	1/10 of most	Most

put. This translation output is then further translated via an appropriate FORTRAN compiler. The only requirement for a high-level language is that it can eventually be translated into the 0s and 1s of machine language.

Programmers frequently have a preference for their "mother tongue"—their first programming language. Nonetheless, other languages may be more suitable for some types of application. The manager or computer professional must make a language decision. The choice criteria should balance comparative benefit with the efficiency of total resources—including human and machine time during program development and its anticipated lifetime usage.

FORTRAN *Formula Translator* was the first broadly accepted standard compiler language. It was originally developed in 1957 to reduce the task of preparing programs for the IBM 704 computer. At that time—and still today—most of the cost and nearly all of the human time in solving scientific or engineering problems on computers were spent on planning, writing, and debugging the programs.

Objectives FORTRAN was developed to simplify the programming of mathematical procedures. It permits the user/programmer to state concise, algebralike instructions. The language has been updated, expanded, and improved since the original documentation manual was issued, but it is still primarily formula-oriented.

Design Features FORTRAN, like the other compiler-level languages, lets the user/programmer write workable programs without needing to know about hardware operating details. The language consists of a permitted vocabulary of symbols and words and a set of grammar rules for writing instructions. It uses names up to six letters long and common mathematical symbols. Thus, it is reasonably easy to learn and use, except for certain arbitrary conventions, particularly for specifying input and output.

A sample program—designed to produce certain payroll information—is shown for each language discussed in this chapter. The problem in each case is the same (see Figure 6-2). The programs use a variety of typical input layouts and output displays.

Statement Types FORTRAN uses six basic types of statements. Each has its own particular function in the input-processing-output cycle.

1. Input/output. I/O statements instruct the computer to seek and read input data from a specified input device and to write output on a specified output device. Input sources include punched cards accessed through a card reader; magnetic tapes read by tape drives; disk packs mounted on disk drives; and direct input from on-line keyboard terminals. Output is frequently printed, although tape, disk, card and terminal outputs are also common.

A representative pair of input statements is shown below. Notice that the format details are specified in a separate statement. Format statements may be referenced by one or more I/O statements, as appropriate. They may specify titles, space out numbers, and so on. The example programming statements in this chapter are usually drawn from the sample program for that language. Thus, we can see their context as well as their syntax.

```
11  READ (5, 12) IEMPLO, HOURS, WAGE, IEXEMP, DEDUCT
12  FORMAT (I10, 2F10.2, I10, F10.2)
```

2. Arithmetic assignment. Computing results and assigning variable names are accomplished by **assignment statements**. Variable names are used to represent all types of data, including alphameric, real, integer, complex and logical variables. The initial letter of a variable denotes whether a real or integer number is intended. Unless specified

Input

The program should accept the following five input variables. Data for two employees is shown.

NUMBER:	Employee number	Employee 1	Employee 2
HOURS:	Number of hours worked	40.0	32.5
WAGE:	Hourly rate of pay in dollars	4.00	2.50
EXEMPTIONS:	Number of exemptions for withholding tax purposes	2	6
DEDUCTION:	Other weekly deductions in dollars	9.20	4.80

Output

The output report should display the following information for each employee:

NUMBER:	NUMBER from input data
GROSS PAY:	Total salary for the week (HOURS × WAGE)
DEDUCTIONS:	DEDUCTION from input data
WITHHOLDING TAX:	Twenty percent of the amount by which gross pay exceeds a nontaxable allowance of $15 per week for each exemption
NET PAY:	Gross pay less withholding tax and deductions

Figure 6-2.   Sample programming problem

otherwise, when the first letter is I, J, K, L, M, or N, the variable is stored internally as an integer; otherwise, it represents a real variable. As in the assignment statement below, arithmetic operations are specified on the right side of the assignment symbol. The computed result is stored in the location represented by the variable name designated on the left.

$$TAKPAY = GROPAY - TAX - DEDUCT$$

3. Specification.   Both the type and format of input and output data can be specified. For example, a DIMENSION statement defines a family of variables sharing a common name, but each having a unique subscript. Other specification statements dictate other data types, such as REAL, INTEGER, and DOUBLE PRECISION. FORMAT statements specify the I/O details, as mentioned.

```
5 FORMAT (10×, EMPLOYEE GROSS DEDUCTIONS WITHHELD
   1NET')
```

4. Control. FORTRAN instructions are executed in sequence unless a **control statement** directs otherwise. A transfer of control may be *conditional* or *unconditional*. A logical test of whether a specified condition exists can be used to **branch**—to transfer from one point in a program to some subsequent instruction. An **unconditional branching** statement always redirects the instructions sequence in some preset, unvarying manner such as GO TO 11. A **conditional branch** redirects the execution sequence only when the specified criterion is met.

IF (TAX.LE.0.) TAX = 0
(LE means "less than" or "equal to".)

5. Iteration. FORTRAN handles repeated processes easily by an **iteration statement**. For example, for values of some index I, ranging from 1 to 50, you might wish to perform the same processing task for each value of I. This task might end with statement number 100. This can be done easily in FORTRAN (although this type of statement does not appear in the sample program).

DO 100 I = 1, 50

6. Subroutine. A **subroutine** is essentially an independent program. It often consists of instructions for performing one particular procedure, usually a repeated one. A subroutine is defined by an initial **declaration statement** that specifies its name. It terminates with a **return statement** that redirects program control back to the point in the main program that called for the subroutine.

Applications FORTRAN is widely used for computation processes. In particular, it deals easily with problems that contain complex formulas or subscripted variables. Its use and acceptance have broadened substantially over the years. It is relatively easy to learn and is essentially independent of machine architecture. Thus, FORTRAN is a good initial language for a person who is becoming acquainted with computer capabilities. A FORTRAN program for the sample payroll problem is shown in Figure 6–3.

COBOL COBOL, which is an acronym for *Common Business Oriented Language*, was developed by 1961. This language was especially designed for business problems. (Algebraic languages like FORTRAN were not designed to handle the large data files and variable-length records typical of commercial applications.) Although COBOL was standard-

```
/PROGRAM SAMPLE
C
C   THIS PROGRAM PRODUCES THE WEEKLY PAYROLL STATEMENT
C
C   ALLOW  - TAX EXEMPT ALLOWANCE AMOUNT
C   DEDUCT - OTHER WEEKLY DEDUCTIONS IN DOLLARS
C   GROPAY - GROSS PAY FOR THE WEEK
C   HOURS  - NUMBER OF HOURS WORKED THIS WEEK
C   IEMPLO - EMPLOYEE NUMBER
C   IEXEMP - NUMBER OF EXEMPTIONS FOR TAX PURPOSES
C   TAKPAY - NET TAKE-HOME PAY
C   TAX    - WITHHOLDING TAX AMOUNT
C   WAGE   - HOURLY RATE OF PAY IN DOLLARS
C
      PRINT 5
    5 FORMAT (10X,'EMPLOYEE        GROSS     DEDUCTIONS      WITHHELD
   1     NET')
      PRINT 6
    6 FORMAT (10X,'  NUMBER         PAY                        TAX
   1     PAY')
   11 READ (5,12) IEMPLO, HOURS, WAGE, IEXEMP, DEDUCT
   12 FORMAT (I10, 2F10.2, I10, F10.2)
      IF (IEMPLO.EQ.999)   GO TO 66
      GROPAY = WAGE*HOURS
   22 ALLOW = IEXEMP*15.
      TAX = (GROPAY-ALLOW)*.2
      IF (TAX.LE.0.)    TAX = 0.
   33 TAKPAY = GROPAY-TAX-DEDUCT
   44 PRINT 55, IEMPLO, GROPAY, DEDUCT, TAX, TAKPAY
   55 FORMAT (8X, I10, 4F13.2)
      GO TO 11
   66 STOP
      END
/GO
EMPLOYEE        GROSS     DEDUCTIONS      WITHHELD          NET
  NUMBER         PAY                        TAX            PAY
         1     160.00          9.20         26.00       124.80
         2      81.25          4.80          0.00        76.45
```

Figure 6-3. Sample problem programmed in FORTRAN

ized and documented in the early 1960s, computer manufacturers' widespread support for it did not occur until the mid-1960s. But, by the early 1970s, it had become the most frequently used language in business organizations. It still is today.

Objectives   COBOL's purpose is to facilitate file processing and to provide accurate arithmetic, data editing, efficient I/O, and self-documentation. The language is essentially machine independent. In short, it is intended to handle the needs of the typical business application.

Design Features   The committee of computer users who met to define COBOL wanted it to be usable on all commercial data processing equipment, regardless of manufacturer or internal architecture. They also devised documenting statements similar to English. Thus each COBOL program is said to resemble a book. Its four required parts, called **divisions**, are analogous to chapters. These division names and purposes are shown below:

1. IDENTIFICATION DIVISION: Identify the program.
2. ENVIRONMENT DIVISION: Describe equipment needs.
3. DATA DIVISION: Detail the format of data and output files.
4. PROCEDURE DIVISION: State what processing steps to perform.

Each COBOL program must have all four divisions in the order shown. The Identification and Procedure divisions can be left virtually unchanged if the program is shifted from one computer to another. The Data division may or may not require revision. The Environment division has to be revised if the program is shifted to a different type of machine since it contains computer-specific information.

Divisions are composed of **sections**. The Procedure division is also organized into groups of **statements**, much as chapters are composed of sections and paragraphs. The syntax uses an A margin and a B margin (columns 8 and 12, respectively). This gives the wordy text an indented appearance. Each statement type begins in a particular margin and ends in a period. Words rather than numbers designate statement sequences. Arithmetic can be stated in words as well. Since commercial problems deal with terms like *accounts receivable*, *withholding tax*, *gross pay*, and *deductions*, COBOL allows variable names as long as 30 characters, including hyphens.

Statement Types   The following sample statements illustrate COBOL. The same problem we saw coded in FORTRAN is coded in COBOL in Figure 6-4. (This program computes net pay for employees from hours worked and wage-rate data.)

The Identification division is short and straightforward. It consists of certain required statements and some optional remarks:

```
IDENTIFICATION DIVISION.
PROGRAM-ID. 'SAMPLE'.
AUTHOR. MADER.
REMARKS. NET PAY PROBLEM
```

```
001010 IDENTIFICATION DIVISION.
001020 PROGRAM-ID. 'SAMPLE'.
001030 AUTHOR. MADER-HAGIN.
001040 INSTALLATION. UPENN-COMPUTER-CENTER.
001050 REMARKS, NET PAY PROBLEM
001060         DOCUMENTED SAMPLE PROGRAM
001070         INPUT AN EMPLOYEE CARD FILE AND
001080         PRINT A PAYROLL REPORT.
001300 ENVIRONMENT DIVISION.
001310 CONFIGURATION SECTION.
001320 SOURCE-COMPUTER. IBM-370.
001330 OBJECT-COMPUTER. IBM-370.
001340 INPUT-OUTPUT SECTION.
001350 FILE-CONTROL.
001360     SELECT EMP-CRD-FILE  ASSIGN TO UT-S-SYSIN.
001380     SELECT PAYROLL-PRINT ASSIGN TO UT-S-SYSPRINT.
001400 DATA DIVISION.
001410 FILE SECTION.
001420 FD  EMP-CRD-FILE
001430     RECORDING MODE IS F
001440     BLOCK CONTAINS 40 RECORDS
001460     RECORD CONTAINS 80 CHARACTERS
001470     LABEL RECORDS ARE OMITTED
001480     DATA RECORD IS EMPLOYEE-PAYROLL-CARD.
001500 01  EMPLOYEE-PAYROLL-CARD.
001510     02   NAME        PICTURE X(12).
001520     02   FILLER      PICTURE XX.
001530     02   HOURS       PICTURE 99V9.
001540     02   FILLER      PICTURE XX.
001550     02   WAGE        PICTURE 99V99.
001560     02   FILLER      PICTURE XX.
001570     02   EXEMP       PICTURE 99.
001580     02   FILLER      PICTURE XX.
001590     02   DEDUCTIONS  PICTURE 99V99.
001591     02   FILLER  PICTURE X(47).
001600 FD  PAYROLL-PRINT
001610     RECORDING MODE IS F
001620     RECORD CONTAINS 133 CHARACTERS
001630     LABEL RECORDS ARE OMITTED
001640     DATA RECORD IS PRINTED-INFO.
001650 01  PRINTED-INFO.
001660     02   FILLER PICTURE X.
001670     02   PRINTED-LINE PICTURE X(132).
001690 WORKING-STORAGE SECTION.
001700 77  GROSS-PAY  PICTURE 999V99.
001710 77  NET-PAY PICTURE 999V99.
001720 77  WITHHOLDING PICTURE S9999V99.
001730 77  STORE-1 PICTURE 999V99.
001733*    STORE-1 HOLDS THE SUM OF WITHHOLDING AND DEDUCTIONS
001734*        WILL SUBSEQUENTLY BE SUBTRACTED FROM GROSS-PAY
001737*        YIELD NET-PAY.
001735 01  INFO-TO-PRINT.
```

Figure 6-4. Sample problem programmed in COBOL

```
001740      02  FILLER  PICTURE X VALUE SPACE.
001750      02  P-EMP-NAME PICTURE X(12).
001760      02  FILLER PICTURE X(4) VALUE SPACE.
001800      02  P-GROSS-PAY   PICTURE ZZ9.99.
001810      02  FILLER  PICTURE XXXX VALUE SPACE.
001820      02  P-NET-PAY PICTURE ZZ9.99.
001830      02  FILLER PICTURE X(10) VALUE SPACE.
001840      02  P-WITHHOLD  PICTURE ZZ9.99.
001850      02  FILLER PICTURE X(12) VALUE SPACE.
001860      02  P-DEDUCT   PICTURE ZZ9.99.
001870      02  FILLER PICTURE X(66) VALUE SPACE.
001900 01  HEADING-1.
001910      02  FILLER PICTURE X VALUE SPACE.
001920      02  FILLER PICTURE X(27) VALUE '     NAME      GROSS PAY  '.
001940      02  FILLER PICTURE X(26) VALUE 'NET PAY    WITHHOLDING TAX'.
001950      02  FILLER PICTURE X(14) VALUE '    DEDUCTION'.
001960      02  FILLER PICTURE X(67) VALUE SPACE.
002010 PROCEDURE DIVISION.
002020 START-RUN.
002030      OPEN INPUT EMP-CRD-FILE.
002040      OPEN OUTPUT PAYROLL-PRINT.
002050 TITLE-PRINT.
002060      WRITE PRINTED-INFO FROM HEADING-1 AFTER ADVANCING 9 LINES.
002062      MOVE SPACES TO PRINTED-LINE.
002064      WRITE PRINTED-INFO AFTER ADVANCING 2 LINES.
002080 READ-A-CARD.
002085*    THERE ARE FEW COMMENTS
002090      READ EMP-CRD-FILE AT END GO TO EOJ.
002100      MULTIPLY HOURS BY WAGE GIVING GROSS-PAY ROUNDED.
002110      MULTIPLY EXEMP BY 15 GIVING WITHHOLDING.
002120      SUBTRACT WITHHOLDING FROM GROSS-PAY GIVING WITHHOLDING.
002130      IF WITHHOLDING > 0.00 MULTIPLY .2 BY WITHHOLDING.
002132         OTHERWISE MOVE 0.00 TO WITHHOLDING.
002150      ADD DEDUCTIONS, WITHHOLDING GIVING STORE-1.
002160      SUBTRACT STORE-1 FROM GROSS-PAY GIVING NET-PAY.
002165*    ALL PRINT DATA-NAMES BEGIN WITH 'P'.
002170      MOVE GROSS-PAY TO P-GROSS-PAY.
002180      MOVE WITHHOLDING TO P-WITHHOLD.
002190      MOVE NET-PAY TO P-NET-PAY.
002200      MOVE DEDUCTIONS TO P-DEDUCT.
002210      MOVE NAME TO P-EMP-NAME.
002230      WRITE PRINTED-INFO FROM INFO-TO-PRINT AFTER ADVANCING
002240          1 LINES.
002250      GO TO READ-A-CARD.
002270 EOJ.
002280      CLOSE EMP-CRD-FILE, PAYROLL-PRINT.
002290      STOP RUN.
```

NAME	GROSS PAY	NET PAY	WITHHOLDING TAX	DEDUCTION
EMPLOYEE 1	160.00	124.80	26.00	9.20
EMPLOYEE 2	81.25	76.45	0.00	4.80

Figure 6-4. Sample problem programmed in COBOL (cont'd.)

The Environment division notes the computer(s) used to compile and execute the program. Memory size requirements, number of tape units, hardware switches, I/O device assignments, and so forth, are among many hardware factors that are designated here. This division has two parts: a CONFIGURATION SECTION concerned with computer specifications and an INPUT-OUTPUT SECTION concerned with I/O devices. Figure 6-5 shows sample statements for the payroll problem.

The Data division describes data files, records, and fields. Every item of data processed must be described by name in the Data division. In contrast, the FORTRAN statement $Y = A * X + B$ defines the variable Y. In COBOL Y must be described in terms of its number of digits and decimal point location. Thus, COBOL's data descriptions are more tedious than FORTRAN's, but they are more convenient for file manipulation. They also provide excellent documentation and impose a standardized organization of data. The Data division is composed of up to four sections:

1. FILE SECTION: Describes I/O files, including names and layouts of records and fields.
2. WORKING-STORAGE SECTION: Describes areas in memory where intermediate results are stored.
3. CONSTANT SECTION: Defines data items whose values remain constant throughout the program.

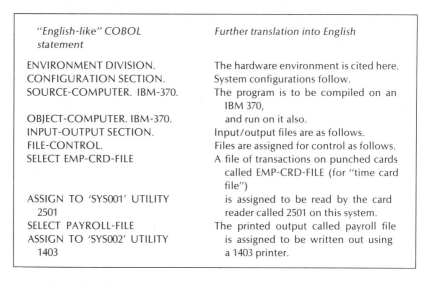

"English-like" COBOL statement	Further translation into English
ENVIRONMENT DIVISION.	The hardware environment is cited here.
CONFIGURATION SECTION.	System configurations follow.
SOURCE-COMPUTER. IBM-370.	The program is to be compiled on an IBM 370,
OBJECT-COMPUTER. IBM-370.	and run on it also.
INPUT-OUTPUT SECTION.	Input/output files are as follows.
FILE-CONTROL.	Files are assigned for control as follows.
SELECT EMP-CRD-FILE	A file of transactions on punched cards called EMP-CRD-FILE (for "time card file")
ASSIGN TO 'SYS001' UTILITY 2501	is assigned to be read by the card reader called 2501 on this system.
SELECT PAYROLL-FILE	The printed output called payroll file
ASSIGN TO 'SYS002' UTILITY 1403	is assigned to be written out using a 1403 printer.

Figure 6-5. Sample statements in COBOL

4. REPORT SECTION: Describes the content and layout of reports to be generated by the report generator capabilities.

In the File section of Figure 6–4, the notation FD in the A margin indicates a *file description* statement. The file is named EMP-CRD-FILE. The recording mode is either variable length (V), fixed (F), or undefined (U). Here all the records are the same length—the 80 characters of a punched card. The 01 level statement shows the record description. The 02 level defines the fields that compose this record. Their data names and "pictures" are given. Thus, the data is structured into a hierarchy. The file itself is specified at the FD level while records are cited as the 01 level. Succeeding levels (groups of fields, individual fields, or subfields) are given larger numbers, usually 02, 03, 04, and so forth. An item that is further subdivided is called a **group item**; otherwise, it is an **elementary item**. An entry named FILLER must be used to indicate unused portions of the record, since the record must be completely defined.

The word PICTURE has a special meaning in COBOL. The language requires a symbolic picture of each data element. Each character of a data element is represented by a code describing it. Thus, an item's PICTURE in COBOL is similar in concept to its FORMAT in FORTRAN. The following PICTURE characters are used:

9	A numeric digit
A	An alphabetic character
X	An alphameric character
V	An assumed decimal point
S	A sign
9(3)	A 3-digit integer ⎫ equivalent alternatives
999	A 3-digit integer ⎭
Thus, 999V99	A 5-digit number with two decimal places
X(65)	Any 65 alphameric characters

Commercial applications often require dollar signs, commas, decimal points, and so forth, at appropriate locations. Some of the editing characters used in the PICTURE of an item follow:

PICTURE	DATA	SYMBOL and MEANING	PICTURE	OUTPUT
9999	0025	Z suppresses leading zeros.	ZZZ9	25
999V9	1968	V inserts a decimal point.	999.9	196.8
999V99	12345	$ locates a right-adjusted dollar sign.	$999.99	$123.45

The Procedure divison specifies the processing **algorithm** (logical steps to be executed). It begins by "opening" the input files described in the Data division. This prepares them for processing. The last procedure steps are to "close" them. Procedures are described by groups of statements, each containing Englishlike words followed by a period. Sample words are MULTIPLY, SUBTRACT, IF, and EQUALS.

The COBOL character set (alphabetic, numeric, and special) can be used for words, punctuation, editing, formulas, and relations. A COBOL word must have at least one alphabetic character (no blanks) and consist of no more than 30 characters. COBOL programs consist of sentences comprised of such words, data, and operators.

Examples of COBOL sentences drawn from Figure 6–4 include:

OPEN INPUT EMP-CRD-FILE.
MOVE SPACES TO PRINTED-LINE.
MULTIPLY HOURS BY WAGE GIVING GROSS-PAY ROUNDED.

Applications COBOL is used for file processing. It is the most popular language for commercial applications. Business-type problems typically involve large volumes of input and output with repeated reference to files and their component records and fields; they also require output editing and program documentation. A majority of the programs currently in use by business firms are COBOL programs.

PL/1 PL/1 (*Programming Language 1*) is a newer high-level language than FORTRAN or COBOL. As such, it benefits from users' early experiences with other languages. PL/1 was originally developed by IBM to complement its System/360 line of computers. It has since been supported by a few other manufacturers as well.

Objectives PL/1 is a multipurpose language that combines the features of FORTRAN and COBOL with additions from other languages and its own innovations. It was designed to be suitable for scientific problems; data management; commercial file processing; character-string manipulation and list processing. Previously, separate languages were tailored to each of these types of application. The reasons for PL/1's modular yet comprehensive design are:

1. To cater to previous users of FORTRAN and COBOL who need comparable capabilities in PL/1.
2. To create PL/1 subsets that can be compiled and run even on small machines.

3. To permit the programmer to begin simply but graduate to more powerful techniques—within the same language.

Design Features

Other important design features include:

- free-form formatting of I/O
- the possibility of multiple statements per line
- no restrictions on the mixing of data types

A PL/1 program is a series of elements within statements. These statements are combined into groups, identified with name labels, and structured into procedures and blocks. A statement is a string of characters terminated by a semicolon. Variable names may be up to 31 characters in length. Compound words that use the break character (as in NET_PAY) make PL/1 variables very readable.

Statement Types

PL/1 uses several statement types, cited below. (It also uses other statements, such as READ, WRITE, BEGIN, ENTRY, LOCATE, REWRITE, OPEN, CLOSE, ALLOCATE, DELETE, END, and so forth.) The major statement types are:

DECLARE	IF
GET	DO
PUT	CALL
GO TO	RETURN

The DECLARE statement is used to define variable names (as in Figure 6-6—our sample payroll program):

DECLARE (HOURS, WAGE_RATE, DEDUCTION)
FIXED DECIMAL (5,3);

The variable names within the parentheses are data descriptions. The FIXED DECIMAL (5,3) portion of the DECLARE statement tells the computer how many places to allow before and after the decimal point. Another statement specifies calculations to be performed using the declared variables. An example from the sample program follows:

GROSS_PAY = HOURS * WAGE_RATE;

The GET statement is used to read in data. Executing this statement "gets" new input data for each variable named, as illustrated in the sample program:

GET LIST (N, HOURS, WAGE_RATE, EXEMPTION, DEDUCTION);

```
PAYROLL:PROCEDURE OPTIONS (MAIN);
DECLARE ( HOURS,WAGE_RATE,DEDUCTION ) FIXED DECIMAL (5,3);
DECLARE (N,EXEMPTION) FIXED DECIMAL (3,0);
DECLARE ( GROSS_PAY,NET_PAY,WITHHOLDING_TAX) FIXED DECIMAL (6,3);
N = 0.0 ;
PUT PAGE;
 LOOP:   GET LIST (N,HOURS,WAGE_RATE,EXEMPTION,DEDUCTION);
         IF N = 999 THEN GO TO STOP;
         GROSS_PAY = HOURS * WAGE_RATE ;
         NET_PAY = EXEMPTION * 15.0 ;
         IF GROSS_PAY  > NET_PAY THEN
         WITHHOLDING_TAX = 0.2 * ( GROSS_PAY - NET_PAY ) ;
         ELSE WITHHOLDING_TAX =0.0 ;
         NET_PAY = GROSS_PAY - ( WITHHOLDING_TAX + DEDUCTION ) ;
         PUT SKIP (4) EDIT
         ('EMPLOYEE','GROSS','NET','WITHHOLDING','DEDUCTIONS'
         ,'HOURS','NUMBER','PAY','PAY','TAX','WORKED')
         (X(35),A(8),X(4),A(5),X(4),A(3),X(5),A(11),X(4),A(10),X(4),
         A(5),SKIP,X(35),A(6),X(6),A(3),X(6),A(3),X(7),A(3),X(24),A(6));
         PUT SKIP (2) EDIT
         ( N,GROSS_PAT,NET_PAY,WITHHOLDING_TAX,DEDUCTION,HOURS )
         ( R ( OUTPUT )) ;
 OUTPUT : FORMAT ( F(40),F(12,2),X(1),F(6,2),X(3),F(10,2),X(3),
 F(9,1),X(8),F(7,2));
```

EMPLOYEE	GROSS	NET	WITHHOLDING	DEDUCTIONS	HOURS
NUMBER	PAY	PAY	TAX		WORKED
1	160.00	124.80	26.00	9.20	40.00
EMPLOYEE	GROSS	NET	WITHHOLDING	DEDUCTIONS	HOURS
NUMBER	PAY	PAY	TAX		WORKED
2	81.25	76.45	0.00	4.80	32.50

Figure 6-6. Sample problem programmed in PL/1

A PUT statement transfers results from storage to other media. In the sample program, this is accomplished by the statement:

PUT SKIP (2) EDIT
(N, GROSS_PAY, NET_PAY, WITHHOLDING TAX,
DEDUCTION, HOURS)
(R (OUTPUT));

There must also be ways to transfer program control. This is accomplished by the GO TO and IF statements. In the sample program, an employee number of 999 implies a cutoff signal. Thus, the IF and GO TO statements are combined as follows:

IF N = 999 THEN GO TO STOP;

The structure of a program often requires linking several statements together so that they can be executed as a single procedure. One method for this uses a DO statement to initiate the statement group and an END statement to conclude it. The CALL statement initiates the transfer of control of some named subroutine. It may then return control when specified conditions are met. This is done using the RETURN statement.

Applications   PL/1 is probably the most versatile and comprehensive language to date. It combines the advantages of FORTRAN and COBOL and makes several of its own improvements. It is used in situations where both computational and data processing problems must be solved and where a single language is desired for consistency within the computer user's operations. Unfortunately, PL/1 has not been universally supported by hardware manufacturers and is only slowly gaining acceptance. However, when adopted, it often becomes the standard language used for all of an organization's programming problems.

RPG   RPG, or *Report Program Generator*, is a report-oriented language rather than a procedure-oriented one. As its name suggests, RPG literally produces a program from a report specification; it does not require definition of a set of procedure-oriented instructions. In other words, the programmer describes the report the computer is to produce without writing the detailed steps required. The object program produced by RPG has a fixed logic adapted to problems that are frequently encountered in commercial applications.

Objectives   RPG is tailored to users who need an easy way to specify computerized transaction processing and report preparation. It is widely used with small computers and for straightforward business reporting requirements. It is relatively easy to learn.

Design Features   RPG programs are created on special RPG specification forms. During program generation, these defined specifications are inputs that become the object program. There are several basic types of specification forms. When read in by the RPG compiler, a suitable object program is generated.

Statement Types   One specification form is for *file description*. In RPG, a file still refers to a collection of logical records, but it also refers to the type of I/O device handling the data file. A deck of cards, a reel of tape, a magnetic disk, and even a line printer can be interpreted as an I/O file. File description specifications identify the file as input and/or output and relate it to an I/O device. This specification form is illustrated in the RPG program listing for the sample problem (Figure 6–7).

Input is another specification form. It identifies each record within the file and describes the various fields to be processed. This includes defining the length of each field and its position in the record.

Calculation, a third form, indicates the operations that must be performed. An Englishlike verb, such as "mult" for multiply, is used for specifying these calculations.

The *output* form specifies the display of output. Like the input specification sheet, it indicates record identification and field description.

There are two more forms for special situations. The *file extension specification* provides ability for chaining, tables, and direct access files. The *line counter specification* handles line control for reports stored on tape or disk for subsequent printing.

Applications   RPG I is designed for use on relatively small computers such as IBM's System/3 or the newer System 32. The most common uses of RPG II include transactions processing and file updating for accounts receivable and payable, payroll, general ledger, and inventory status. Other uses include sales analysis, budgeting, and distribution planning.

BASIC   BASIC (*Beginners All-purpose Symbolic Instruction Code*) was developed in the 1960s at Dartmouth, with the support of General Electric. At the time, Dartmouth was emphasizing student computer use in many subject areas. BASIC was designed to be an easy-to-learn language much like a simplified subset of FORTRAN. A few distinct versions have since evolved, including "basic" BASIC and "extended" BASIC.

Objectives   The developers of BASIC wanted I/O and arithmetic to be specified with a minimum of restrictions or fixed conventions. Thus, BASIC is especially suitable for interactive terminal use and for short, computationally oriented problems as encountered by students, engineers, and researchers.

Design Features   Input and output statements need not have the FORMAT statements, as in FORTRAN. Instead, BASIC uses a standard format of orderly col-

referring to its line number. After the line number, each statement must begin with a legal command. However, the computer ignores the command REM, so that programmers can insert lines of remark or documentation among other lines of code.

Other command words have defined meanings in BASIC. These include:

LET	IF-THEN
INPUT	FOR
READ	NEXT
DATA	GOSUB
PRINT	RETURN
GO TO	

The LET command calls for the calculation of some expression stated to the right of an equal sign. The calculated result is then placed into a storage location identified by the variable name cited to the left of the equal sign. Thus, two variables H and W can be multiplied and the result stored in a third location G by stating:

$$40 \ \ \text{LET } G = H * W$$

Data items are defined by either the INPUT or READ command. An INPUT command calls for data items to be entered via a terminal; processing waits until this is done. The READ command calls for data items specified by a DATA statement. The DATA command, in turn, defines these data values in the same order, separated by commas. Thus, the sample problem programmed in BASIC includes the lines:

$$30 \ \ \text{READ N, H, W, E, D}$$
$$200 \ \ \text{DATA 1, 40, 4.00, 2, 9.20}$$

Output items, whether text or numbers, can be printed by using the PRINT command. Titles or other alphameric data to be output can be cited in quotation marks. Output variables are listed with items separated by commas, as illustrated in Figure 6–8.

Transfer of control capability (that is, altering the sequence of program execution) is provided by the GO TO command. It specifies the line number of the instruction to be executed next. The IF-THEN statement allows for conditional transfer of control based on some defined condition. For example, the following statements set T (for tax withheld) to zero if the computed amount is negative:

$$70 \ \ \text{IF T} > = 0 \ \text{THEN 90}$$
$$80 \ \ \text{LET T} = 0$$
$$90 \ . \ . \ .$$

Iteration—repeating a group of instructions—is accomplished by using the FOR command coupled with the NEXT command. Thus, to repeat certain instructions 12 times, one could write:

```
20 FOR I = 1 TO 12
 *
 *   (Instructions to be repeated)
 *
150 NEXT I
```

```
SAMPLE      31 JAN 74   14:25

10 REM SAMPLE PAYROLL PROGRAM
11 REM    N   IS NUMBER
12 REM    H   IS HOURS
13 REM    W   IS WAGES
14 REM    E   IS EXEMPTIONS
15 REM    D   IS DEDUCTIONS
16 REM    G   IS GROSS PAY
17 REM    U   IS UNTAXED PAY
18 REM    T   IS TAX WITHHELD
19 REM    P   IS NET PAY
20 FOR I = 1 TO 2
30 READ N,H,W,E,D
40 LET G=H*W
50 LET U=E*15
60 LET T=.20*(G-U)
70 IF T >= 0 THEN 90
80 LET T=0
90 LET P=G-T-D
100 PRINT "EM NUM","GROSS","TAXES","DEDUCTS","NET PAY"
110 PRINT N,G,T,D,P
150 NEXT I
200 DATA 1,40,4.00,2,9.20
201 DATA 2,32.5,2.50,6,4.80
210 END
READY


RUN


SAMPLE      31 JAN 74   14:26

EM NUM      GROSS       TAXES       DEDUCTS     NET PAY
 1          160.        26.         9.2         124.8
EM NUM      GROSS       TAXES       DEDUCTS     NET PAY
 2          81.25       0.          4.8         76.45
```

Figure 6-8. Sample problem programmed in BASIC

The commands GOSUB and RETURN are used together. They cause transfer to a line number stated after the GOSUB. Subsequent encountering of RETURN causes transfer back to the original sequence (that is, to the next instruction in the sequence after the GOSUB). Thus, execution proceeds in this order:

```
        *                                          (First)
        *
 50  GOSUB 100
 60  LET Z = A
        *                                          (Third)
        *
      etc.
100  LET A = B + C
        *                                          (Second)
        *
150  RETURN
```

Applications Since BASIC is a terminal-oriented language, it is especially suitable for short calculation-oriented tasks with little input or output. Since it is deliberately simplified, it is easy to learn. With the availability and growth of interactive computer use, BASIC has continued to be heavily used in education, engineering, management science, and more in business now that its file processing features have been enhanced.

APL APL (*A Programming Language*) has evolved from work done by Ken Iverson and others, initially at IBM. APL has a powerful notation scheme that includes several unique operators.

Objectives APL seeks to provide quick, powerful computation for terminal-oriented users. The language is interpreted instruction-by-instruction, so that writing many statements or detailing formats is not required.

Design Features APL uses a keyboard with certain special symbols. Parameters and variables are easily specified, stored, processed, and recalled. Simple calculations can be stated with no required instructions for I/O or file description, just by keying 2 + 2 = , for example. On the other hand, the single instruction A = B * C is designed to work even if B and C are previously defined as matrices, not just single values.

```
[1] 'please enter each employee number, hours worked, wage rate, number of
    exemptions, and deductions amount.'
[2] 'if more than one employee, enter data with a space between each entry.'
[3] EMPNUM ←□
[4] HOURS ←□
[5] WAGE ←□
[6] EXEMPT ←□
[7] DEDUCT ←□
[8] GROPAY ← HOURS × WAGE
[9] TAX ← .2 × (GROPAY − (15 × EXEMPT))
[10] (TAX ≥ 0) × TAX
[11] NETPAY ← (GROPAY − TAX) − DEDUCT
[12] 'NUMBER:', EMPNUM
[13] 'GROSS PAY:', GROPAY
[14] 'DEDUCTIONS:', DEDUCT
[15] 'WITHHOLDING:', TAX
[16] 'NET PAY:', NETPAY
```

Figure 6-9   APL payroll program

Statement Types   The statements shown in Figure 6–9 are an APL listing for calculating our sample payroll problem. Each statement is numbered. The quoted text is typed automatically by the terminal as a prompting aid to the program user, who then types in the indicated data values, as requested. Statement for executing the appropriate payroll calculations follow this input. Then labels and numerical results for specified variables are printed.

Applications   APL provides the terminal user with a compact notation for expressing computational problems. It aids interactive use, and, while powerful in specifying computations, can be learned easily in stages. More recently, its capability has been extended to support report formatting; typical file processing applications; and repeatedly run programs in addition to one-shot calculations.

SUMMARY   While hundreds of high-level languages exist, only a few are widely used. Programming in any language involves decomposing a problem into a series of relatively elemental steps and then coding and debugging the appropriate instructions. Documenting how to use a program and how it was coded are important for ongoing use of the program. A good program should also feature correctness, efficiency, sensible I/O layout, modularity, generality, flexibility, and orderly structure.

High-level language programs must then be translated—assembled or compiled—into 0 and 1 codes suitable for computer storage and execution. The comparative advantages and disadvantages of six high-level languages are listed in Table 6.2.

TABLE 6.2 SUMMARY COMPARISON OF SIX HIGH-LEVEL LANGUAGES

Language	Advantages	Disadvantages
FORTRAN	Widely known and supported Algebraic notation Relatively easy to learn	Arbitrary format conventions Restrictive variable names Inadequate file commands Poor editing capability Arithmetic precision limits
COBOL	Wide commercial support File processing capability Self-documenting Fnglish- & booklike Excellent editing Arithmetic precision	Wordy, lengthy Somewhat difficult to learn Lengthy compilation
PL/1	Comprehensive capability Modular subsets Many data types Free-form formats List processing Relatively easy to learn	Large memory needed Compiler lengthy for all modules Complex at advanced level
RPG	Easy to learn & use Suitable for small computers File-oriented	Limited capability Preset processing may be inefficient Not uniformly supported
BASIC	Easy to learn Terminal-oriented Format-free options Concise algebra notation	Limited I/O capability Weak file processing without extended features
APL	Powerful operators Terminal-oriented Matrix capability Concise notation	Specialized notation Slow execution Special equipment needed

CONCEPTS

syntax
numerical analysis
source program
object program
assembly-level
  language
assembler
compiler-level
  language

compiler
quick-and-dirty compiler
optimizing compiler
assignment statement
control statement
branch
unconditional branch
conditional branch
iteration statement

subroutine
declaration statement
return statement
division
section
statement
group item
elementary item
algorithm

QUESTIONS

1. What is meant by the term *syntax* when it is applied to computer languages?
2. Describe the attributes you feel would be important to a person's success as a programmer.
3. Discuss the trade-offs between programming cost and program translation cost. Between translation cost and execution cost.
4. FORTRAN was the first widely adopted high-level language. What particular limitations does it have?
5. How does COBOL relieve many weaknesses of FORTRAN? What are COBOL's comparative disadvantages?
6. Why has PL/1 not been broadly applied, since it is generally acknowledged to be comprehensive, convenient, and modular?
7. Why is RPG II especially useful to the small business-oriented computer user?
8. Why might BASIC and APL become the most widely known and applied languages?

Part Three

Methods of Processing

Chapter 7   **Sequential Processing**

Among the several ways of processing data, sequential access to one data item after another has been most frequently used. It is often easiest and cheapest.

Chapter 8   **Direct Access Processing**

Quick retrieval of timely data is a powerful capability, making possible many applications and efficient, satisfying results for people.

Chapter 9   **Database Processing**

Data can be promptly updated, centrally stored, and universally accessed by different applications using database processing and appropriate data management software.

Chapter 10   **Distributed Processing**

Minicomputers and communications, plus convenient access procedures, let users everywhere process and share data and programs.

Chapter Seven

**Sequential
Processing**

7

One major use of computers, particularly in businesses, is for maintaining up-to-date data to support people's information needs. When pertinent events occur—such as a sale, a receipt of purchased goods, or an employee working an hour of overtime—data about them must be captured and processed. Such **transactions processing** frequently drives the organization's **management information system (MIS)** used to support decisions. For example, processing a sales order may trigger the proper shipment, cause printing and mailing of an invoice, record the payment due, credit the salesperson's commissions, and then be input to a computer-aided sales forecast used for managerial decision making.

Traditionally, file updating involved **sequential processing**. Indeed, until the expanded hardware and software capabilities of third-generation and later computers, this method was used almost exclusively. It still finds widespread application. However, the design of computer applications has become more complicated because other processing schemes are now available. Thus, after our consideration of sequential processing, we will discuss direct access processing (Chapter 8). Then, in Chapter 9, we will examine database processing for managing and accessing large amounts of data. In Chapter 10, we will look at distributed processing.

FILE ORGANIZATION

Files are groups of records composed of fields. They are usually large hierarchies of separate data items, all of which pertain to similar transactions. For example, an inventory file for a large organization might contain 10,000 or more records, one per product, including variations. Similarly, customer files may have tens of thousands of records. Magazine subscription lists involve literally millions of names, addresses, zip codes, and other data items. Large banks or savings institutions may have hundreds of thousands of customer accounts, some of which are active almost daily.

It would be desirable to have all of an organization's files stored in its computer's main memory, ready for microsecond access and processing. However, main memory costs make this uneconomical. Consequently, secondary storage devices (such as those discussed in Chapter 4) are used to store files or programs at relatively low cost. As we have seen, secondary storage—principally magnetic tapes and disks—allows economical storage of massive data files. When the physical media that store these files are needed for processing by some program, they can be mounted on appropriate drives and made accessible to the computer.

The data in a file can be organized in different ways called **file organization methods**. These have different efficiencies for different usage patterns. By anticipating the use to be made of a file, the information system designer can choose the most economical file organization method.

There are three traditional file organization methods:

- sequential
- direct
- indexed-sequential

Each method has its relative economic and technical advantages in various types of applications. Sequential processing relies mainly on sequential file organization with tape or disk storage. We will first take an in-depth look at sequential processing and then consider the other two file organization methods in detail in the next chapter.

Sequential file organization is a data storage method in which all records in a given file are arranged in a specified order. This sorting or sequencing is done according to the contents of some particular field—called the **key field** or **control field**—within each record. Files are frequently sequenced in ascending order of some numeric field; for example, by account number in a credit card file. It is desirable and usually necessary to have a unique key field value for each record. Thus, the key field identifies the record and is used to find it.

Files may be organized sequentially according to any of several possible key fields. However, once a file is created in a particular sequence, it will almost certainly be out of sequence by any other field. For example, an employee file may be ordered by ascending employee numbers or alphabetically by last name, but usually not by both. A copy of a file resequenced according to another key field is really another file. For example, telephone information operators have a "white pages" file that lists telephone numbers alphabetically by subscriber name and a separate file for which the key field is the street address.

The systems analyst's file organization decision used to be easy. For example, in a tape-only computer system, sequential organization was the only choice. Choosing the key field and whether to sequence in ascending or descending order was an issue, however. Also, analysts had to determine the data fields to be stored in each record and what their layout should be. For instance, should a last name field be of variable or fixed length? If fixed, how many characters should it be? If variable, how should each field's length be indicated—by a prefix noting its length or by a trailing code indicating its end?

OVERVIEW OF SEQUENTIAL PROCESSING

Data on a magnetic tape or even in a disk-based sequential file can be retrieved only by having the computer read the file in sequence from the beginning. As each record is read, the computer compares its key field to that of the desired record. A matching of key fields indicates that the desired record has been found.

Finding a single record in a sequential file is thus a rather tedious process—start at the beginning and keep searching until the record is found. If only one data record is being sought, probably about half of the file must be read to locate it. It is desirable, therefore, to batch transactions of a similar type. They can then be processed together in one run of the file. If the batched transactions are sorted in the *same* order of the *same* key field as the file being updated, then the **batch processing** requires only a single run of the file. That is, updating a *single* record takes the time to read half the file plus process one record. But updating *every* record via batch processing takes only the time necessary to read the full file once plus the processing time for each record.

Reading the full file only once per batch is an important advantage. Input/output, not processing, is often the throughput bottleneck. Batching and sorting transactions reduce the computer time required per record processed. In addition, time is needed to read a program into main memory, particularly if the program must be compiled from a source deck. Therefore, processing many transactions via that program is desirable. This also encourages batching. Figure 7–1 illustrates sequential processing; Figure 7–2 shows a tape-oriented data processing center.

In sequential processing, inputs consist of an **old master file** that is to be updated. A batch of recent transactions are sorted into a sequence

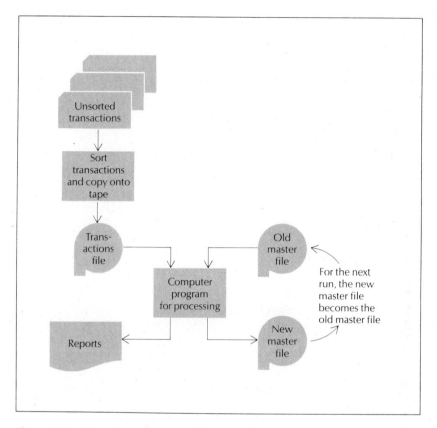

Figure 7-1. Overview of sequential processing

corresponding to that of the master file. The outputs are a **new master file** and reports. These reflect the input transactions and appropriate responses. The responses may include error reports and reports of exceptional conditions; or action notices, executive summaries, and comprehensive listings. The new master file is output on a separate storage file. Thus, even a record that does not have any transactions pertaining to it must be read in sequence, matched against the record being processed, and copied unchanged onto the new master file. This ensures that the new file is complete as well as current.

SEQUENTIAL PROCESSING WITH MAGNETIC TAPES Since magnetic tape can only be read in sequence, sequential processing is strongly favored. Thus, the program for such processing assumes that records will be read from the sorted transaction file and the old master file in a proper order for matching. The program com-

Figure 7-2. A tape-oriented data processing center

pares the transaction record, using its key field, with the master record. If a match is found, the transaction data applies to that master record and the desired processing is then executed.

A mismatch between the transaction record and the master record usually indicates that there is no transaction for that master record. In such cases, the master record is copied unchanged onto the new master file. New master records can also be created, in their proper sequence, as processing proceeds through the file. This would usually be indicated by a transaction record that had no corresponding master record—thus causing one to be created. Depending on the comparison of keys, however, an error may also be indicated by a key mismatch. This usually triggers special diagnostic processing or calls for manual intervention. A detailed flowchart of the programming logic for batch

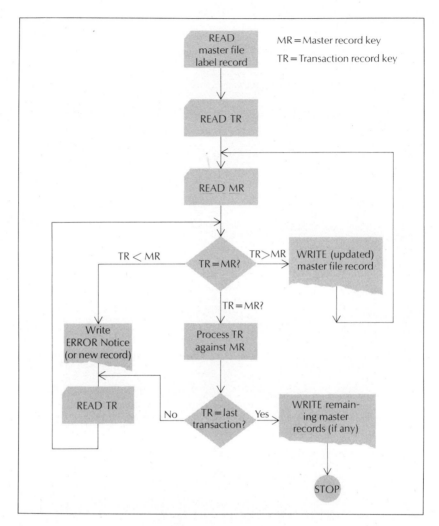

Figure 7-3. Logic flowchart for sequential file processing

processing is illustrated in Figure 7-3. This processing logic is widely applied, especially in routine business applications.

As noted in Chapter 4, a magnetic tape must be in motion past the read/write heads in order to be read or written on. Thus, to read a tape, it must be physically accelerated by its tape drive from zero velocity to its precise transport speed. Similarly, it must be stopped after the read operation. Otherwise it may physically bypass the next data item before the program has called for it to be read. Reading or writing is not practical while the tape is accelerating, decelerating, or stopped.

Therefore, a standard-sized gap of blank tape (often .6 inch) is allowed for starting and stopping between read or write commands.

This **interrecord gap (IRG)** permits the tape to be stopped and started between read or write operations. But, suppose that the amount of data stored as one continuous record is only the 80 columns of one punched card. Then, with 1600 bytes per inch (bpi) recording density, only 1/20 inch of tape is needed to record these 80 characters of data. If such a small amount of data is followed by a .6-inch interrecord gap, the tape will be over 90 percent blank space. It is clearly desirable to record more than 80 characters in a single continuous data group on tape before incurring a blank space.

Suppose on the other hand, that a particular file's **logical records**—meaningful data units—are truly 800 characters long. However, the **physical record** length of most punched cards is only 80 columns (96 columns for cards used by certain IBM and Burroughs computers). Many card records would have to be used to store the one 800-character logical record. But such a large logical record is easily stored on tape, where it can be treated as one continuous entity. In fact, blocking several logical records together allows the tape to contain even more continuous data between interrecord gaps. Then the blank tape space between such blocks is sometimes referred to as an **interblock gap**. This is illustrated in Figure 7–4.

The program that reads data stored on a magnetic tape must properly specify the file's actual blocking factor. Then, the tape drive can read or write a full block of data in one command. There is no interim blank tape within which to pause. Once the records are in main

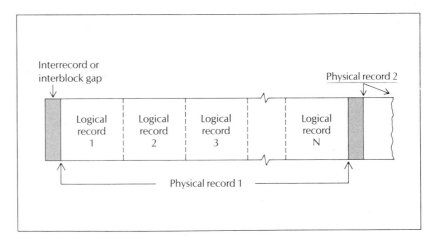

Figure 7–4. Blocking of logical records on magnetic tape

storage, however, the program can separate them into the logical data records and the fields in the block.

When a file layout for tape storage is designed, the blocking factor must be taken into consideration. It can have a large impact on the system's overall reading-processing-writing speed. Ten, twenty, or forty logical records per physical block are common blocking factors. Having large numbers of records per block conserves magnetic tape by reducing blank spaces. It also improves reading and writing speed and therefore the processing economics. A limiting factor on block size is the size of the buffer area in main memory reserved for storing these I/O blocks.

Ongoing improvements in magnetic tape technology are being made. Its cost over the past decade has fallen by more than half while its quality and data storage capacity have been increased. Even higher density recording surfaces are being developed. Small cartridge tapes have also been developed for storing small amounts of data. Programs, which also are sequences of characters, are easily stored on these small tapes. Tape will continue to play an important, although perhaps diminishing, role in information systems.

SEQUENTIAL PROCESSING WITH DISK STORAGE

Sequential processing can also use magnetic disks for secondary storage rather than magnetic tape. In fact, since the late 1960s, expenditures for disk-based storage and retrieval have outstripped those for tape-based methods. As discussed in Chapter 4, disks allow direct access. This eliminates the need to read sequentially. Instead of reading all data in a file, just the data sought can be retrieved and processed—*if* the file has been organized in a manner that supports such retrieval.

Sequential processing usually involves many transactions. Finding the corresponding data in a file is often most easily done by sorting the transactions into the same sequence as the file and then sequentially reading the entire file. Reading a tape or disk in sequence occurs rapidly because of the device's motion. Little stop-start of read/write-head-movement time is required relative to the large quantity of data read per second. Thus, even though all records are not needed, little is lost in reading the full sequence anyway.

The most efficient way to store records on a disk, given that they will be read in sequence, is to write them in this same sequence on each track of the disk. When one track is filled, the same track number on another surface should be filled next. When all tracks in a single cylinder are used, subsequent data should fill the adjacent tracks. This pattern permits retrieval at the disk's maximum transfer rate, with minimum need for mechanical movement of read/write heads. (Storing a sequentially organized file on a disk pack is illustrated in Figure 7-5.)

Notice that in using disks to support sequential batch processing, the direct access capability of disk is really not utilized. Other than accessing the beginning of the file directly, data is read in sequence without performing direct access. Furthermore, this storage strategy *could not support* direct access of a particular record—the system doesn't know in advance where any specific record is. Its only retrieval mode is: start at the beginning and search in sequence. Thus, using a disk in this manner is logically very much like using tape. It has the same economics of sequential processing, as discussed below.

ECONOMICS OF SEQUENTIAL PROCESSING

The efficiency of file processing depends on the application and the file organization method used. How a data file is used determines which file organization method is most appropriate. Several *processing criteria*—descriptive aspects of the nature of the application—have an

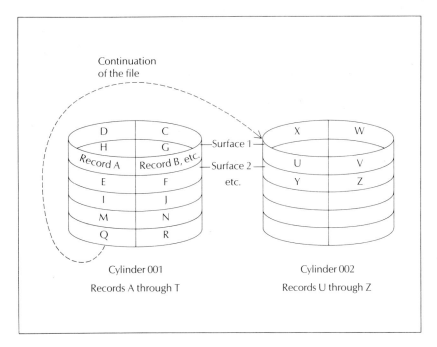

Figure 7-5.   A sequentially organized file stored on disk

important impact on the economics of file processing. The six processing criteria used to describe an application are:

- activity
- response time
- volatility
- size
- integration
- security and backup

(The next chapter will apply these same criteria to determine the effectiveness of direct access processing.)

Activity The **activity** of a file is defined as the portion of records in it that require processing. A master file record is said to be active if it requires retrieval and processing during a particular use of the file. Records with no transactions need not be updated and are considered **inactive**. However, the programming logic of sequential processing still requires that each record be read in, be compared to some transaction record, and be written out.

Only active records have transactions bearing on them. Processing a single transaction or inquiring about only one record are examples of the least possible activity of a file. In contrast, payroll processing is usually a high-activity application. Nearly all personnel submit time cards during each processing cycle, and, consequently, nearly all the personnel records require processing.

The efficiency of sequential processing depends heavily on the file's **activity ratio**—the number of active records divided by the total number of records in the file. It is often expressed as a percentage. Thus, an inquiry for one record from a file of 10,000 records represents a .01 percent activity. In another use of the file, a payroll application might need 90 percent or more of the records. This is high activity. Since a tape sequential file must be completely read and rewritten just to update a single record, its use for low-activity applications is very expensive per transaction.

Furthermore, input/output is frequently the bottleneck anyway. Thus, an entire file can be processed and each record updated in little more time than it takes just to read and process only a few transactions. The computer time necessary is largely fixed. It rises little as additional transactions are included in the batch. Thus, computer time per transaction declines as activity rises. To paraphrase Benjamin Franklin, "(Computer) time is money." Therefore, cost per transaction also declines with higher activity. This is summarized in Figure 7–6.

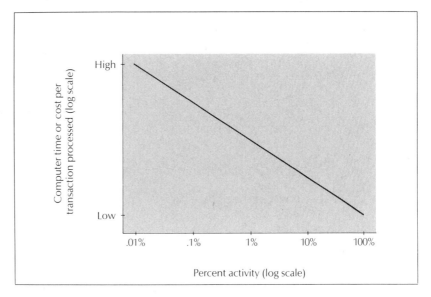

Figure 7-6. Cost per transaction processed versus activity

The scale of costs depicted in Figure 7-6 is stated in relative terms. The exact time or cost per transaction depends on the files, the sizes of the records and blocks, the amount of processing versus I/O, the capabilities of the computers used, and other factors. But, remember, sequential processing of very low activity applications is usually not economical.

To lower the cost per transaction, the activity ratio must be increased. This can be done by lengthening the **batching cycle**—the time period between updating runs. Suppose the transactions that need posting to a file occur fairly uniformly over time. Lengthening this batching cycle will create a larger transactions batch. Then, more records will be active when the file is updated. This lowers the processing cost per transaction. The relationship of average batch size and the batching cycle is shown in Figure 7-7. However, the disadvantage of lengthening the cycle is that, on the average, the file is half a batch cycle out of date. Thus, although long batching cycles produce economical data processing, they create out-of-date files and processing delays.

Response Time The second major criterion of an application that affects its overall economics is **response time**. Response time is defined as the elapsed period between a demand for processing and its fulfillment. The response time of transactions processing involves both the waiting time

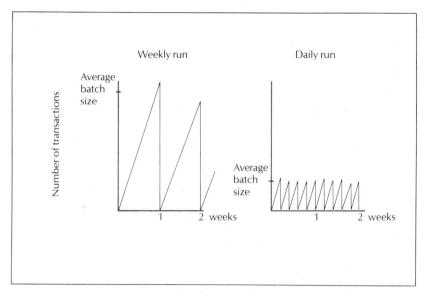

Figure 7-7. Average batch size and the batching cycle

until a batch is run and the processing time itself. As indicated in Figure 7-7, frequent processing of files improves response time. Information is then more available and more current.

Generally, faster response time is more expensive. However, the value of quick or up-to-date information very often justifies the added cost per transaction. The response time of sequential processing is always at least a few minutes long because, on the average, half or more of the file must be read. In fact, a response time of a few hours is short when we consider tape handling requirements, batch size economies, job priorities, and so forth. Frequently, a daily, weekly, or even monthly batch cycle is used. If there is little or no loss of information usefulness with time, economies may be gained from the higher activity of longer batching cycles. Also, fewer job setups are required if each run processes more data. Response time's effect on sequential processing is indicated by the general relationship diagrammed in Figure 7-8.

Volatility   A third criterion by which applications can be measured is **volatility** —the proportion of records added to or deleted from a file over time. For example, in an employee file, volatility would depend on employee turnover. Each time an employee is hired, an employee record has to be added to the file. Some files are inherently more volatile than others. File volatility affects the economics of data processing because

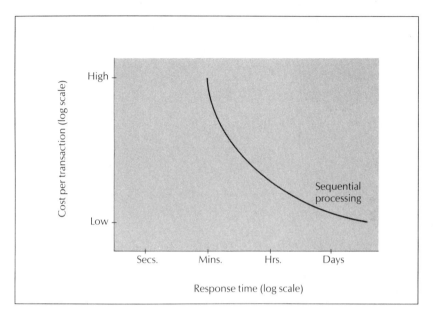

Figure 7-8.   Cost impact of response time on sequential processing

each file organization method involves somewhat different processing tactics to add or delete records.

In sequential processing, it might seem difficult to add a record in its proper point in sequence. That point would have to be found and subsequent records would all have to be repositioned or "bumped" down the list. Similarly, deleting a record would require that it be omitted and the sequence of records bumped up. In fact, such volatility is easily handled as a byproduct of normal transactions processing. It is easy and economically painless to splice in a new record on the new master file or to delete one, as we shall see.

To create a new record, an "add-a-record" transaction is sorted into the transaction file. When the proper point in the sequence is found during normal file processing, the new record is written out on the new master file. Existing records that are processed after this added record naturally follow it. Thus, the new master file contains the added record in proper sequence.

Deleting a record is also straightforward. In response to a transaction that calls for eliminating a particular record, processing simply involves not copying that record onto the output master file. (It is wise, therefore, to establish precautions against erroneous "delete-a-record" transactions that could cause the loss of valuable data.)

Size **File size** is usually measured by the total number of characters. This can be determined as the number of records in the file times the average record length. File size is a measure of the amount of processing required. Very small files probably will not require a great deal of meticulous effort in file and processing design. However, large ones require careful design. Such aspects as split files, split batch cycles, blocking, run operation details, and so forth must be considered. For example, a **split file** might separate the more active records from the less active ones. Alternately, the contents of each record might be split into more active and less active fields. In effect, these techniques create two files.

The file's initial size plus its growth over time dictates its future size. Files can grow in two dimensions—more records and more characters per record. It is common for them to grow both ways, often more rapidly than anticipated. For example, once file processing is automated, users often find it desirable to add more data to each record and/or more records to the list currently in the file.

Integration **Integration** of files or applications refers to the extent to which they are made interdependent. The degree of integration is the fifth criterion that affects the economics of file processing. Highly integrated applications allow several files to be updated during one run operation. However, the complexity of programming and file design generally increases with such integrated processing.

Sequential processing usually updates one file at a time, each by a separate program. Transactions usually must be sorted according to a new key field sequence between these separate runs. For example, a sales transaction might be run first against a credit/accounts receivable file, then against a sales commission file, and then against a shipping order file. Each file run would be separate, and the batch of sales transactions would require resorting by a different key for each file. In direct access processing, this overall operation can be more easily integrated into a single run.

Security and Backup The **security** requirements of an application dictate appropriate **back-up** procedures and hardware. Security needs are specific to a particular information system. However, it should be noted that, in general, sequential processing provides a good measure of built-in data back-up. Since a new master file copy is made each run, keeping prior copies (called the **father file**, the **grandfather file**, and so forth) together with the transactions files provides a way to reconstruct an updated file if it becomes missing, destroyed, or exposed to errors—deliberately or accidentally.

Data security is more vulnerable with other file processing methods, particularly online processing. However, no matter what method of file organization is used, specific steps should be taken to provide security and backup for both physical and logical threats to the system. For example, copies of critical files and programs can be made periodically and stored away from the computer center. Restricting access to data and logging certain types of changes are other common procedures. In addition, hardware reliability and fallback processing capabilities are aspects of security the system designer should not ignore.

DISK VERSUS TAPE SEQUENTIAL PROCESSING

Sequential processing can use either tape or disk (or both) as storage media. While, in general, the economics are similar, disk offers some advantages (and disadvantages) relative to tape.

Sequential file organization essentially does not use the disk's direct access capability. Only one record, the first, is directly retrievable. All other records are found by a sequential or other search pattern from that single known starting point. Like tape sequential files, disk sequential files cannot provide very short response times. Nonetheless, disk may be faster and have other advantages over tape, even for storing sequential files. Its comparison to tape is summarized and discussed below:

Disk Advantages

- typically has a higher data transfer rate
- "Rewindable" quickly
- Unchanged records may not need recopying
- Costs are comparable when online
- Multiple files are easily stored and accessible on one pack

Disk Disadvantages

- Adding or deleting records requires recopying
- Offline data storage is more costly
- Security and backup are more difficult

Disk data transfer rates are generally faster than tape. Disk sequential files can be read at maximum speed because all the records sought are aligned for speedy retrieval *in that sequence*. Improving the I/O transfer rate helps lower overall processing cost.

A disk sequential file is rapidly "rewindable." That is, its fast rotation time (typically, 60 rps) allows a particular location on the file to be reaccessed quickly. In contrast, a tape should not be backspaced frequently and may require 2 minutes for complete rewinding if the file needs to be reprocessed or even just dismounted.

It is also possible, if desired, to update a disk sequential file without recopying the entire file; for example, an updated record can be written onto the original file copy to supplant the old one. However, a full disk rotation or more is required to read and update the record before it can be written out beginning at the same location. With large records (nearly a full track) this limitation may be unimportant. But, with this processing logic there can be no additions or deletions of records (volatility). Thus, adding or deleting records in a disk sequential file requires that the file be recopied, as is noted in the disadvantages.

To use the data on a disk or tape it must be mounted on an appropriate drive unit capable of accessing its stored contents. High-speed tape and disk drives cost roughly the same—about $10,000 to $20,000 per unit depending on current technology and features. The cost of the storage medium itself—the disk pack or magnetic tape—is nominal compared to a disk or tape drive's cost. Thus, when disk storage is online, its full cost is comparable to that of an online tape. However, since disk data transfer is usually faster than tape, the processor might actually be tied up for a shorter period with disk. Furthermore, by not recopying the file or by storing more than one file per pack, fewer drives may be needed than with tape processing.

One disadvantage of disk versus tape is the cost of offline data storage. A magnetic tape costs only about one-tenth as much and is more compact than a disk pack of comparable capacity. For example, data that fill 1000 card boxes, each holding 2000 punched cards, occupy over 300 cubic feet of space. In contrast, the same quantity of data can be stored in about 1 cubic foot on disk or in somewhat less using tape reels. The cards would cost a few thousand dollars and are not reusable (although they make excellent scrap for recycling). A disk pack of this capacity would cost about $500. But suitable magnetic tapes might cost under $100. Thus, storing data on the shelf, or *offline*, is substantially cheaper with magnetic tape than with disks or cards.

Another disadvantage of disk sequential processing is the need for security and backup. If a new copy of the file is not made each time the file is processed, there will be no backup file in case of loss. Instead, disk files are often periodically recopied onto tapes, which are then stored away from the computer installation. Also, an **audit trail**, or journal of file changes, may be necessary for the security and assured integrity of the data.

SUMMARY   The choices of a processing method, of a corresponding file organization method, and of a secondary storage medium have significant impact on the economics of data processing. The choice of sequential processing on magnetic tape or disk depends on the nature of the application. Several processing criteria are helpful in classifying a particular application. Activity, response time, volatility, size, integration, and security and backup are all important factors.

Efficient systems are based on good decisions. This requires awareness of alternative designs and their performance levels and costs. For example, properly blocking records on tape to balance processing with I/O can reduce costs. In general, sequential processing is economical, but only if the user can wait for batching and updating and can tolerate delays.

CONCEPTS

transactions processing	batch processing	batching cycle
management information	old master file	response time
system (MIS)	new master file	volatility
sequential processing	interrecord gap (IRG)	file size
file organization	logical record	split file
method	physical record	integration
sequential file	interblock gap	security
organization	activity	backup
key field	inactive	father file
control field	activity ratio	grandfather file
		audit trail

QUESTIONS   1. Why has sequential processing been the traditional technique for data processing involving file updating?
2. When preparing for sequential processing of files stored on magnetic tape, what factors of file design must be decided on?
3. Explain, in words, the logic of sequential processing.
4. Why is a long batching cycle helpful in lowering processing costs but detrimental to users needing the processed results?
5. Define several processing criteria that affect the economics of processing and are used to evaluate an application.
6. How do these criteria affect sequential processing using either magnetic tape or magnetic disk for file storage?
7. Why is sequential processing using disks often more advantageous than using tapes?

Chapter Eight

**Direct
Access
Processing**

Direct access processing, employing disks and other direct access storage devices, has increased dramatically in the last dozen years. Such processing, in contrast to sequential processing, allows quick access to stored data. This permits timely updating as well as prompt response to inquiries. Thus, data can be both up-to-the-minute and quickly retrieved, a powerful capability for many applications.

DIRECT ACCESS STORAGE AND RETRIEVAL

Direct access storage devices (DASDs) are so named because of their capability to store data and access it directly. The term *direct access* implies the ability to retrieve data without having to read any unwanted data. Direct access storage devices must sometimes read a modest amount of unwanted data, but, for most practical purposes, they can directly access the data sought.

A disk, drum, or mass storage system uses some addressing scheme that defines the available physical locations. To read data directly, the DASD must be commanded to access the specific address of the storage location holding the data to be retrieved. This address specifies the device and the location on it that should be read.

Some form of file organization is needed so that when a data item is sought, its address can be determined. Imagine a manual filing system accessed through a knowledgeable and diligent secretary. The user need not know, or care, where particular items are stored, so long as a convenient intermediary exists to retrieve them on command. The computer, its operating system, and some chosen file organization method perform the role of the manual system secretary.

When direct access is desirable, files are commonly organized in one of two ways: *random* and *indexed sequential*. Both of these schemes have the property that, when a data item is properly specified, the information system can retrieve it almost immediately. This chapter discusses the logic and technology supporting this capability and the economics, advantages, and limitations of its use.

RANDOM (DIRECT) FILE ORGANIZATION

If the anticipated use of a file involves only low activity or requires instantaneous response, then the **random** (also called **direct**) **file organization** method is likely to be the proper choice. **Random access** refers to the ability to read any "next" item directly, without reading other intervening items. Main computer memory is a random access device. It can access any of its storage locations with equal ease and speed.

Disks, drums, and mass storage are called **direct access** devices. Although they can read items in any random sequence, the time between successive retrievals depends heavily on the actual locations accessed. For example, if data are aligned in sequence on the same surface in the same cylinder, the second item can be read only microseconds after the first. However, if the read/write arm must move and the disk must rotate, the time required to read the second item might be 100,000 microseconds, even though access to it is direct. In practice, the terms *random* and *direct* are often used interchangeably in referring to access, to file organization methods, or to storage devices.

Random (direct) file organization uses the disk's full capability for direct access and quick response time. When a user requests a data item, the system must determine its DASD address. The data item sought from this location is then retrieved by proper head movement and selection. But some means of generating the data item's address is needed, given each retrieval request.

In the random file organization method, a record's key field acts as its identifier. Given this key, the computer must be able to generate its disk address. The key is called the record's **external identifier** while its storage address is called its **internal identifier**. Two general methods—*direct* and *indirect* addressing—are available for relating these external and internal identifiers.

Direct addressing in random file organization is an awkward, outdated technique. With this scheme, the record key is the internal disk address. This means that key fields must have a format and numeric range identical to those of the available disk addresses.

Changing a record's disk address or adding and deleting records is cumbersome and wasteful of storage. As a practical matter, it is almost always better to have recognizable, useful, mnemonic, and meaningful record keys rather than to use arbitrary disk addresses as external identifiers. All things considered, this method of generating a disk address from the key (that is, having the address be identical to the key) has been discredited by trial.

Direct addressing may also be accomplished by deriving a disk address via a simple, unique, one for one correspondence of key field values and disk addresses. For instance, items numbered from 0001 to 5000 might be stored in disk addresses 20001 to 25000. Generating a suitable disk address would merely involve adding 20000 to each key field's contents and using the derived number as that record's internal disk address. This technique is often useful. In system programming, for example, the records being stored might be programming statements with statement numbers as keys.

Indirect addressing in random file organization is quite common. This technique uses a **transform** to generate the internal disk address of a record from its key field contents. A transform is an **algorithm**—a short series of procedural steps—that accepts a key field's contents as input and then outputs an acceptable disk address. Thus, the key field value need not be a disk address itself. It can be some meaningful data item such as a last name, social security number, or product code. Given this record key, the transform then computes the disk address at which that record should be stored.

When a file is originally organized and stored on disk by this technique, the key field value of each record is transformed to produce an acceptable disk address. The computer then stores the full record beginning at the disk address indicated by the transform. When there are requests for retrieval of the record, only the key need be supplied. The computer then generates the record's disk address by again applying the transform to this key field value. The record can then be retrieved by direct access—*now that its address is known to the system.*

To create a randomly organized file, each record's key is successively transformed and the full record stored in the corresponding storage location. It sometimes happens that two different key field values will generate the same disk address when transformed. In this somewhat undesirable event, the records are called **synonyms** because their transformed keys are the same. Since two records cannot be stored at the same disk location, this situation generates an **overflow**. The overflow record must be stored in an auxiliary location.

Overflow records are handled by **chaining** them into an **overflow area**. Chaining consists of logically linking one storage location to another. One method is simply to use the next location in sequence. Another linking method uses a specially reserved portion of the disk as an overflow area. In this case, the overflow location's address is then stored as part of the contents of the first location.

Thus, an overflow record is not found at its transformed address. Rather, the chaining scheme redirects access appropriately. Typically, an overflow area is set up in each cylinder, so that the redirected search for the record does not cause head movement delay. A comparison of the desired key with the synonym and subsequent keys, or with the keys of records stored in the overflow area, assures a correct matching and retrieval.

The number of overflows actually generated in initially storing a file depends on the nature of the transform and any patterns present in the key field values. Sometimes, transforms that use storage capacity quite efficiently can be devised. For example, a particular transform might generate few overflows and leave few vacant disk locations, if the file had a specific set of keys. However, if the pattern of keys were to change either by chance or design an inordinately high number of overflows might be generated.

Some transforms are designed to be **randomizing transforms**. These generate addresses by using essentially random conversions of the key field values. The resulting disk addresses span some predetermined ample storage capacity on the disk. For example, a record might have its key transformed into any of the addresses allocated for the file.

A randomizing transform has the advantage that the probable number of overflows is statistically predictable. Accordingly, the necessary overflow capacity can be predicted and allocated when the file is initially organized. Upon subsequent retrieval, given any record's key, applying the same transform will always produce the same disk address for that record. It can be directly accessed at its designated location (except that overflow records must then be sought out in the overflow location).

The records stored via the random (direct) file organization method seem to get scattered about randomly on the disk, as illustrated in Figure 8–1. They certainly are not in neat sequence by track and within cylinder. However, each record is in a particular physical location. Given the record's key, a known transform can calculate its disk address for direct retrieval.

Notice that some vacant storage appears in the file. With randomizing transform, there is a trade-off between the excess space allowed and the likely number of synonyms. It is desirable to allocate some extra storage capacity beyond what will actually get filled. This vacant space keeps down the number of synonyms and resultant overflows. Each record is more likely to be uniquely transformed.

The example below illustrates a file organized and stored via the random (direct) method using a randomizing transform. This method

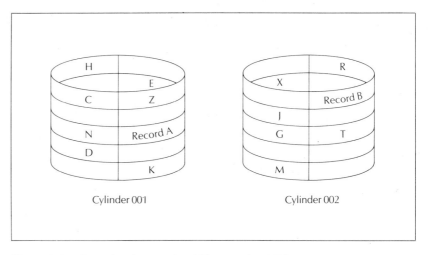

Figure 8-1. A randomly organized file stored on disk

of generating internal identifiers (addresses) from external ones (keys) is also called **hash coding** or **hashing**. Specifically, the example includes the issues of:

- organization and storage of a random file
- nature of randomizing transforms
- generation of overflows
- allowance for vacant storage capacity
- subsequent retrieval from the file

Suppose the file in our example contains only four records. Each consists of a three-digit key followed by data. The file will be stored with one record per disk track. The file's anticipated use is for *inquiry* —a low-activity use, since only one record is sought on each processing of the file. Therefore, it is desirable to store the file online using the random file organization method.

Suppose that seven tracks of disk capacity plus one track for overflow are allocated for storage. Thus, the reserved capacity is eight tracks, twice what will actually be used for storing the four records. A randomizing transform is needed. The record keys need to be converted into any one of the seven primary disk addresses. If the key fields are three-digit employee numbers, then a suitable transform might have the following algorithm:

Transform Step	*Example*
Note record key	894
Divide key by 7	127 carry 5
Note remainder	5
Add 200 for displacement	205
The result is the disk address	205 is the address

When the file is loaded, this transform is applied to each record's key. This determines the address at which that record should be stored. Dividing keys by the number 7 produces a remainder between 0 and 6. When such division is by a prime number, the remainders will tend to be randomly distributed. Each remainder is then added to a displacement value equal to the initial address allocated for the file. The displacement value 200 means that the file begins with the two hundredth track. Assuming 10 tracks per cylinder, the transform-generated address 205 means track number 5 on cylinder number 20. This transform is illustrated in Figure 8–2.

Applying the transform to each record's key in this example results in an overflow for the third record. Also, four tracks remain vacant in the **prime storage area**—the main reserved locations, excluding overflow.

Retrieval from the file can now be made directly. This unique attribute of random file organization results from being able to compute the proper disk address each time a key is provided. Other file organization methods have to search in sequence or otherwise for the given key. With random file organization, the exact record address, subject to overflow, can be computed in a few microseconds. The movement of the read/write heads to the indicated track (*seek time*) takes only about 30 milliseconds, on the average.

In summary, to retrieve a record from an online, randomly organized file, just furnish its key. Then, the transform is applied to this key and a disk address is generated. The disk makes the necessary switching and head movements and reads through some rotational delay period until the desired record is found. A matching of keys assures that the desired record has been retrieved. A mismatch of keys directs the computer to the related overflow area. This is then searched sequentially by comparing the keys of overflow records with the key being sought. This process locates the desired record. Overflow need not involve an extra read/write head movement if the overflow area is in the same cylinder as the first address.

ECONOMICS OF RANDOM FILE PROCESSING

With random file organization, records can be retrieved in any order. Actually, even if they are sought in some known order, each one must be individually retrieved since they are scattered around the disk. That

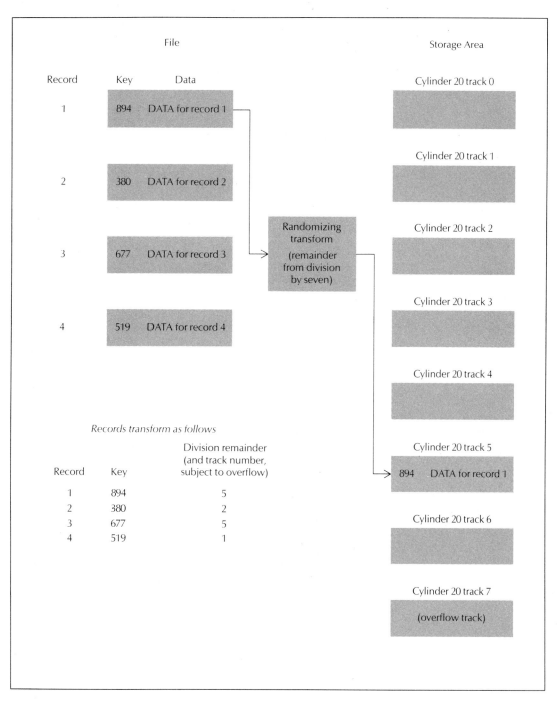

Figure 8-2. Loading a file using random organization and a randomizing transform

is, each record retrieval will likely necessitate a read/write head repositioning as well as some rotational delay. Thus, the time and cost per record accessed will not be improved by batching.

Activity

Since batching provides few economies, it is not necessary to sort transactions data. There is no preferred sequence for input. Thus, random processing has a cost per transaction with respect to activity as depicted in Figure 8–3.

Note that each transaction with the random file essentially has a fixed cost. By contrast, sequential processing has a declining unit cost as activity rises. The crossover point typically occurs around 1 percent activity. However, this figure depends significantly on file size, average record length, disk drive performance, processing time required per record, and other variables. The cost per transaction difference at either extreme of activity may be as much as 100 to 1. Inquiry into a large sequential file is prohibitively expensive. Similarly, high-activity processing of a random file is wastefully time consuming versus having the file organized sequentially.

Response Time

An online random file permits virtually immediate retrieval. However, little processing advantage or cost reduction is available from batching or sorting. Thus, the criterion of response time affects random processing economics differently than it does sequential files, as shown in Figure 8–4.

Volatility

A file's volatility also affects the overall economics of a particular method of processing. In a random file, the processes for adding and deleting records are relatively painless. For adding, the record key and the data are supplied to the computer. Then, the transform governing access to the file generates an address for this record. The record is simply stored at the indicated address if it is vacant. If the storage location is occupied, the new record is linked to the first record and stored in the appropriate overflow area. The record is now a part of the file and available for retrieval.

Deleting records vacates storage space. However, some records may still be in the overflow area after their synonym records have been deleted. And, if many records are added, an uncomfortably high number of overflows may be generated.

For these reasons, after substantial volatility has occurred, a random file is often **purged**—that is, cleaned up by being re-created. The file may be reloaded into a somewhat larger or smaller total storage area. The objective of this cleanup effort (sometimes called **garbage collecting**) is to remove gaps in overflow chains and thus reduce the number of overflows. This also reduces the access time to many records.

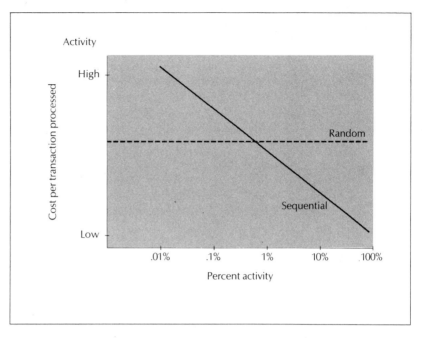

Figure 8-3. Economic impact of activity on file organization method

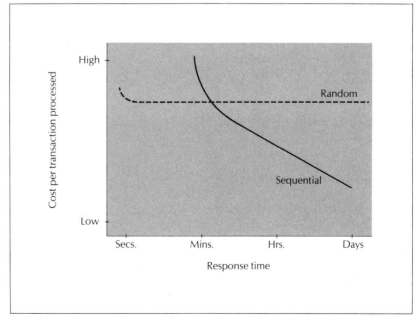

Figure 8-4. Economic impact of response time on file organization method

Sometimes thee most frequently sought records can be loaded first, which tends to minimize their likelihood of overflowing. Thus, a **frequency loading** technique also lowers the file's average access time.

Size File size partly determines whether a detailed system design should be made. In the four-record file in Figure 8-2, only a single cylinder of storage is needed. Since the read/write heads do not have to move to read the entire file, its organization is relatively unimportant. In large files, of course, the organization method together with the file's usage pattern is a major determinant of processing costs and performance.

Integration All the files affected by a particular transaction can be updated immediately with online processing of random files. A transaction, such as an order to buy a certain product, will possibly require posting to such files as customer accounts receivable, product inventory-on-hand, warehouse shipment notices, delivery truck routing lists, sales commissions, open invoices, perhaps backorders, and so forth. With random files, this transaction can be entered and—without batching, sorting, or manual intervention—all these relevant files can be updated to reflect it. Furthermore, multiple files and programs can be stored on a single disk, which enhances opportunities for highly integrated processing.

Security and Backup Random files are inherently in great danger of security and backup problems. Often, special techniques must be used to ensure correctness and recovery from errors. For example, data written on a disk are sometimes immediately read back just to check their validity. Further precautions are separately recording all requested file changes and periodically recopying the file onto tape. Access to the system may be protected by passwords and authorizations at various levels. Security and backup are growing in importance due to the needs for privacy protection and fraud prevention.

INDEXED-SEQUENTIAL FILE ORGANIZATION Sequential processing provides the lowest cost per transaction processed when activity is high for each use of the file. But, to have high activity, a significant batch of transactions must be accumulated before each run. Typically, this means that sequential processing is not practical when quick response or up-to-the-minute data are required.

Random processing provides the most economical way to retrieve a few records from a large file. Thus, if the application demands that a file be accessed as transactions or inquiries occur, then the random method will likely be best. The time delay of a sequential search would be too long. Also, the lag between event and processing, if done by batch, would be intolerable.

The selection of the sequential or random file organization method is an either-or proposition. If a file is organized to be processed sequentially, records within it cannot be accessed directly. Each record's location is simply not known. Conversely, a file that is organized for random access via transforming keys cannot be processed sequentially. Records can be gotten at in any sequence, but only by directly retrieving each record one by one. This takes as long as 100 milliseconds per record accessed. The decision between these two techniques must be made on the basis of expected activity, response time, and other criteria of the file's anticipated use.

Unfortunately, this file organization and processing decision is not always clear-cut. It is often advantageous to process a file sequentially after periodic batches of transactions have been accumulated *and* to make direct access inquiries into it between these high-activity runs. A file organization method called the **indexed-sequential access method** (**ISAM**, pronounced I SAM) helps in this case. It provides the essential benefits of both the sequential and random methods—it permits economical sequential access for high-activity batch processing *and* the convenience of direct access when activity is low and fast response is useful.

We can understand ISAM by considering how one might retrieve telephone numbers from a phone directory if forced to behave like a computer. With only sequential processing logic, one would have to read each record in order from the beginning of the phone book. To find a particular name, say Lynnett, each record would be read until Lynnett is found or the place it belongs is passed. On the average, one would have to read half the phone book.

Suppose that instead of one large directory there are 20 subbooks, indexed and stored in sequence as shown in Figure 8–5. (The name on the edge of each book is the last name appearing in it.) A glance at the figure suggests the advantage of indexed-sequential organization. This **index**, or group of periodic key fields, can be searched first. In this example, a short sequential search can indicate the subbook of interest. Having selected the proper subbook, one can sequentially search it in about one-twentieth of the search time it would take using the full nonindexed file.

Such subbooks can be further divided into sections. Thus, we can think of the procedure for locating a record in an indexed-sequential file as:

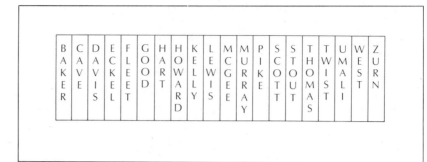

Figure 8-5. Indexed-sequential telephone subbooks

1. Sequentially search the subbook index.
2. Go to the subbook of interest.
3. Sequentially search the section index.
4. Go to the section of interest.
5. Sequentially search that section.

It should be clear that the basic file is stored sequentially. In addition, an index is created and stored. This way, a good beginning search point can be quickly determined. Usually, the search point is not the first record in the file. Thus, ISAM avoids much unnecessary record reading and key comparing. The advantage of indexed-sequential files over pure sequential ones is that the time required to locate an item of interest is drastically reduced. Their main disadvantage is the overhead cost of creating, storing, and maintaining the indexes.

The organization of an ISAM file on disk is merely an extension of the directory–subbook–section analogy. In hardware terms, this becomes:

- telephone directory—file
- subbook—cylinder
- section—surface

This index hierarchy can be illustrated by tracing through an example. Suppose we want to retrieve the record with the last-name key of LYNNETT from a telephone directory stored on a disk. The following sequence of events takes place:

- The file's cylinder index, which is known to be on a particular track, is read sequentially. For example, it might contain:

Last name on cylinder	Cylinder number
*	*
*	*
LUMP	40
LYNAS	41
LYTLE	42

- The record key being sought (LYNNETT) should be on cylinder 42 because it is between LYNAS and LYTLE. Therefore, the read/write heads are moved to cylinder 42, which has three groups of surfaces, as shown in Figure 8-6.

- The first track on cylinder 42 contains the start of the surface index. This is read sequentially until LYNNOT. Since LYNNETT should precede that key, it must therefore reside on surface 4.

- Read head 4 is selected. The records on track 4 within cylinder 42 are read sequentially in search of the record with the key LYNNETT.

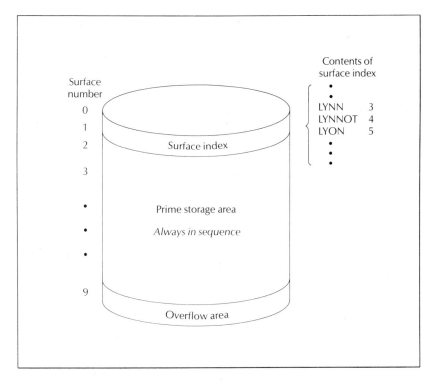

Figure 8-6.   One cylinder of an ISAM file stored on disk

Note the cylinder overflow area shown in Figure 8–6. Its use can be illustrated by considering what happens when a record like LYNNETT is added to the file. The problem with such additions stems from the fact that the sequential order of the prime area must be preserved. The addition of a record for LYNNETT would proceed as before:
- The cylinder index says LYNNETT belongs on cylinder 42.
- The surface index for cylinder 42 says that LYNNETT belongs on surface 4.

At this point the "add-a-record" procedure is different from the "find-a-record" procedure.

- The contents of track 4 are read into main storage.
- These contents are written back onto track 4 with LYNNETT's record in its proper sequence.
- With the addition of LYNNETT's record to the track, there is no room for the previous last-place record, which is LYNNOT.
- This *overflow record* from track 4 is stored in the overflow area—track 9. Notice that this movement of a record to the overflow area did not necessitate a movement of the read/write heads to another cylinder, since an overflow area is set up for each cylinder.

- Two things are now wrong on the surface index—track 4 has a new "last record" and the old last record has been moved to the track reserved for overflow. The surface index is therefore revised to:

LYNN   3
LYNNFIELD   4
LYNNOT   9
LYON   5

- Notice that the surface index is still in sequential order, but it is now longer. Any record in the cylinder can still be accessed without moving the read/write head mechanism.

ECONOMICS OF ISAM PROCESSING

The economics of indexed-sequential file processing is favorable for many business applications, as contrasted with sequential and random processing in the sections below.

Activity

Notice in Figure 8–7 that indexed-sequential processing is less economical than the better of either purely sequential or purely random

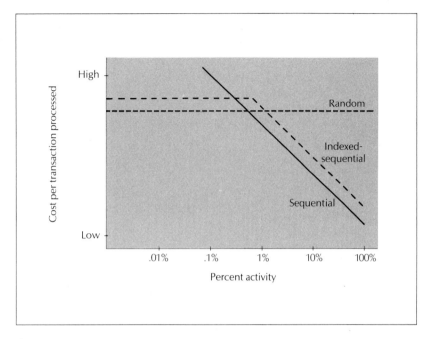

Figure 8-7.   Economic impact of activity of ISAM file processing

processing for any single activity level. Its advantage lies in economic access to records in the same file both sequentially *and* directly.

For example, at high activity, an ISAM file can be processed in sequence. This is less efficient than strict sequential processing because the indexes have to be created, stored, and maintained. These indexes are then ignored when the ISAM file is used for sequential processing—resulting in an indexing cost with no benefit.

Similarly, ISAM is less efficient than strictly random processing for low activity. The reason is that ISAM must access an index (or two) in order to determine the required cylinder and surface. This probably requires two or more head movements. The random method, by contrast, computes the sought record's exact address in microseconds and usually requires only one head movement to retrieve it. However, keeping a portion of the index in main memory and organizing the rest wisely on the disk can reduce index processing time. Furthermore, ISAM's ability to provide reasonable economics for both sequential and direct access often offsets its overhead penalty for either one.

Response Time   In terms of response time, ISAM provides a middle-ground performance, as shown in Figure 8-8. This results mainly from the effect of

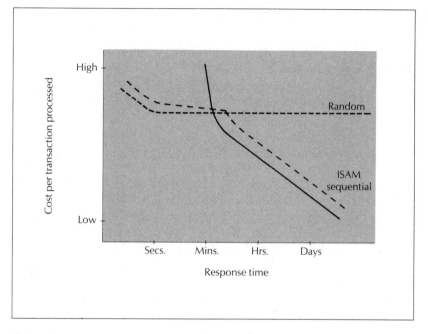

Figure 8-8. Economic impact of response time on ISAM file processing

batching time, together with ISAM's ability to retrieve individual records rapidly via its indexes or to read all records rapidly in sequence.

If ISAM files are very volatile, excessive overflows and/or vacant storage locations are generated. The overflow areas can themselves overflow to other cylinders and thus cause much read/write head movement. When this kind of overflow becomes a problem, the file must be purged. This process resequences the prime storage area, creates new indexes, and sets aside vacant overflow areas.

ISAM Summary To summarize, ISAM provides good flexibility for users who need both inquiry and high-activity processing of the same file. For either extreme of activity, the economic penalty of ISAM compared to the "best" file organization method is slight relative to the large savings versus the "worst" method. In terms of size, integration, and security and backup, its advantages and disadvantages are like those of random organization. Specifically, for small files the organization choice matters little. ISAM helps file integration potential because it makes rapid access possible via the indexes; however, data vulnerability is high. Recovery procedures and protection from accidental or deliberate loss are needed. Methods to prevent or detect unauthorized access should be embedded in both the processing logic and the operating procedures.

SUMMARY   Direct access processing can provide quick response and up-to-date data. It relies on direct access devices, principally disk. Two methods of file organization—random (direct) and indexed-sequential (ISAM) —are most common. Their costs and performance were discussed in terms of activity, response time, volatility, size, integration, and security and backup. When quick access to up-to-the-minute data is required, random processing is advantageous. When both batch processing and inquiring uses of a file are anticipated, ISAM offers the best overall economy. More advanced techniques for organizing and processing data are discussed in the next two chapters.

CONCEPTS

random file
  organization
direct file
  organization
random access
direct access
external identifier
internal identifier
direct addressing

indirect addressing
transform
algorithm
synonym
overflow
chaining
overflow area
randomizing transform
hash coding

hashing
prime storage area
purge
garbage collecting
frequency loading
indexed-sequential
  access method (ISAM)
index

QUESTIONS
1. What advantages and disadvantages does direct access processing have relative to sequential processing?
2. Cite and discuss two methods for linking external identifiers to internal identifiers.
3. What happens to a synonym record when a randomly organized file is created? How is that record subsequently retrieved?
4. What types of applications favor the use of random (direct) processing?
5. How does ISAM processing occur (including file creation and record retrieval)?
6. How does ISAM tend to combine the advantages of both sequential and random processing? What is its disadvantage relative to each?
7. If forced to organize all files by the same method, which would you select? Compare this to manually maintained records kept in folders in a file drawer.
8. Both random and ISAM processing involve a single key to each record. How can a record be retrieved, in a bank, for example, when a person's account number (record key) is unknown (but he remembers his name)? Should people have to remember such account numbers, which are part of someone else's data processing system?

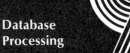

Chapter Nine

Database Processing

The previous two chapters examined sequential and direct access processing and the economics of three commonly used file organization methods. *Sequential file organization*, associated with either magnetic tape or disk processing systems, is the least sophisticated. However, it has economic advantages when used to update high-activity files where rapid response is not crucial. *Random processing systems* usually cost more per record retrieved, but they give terminal-oriented users quick access to stored data. The indexed-sequential access method (ISAM) avoids certain shortcomings of both sequential and random file organizations.

These three file organization techniques allow economical data processing, but they fail to support an essential management information need—interfile inquiry. **Database systems**, which are discussed in this chapter, relieve this shortcoming. They can also simplify creating and maintaining computer applications and their data requirements. As a result, this concept is being rapidly adopted.

DATABASE CONCEPTS As a firm gains experience with computer-based systems, it very likely will desire some applications beyond the realm of traditional data processing. Such applications are usually appropriately classified as part of a **management information system (MIS)**. (This concept will be discussed in detail in Chapter 11.) Two important MIS functions are:

- Processing routine transactions, including updating a database
- Processing data and user requests to aid managerial decisions, including inquiries into the database

Thus, a database is a significant part of an MIS and a key asset of the organization. The database concept treats this pool of data available to the organization as a **resource**—adding it to the traditional list of information systems resources: hardware, software, and people. To be a useful ongoing resource, the database requires content, structure, and management.

A second database concept, beyond viewing data as a resource, is the idea of **logical versus physical storage**. The user or programmer is concerned with the logical relationships of data items. For example, in family health records, parent-child relationships are important to many medical or social services decisions. The user should be able to retrieve, relate, and report data on any family member. A database system lets the computer worry about how to structure and store the data physically on disks or other devices. The user need only be concerned with logical relationships, like the parent-child sequence. It is up to the system to retrieve the records in that sequence, but it doesn't have to store them that way physically.

A third database concept is **reduced redundancy**. In the family record example, the last name and address might be stored only once —others in the family are assumed to have the same last name and address, unless otherwise indicated. Yet, the last name and address are logically a part of each family member's full record and can be presented to the user as such. Reduced redundancy not only saves storage space but also cuts data entry effort.

Data independence is another database concept. Traditionally, programming languages like COBOL or FORTRAN require statements *in each program* that define the data to be processed by that program. A "picture" or "format" layout of the data must be described. This makes the program dependent on the data and vice versa. A change in data formats usually requires a change in the program. And such program changes may require restructuring the data. These problems in program maintenance and modification are aggravated by staff turnover and the mere passing of time. Database systems reduce these problems by unlinking data and programs, making them independent.

A fifth feature of database systems is the **shared-data** concept. Imagine the organization's data resources as a pool into which all computer data flows and from which all seeking information can drink. But this analogy oversimplifies the situation—water is all the same (excluding pollutants). A database user wants particular data, not just any data. Perhaps, then, our database is a soup kettle (alphabet soup, no doubt, or better yet, alphameric). Users ladle out the specific items of interest. In a more realistic example, a university usually keeps each student's name and address in a number of different departmental files—with many records misspelled or out of date. In a database system, this data can be stored once, kept updated, probably correctly, and shared by authorized users.

Also, a database system allows economical **interfile inquiry**. Really, the database itself is a giant file and any of its data elements can be logically related. The traditional technique of separate applications with separate files gives way to the common database that makes all data potentially available to any application. Naturally, a heightened need for user authorization goes with this approach to preserve data integrity, security, and backup.

This chapter describes the methods of processing available with a database system. We examine several levels of user-system interaction and discuss the basic user need—called **content retrieval**—of getting the desired data quickly and economically. Then, we discuss data structures—ways of providing content retrieval capability. We also look at the role of a new specialist position, the **database administrator (DBA)**. Then, **database management systems (DBMS)**—complex software packages for organizing, managing, accessing, and controlling databases—are described. Several of the leading commercial DBMS are then reviewed.

USER-DATABASE INTERACTIONS

Broadly speaking, computer users work with database systems on one or more of eight levels of involvement:

Preformatted inquiry This is the most basic level of database usage. It involves interrogating the database for a particular data item. It is limited to predetermined questions that use preformatted input and output procedures. The system must already include the programming necessary for answering the inquiry. Often, a special-purpose button on a terminal is used for this kind of data request. For example, on a stockbroker's quotation terminal, punching in a stock symbol code and the "last price" button causes retrieval and display of the indicated stock's current price.

Ad hoc inquiry Ad hoc inquiries to the database do not have predetermined procedures; they are specialized but currently pertinent questions. At this level, the user must understand the existing content of the database and be able to use the retrieval procedures embedded in the DBMS. This interaction does not involve changing the database contents.

Routine Updating At this level, clerical personnel revise existing records via the DBMS, thus keeping the database up to date. Personnel who interact with the system at this level are usually unaware of programming. They merely follow established procedures. This procedure changes some data items, but what items are stored and how they are stored remains unchanged.

Routine additions or deletions Here clerical personnel add or delete data items (or entire records). This typically requires a higher level of authority and control than inquiry or updating. Otherwise, an unprincipled programmer, for example, might arrange for a second computer-produced paycheck without the bother of working for it. Adding a falsified payroll record, if unaudited access to the system were allowed, would be easy, technically.

Defining database content At this level, the user and analyst/programmer specify the data items needed to produce the desired computer outputs—for example, inquiry responses or periodic printed reports. To do this, the user-designer team must consider which data fields need to be maintained and what the possible retrieval combinations and interitem relationships are.

For example, consider a university payroll file. Assume that there is also a course file that contains, for each course, the instructor's name and other fields. To answer a straightforward question such as, "What is the faculty salary cost of course X?," the course file must be able to reference the payroll file. That is, the user-designer must have decided to include the instructor's name or employee number in the course file—or there must be other means of linking the two files together. A new job category—database administrator—is often established to control and coordinate the database contents.

Defining database structure At this level, an information systems specialist tries to structure the database to meet all of its design criteria with the least overall cost. The design of the database's content, data relationships, and specified response times must be evaluated against the costs of alternative structures (many of which will be discussed later in this chapter).

Managing the logical database Each user may have a different view of the database contents. For example, one program might call for an employee's hourly wage in dollars while another program expects it in cents. In the first case, BCD data coding might be assumed, whereas the second program might expect a binary representation of the hourly wage data item. These differences of units and coding can be resolved by having the DBMS transcribe the data so that all users get what their programs call for.

In a second dimension, users may want different data items. One program might want name and home address; a second might want name (with last name first) followed by business address. In database jargon, the total database is called the **schema**, referring to its logical content. Each user can then define (for each application) a **subschema**—that subset or particular view of the full database that is required for this application. The database administrator is responsible for authorizing, documenting, and controlling the schema and each user-application subschema. This gives heightened control and security over the important shared resource—the database.

Managing the physical database   At this final and most complex level, systems programmers (perhaps using a purchased DBMS package) are concerned with devising storage allocation and security methods for the database. They must consider both accidental loss and unauthorized tampering, for example.

A database management system can be thought of as a way of insulating data users from the intricacies of data storage. It supports most or all of the functions summarized in Table 9.1. The system retrieves selected data items from the database, on request and without laborious processing. Such a system also simplifies the tasks of data definition, storage, processing, display, and security. Its purpose is

TABLE 9.1   EIGHT LEVELS OF USER-DATABASE INTERACTION

1. Preformatted inquiry	Two levels of inquiry, without changing database contents
2. Ad hoc inquiry	
3. Routine updating	Two levels of changing database values, but not the type of content
4. Routine additions or deletions	
5. Defining database content	Managerial activities of increasing complexity and involvement with systems specialists to set or change what should be in the database and the interrelationship between items.
6. Defining database structure	
7. Managing the logical database	Most complex technical involvement handled by systems specialists and DBMS to change the user view of or actual storage of the database
8. Managing the physical database	

much like that of a high-level language, which insulates a programmer from the nitty-gritty of the machine's details. The database system, designed to operate with the computer's software operating system, insulates the user from many data related details, as illustrated in Figure 9–1.

CONTENT RETRIEVAL

The uses of computers include processing transactions and aiding decisions. In business organizations this means economically updating files and databases and responding quickly to inquiries for data.

The classic problem of file processing—balancing fast data retrieval against economical full-file processing—is shown pictorially in Figure 9–2a. As design criteria are shifted toward providing fast retrieval, economical file maintenance suffers (Figure 9–2b). An economic balance is achieved only if the value to the user outweighs the higher cost of file maintenance (Figure 9–2c). Database management systems minimize the classic imbalance between retrieval and maintenance by shortening the gap between the two functions (Figure 9–2d).

Database management systems also reduce the human effort involved both in constructing new applications and in providing application maintenance. The relationship of DBMS to other software developments that have also reduced user effort is shown in Figure 9–3.

As we have seen, first-generation computers required tedious machine-language programming. Second-generation machines combined improved hardware design with such user improvements as widely adopted assembly languages and input-output control systems (IOCS), the forerunners of today's operating systems. The introduction of third-generation hardware, such as the IBM System/360 series, ac-

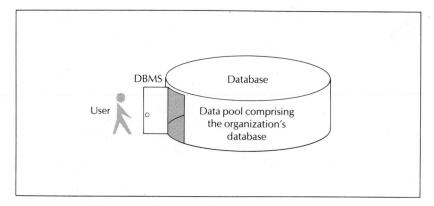

Figure 9–1. Conceptual illustration of a user, a database, and a DBMS

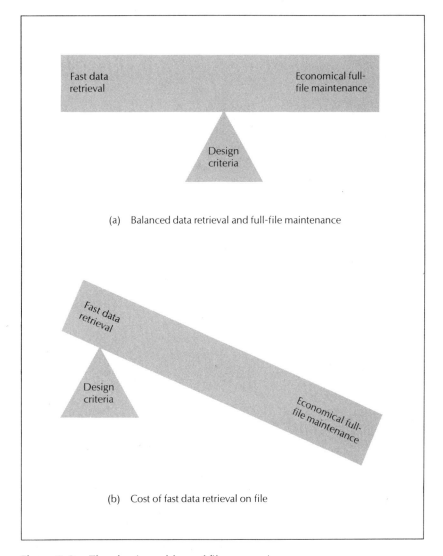

Fast data retrieval

Economical full-file maintenance

Design criteria

(a)   Balanced data retrieval and full-file maintenance

Fast data retrieval

Design criteria

Economical full-file maintenance

(b)   Cost of fast data retrieval on file

Figure 9-2.   The classic problem of file processing

celerated the use of high-level languages like COBOL in a program-ming environment controlled by the machine's own operating system. With later hardware, such as the IBM System/370, the management of large and complex databases has become more automated. Database management systems support the user's need to extract content infor-mation from interrelated files, especially for effective decision aiding information.

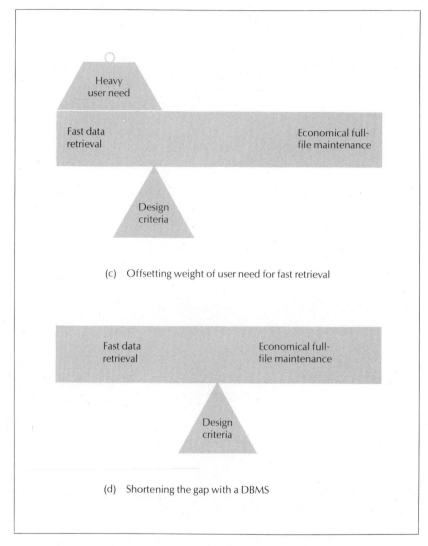

(c)   Offsetting weight of user need for fast retrieval

(d)   Shortening the gap with a DBMS

Figure 9-2.   The classic problem of file processing (cont'd.)

Content retrieval means inquiry based on a sought fact, rather than by specifying a key field. For example, suppose you have an invoice file formatted as illustrated in Figure 9-4. Notice that the file is organized sequentially by invoice number for economical batch processing. However, the problem is that a file can be organized sequentially by only one key. All other content, such as data on a particular customer, is spread throughout the file. Herein lies a major frustration for those

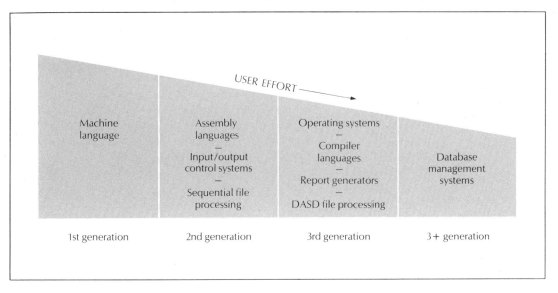

Figure 9–3. Effect of software improvements on user effort

Invoice number	Customer number	Other invoice information
1001	20	XXXXXXXXXXXXXXXXXXXXXXXXX
1002	6	XXXXXXXXXXXXXXXXXXXXXXXXX
1003	20	XXXXXXXXXXXXXXXXXXXXXXXXX
1004	3	XXXXXXXXXXXXXXXXXXXXXXXXX

Figure 9–4. Unpaid invoice file

seeking management information from a system organized for efficient data processing.

The invoice file in Figure 9–4 permits efficient file updating. Yet, managers often need information that is not usually provided during file updating. For example, a manager might need to know the invoice number and total amount due on all unpaid invoices for "customer 20." She knows that the data is in the file and generally cannot understand why it is difficult to retrieve. However, to respond to such an inquiry, this system must be able to perform content retrieval—that is, extract nonkey data elements.

The straightforward way to perform content retrieval is to search the entire file for the desired items. Thus, to find customer 20, each invoice record in the file must be read. Unfortunately, most files are too large for frequent total searches. They force the computer to do an enormous amount of what it does worst—input/output. For example, even at top speed, a few minutes are required to read a full magnetic disk pack just to process a content match for a nonkey field.

Such special-purpose content retrieval runs are very expensive. So, some DBMS provide this capability as a byproduct of routine sequential file updates. In such systems, ad hoc inquiries demanding content retrieval are saved and batched. Then they are run with other transactions during routine file processing. Obviously, however, this content retrieval strategy cannot provide the fast response time that is often vital to decision-making quality and productivity.

DATA STRUCTURES

Database systems that provide quick content retrieval must be able to retrieve nonkey data items directly from large files. The problem is like using your local phone book to find all the names that have addresses on a particular street—without reading the whole book. To perform content retrieval, related data items, such as each customer's invoices or all people living on the same street, must somehow be logically tied together. The methods for structuring these logical relationships among data items are reviewed below.

Sequential, Random, and Indexed-Sequential

In Chapters 7 and 8 we discussed sequential and direct access processing and three methods of organizing data to support such processing: sequential, random, and indexed-sequential. Database processing includes other data structures among its list of options. Based on the user's needs, including the economics of cost versus value of information, these more intricate but more powerful data structures are increasingly being adopted to support content retrieval.

The first kind of DBMS we will illustrate relies on traditionally organized files, but is still able to respond economically to ad hoc requests. For example, suppose we request that a special report be drawn from a sequentially organized file. This can be done easily, *if* the response can be delayed and performed as a byproduct of the next normally scheduled file update run. This technique is attractive because such reports can be made with little marginal processing cost, as measured by system throughput or I/O efficiency. Furthermore, such reports may give management extremely useful information within an acceptable time frame.

The best-selling sequential byproduct DBMS is the MARK IV File Management System of Informatics, Inc. In addition to its content retrieval capability, MARK IV also reduces programmer effort, as illustrated by the following example: Suppose that, when processing a personnel file, sequenced by employee number, a special purpose telephone directory is desired that lists name (in alphabetical order), phone extension, home address, and home phone. Without a DBMS, such a request would require both a special-purpose program and a special run. The cost of either might likely be more than the value of the directory.

But a user of the MARK IV system could communicate such an ad hoc request by merely coding it on an information request form. Complex requests may require additional forms, but the report in this example can be triggered by the short request shown in Figure 9–5.

This request tells the system that as a byproduct of normal work on the file named PERSONEL, extract the PHONEEXT, ADDRESS, and HOMEPHON. When the normal processing of this file is completed, the extracted information is alphabetized. Then, using full English labels such as HOME ADDRESS, rather than the abbreviated field identifiers such as ADDRESS, a nicely spaced report is produced. The resulting report appears in Figure 9–6.

The most common form of file organization has been a file sequenced physically on a single key. Inquiries on the basis of any other data item usually require resorting or passing of the entire file. Thus, a large part of sequential file processing involves sorting and merging—combining of two or more files into one file with the same sequence. Furthermore, sequential processing tends to encourage lengthy batch cycles, extending turnaround time. In turn, this encourages producing voluminous listings in anticipation of possible inquiries. Managers getting such comprehensive file listings rightfully feel inundated with an overabundance of largely irrevelant data.

With a random file structure, any given record's retrieval must also be based on a single key. Therefore, when the existing file key is not relevant to the data sought, the entire file must be searched.

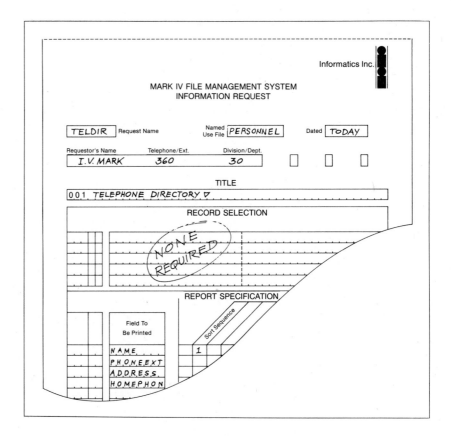

Figure 9-5. Sample MARK IV information request sheet

Similarly, with an indexed-sequential file, there is only one key field for retrieval. There are two access strategies in this case: Read the full file in sequence from the beginning or skip inappropriate parts of the file by consulting the index. In either case, retrieval by content other than the key field requires a time-consuming search of the full file.

One solution to this dilemma is to create many copies of the records, each with a separate access key. But this soon leads to duplication and complicated logical relationships among records. Both of these problems are lessened by means of pointers used to create chains, lists, and rings.

Pointers, Chains, Lists, and Rings   The database concept permits retrieval by contents other than a single key field. The data must be structured, with defined logical relationships, so as to support such retrieval. The major traditional way of relating records is via their physical storage—the next logical record is the next physical record. But what if the dimension of inquiry changes?

```
Feb, 31, 1984              Telephone Directory              Page 1
----------------------------------------------------------------------
                        Phone                Home              Home
        Name            Extension            Address           Phone
----------------------------------------------------------------------

Addams, S.               243        134 Rodda Ave.        781-2345
Blauner, D.              272        1214 Hill St.         345-7829
Bliesner, R. G.          260        891 Westlake Ave.     347-7865
Buettell, T. D.          269        812 N. Orange Ave.    378-2121
Braddock, F.             262        121 National Blvd.    347-8876
Cooper, W. R., Jr.       203        144 E. Grove Ave.     873-4211
Coryell, T.              265        782 S. Brand Ave.     781-9782
Couch, S. J.             247        817 Roscoe St.        871-3131
Cutler, W. C.            250        1218 Standard Ave.    781-9650
Dowkont, A. J.           240        1814 National Blvd.   781-9600
Gatto, A. T.             272        128 Commerce St.      781-2515
Glenn, R. C.             242        130 Aviation Blvd.    347-6430
Haskell, E. L.           245        161 Trade St.         341-9539
Huber, C. L.             248        315 Kimberly Ave.     345-7824
Jacobson, H.             246        170 Allen Blvd.       342-6830
Johnson, N.              253        23 Lambeth Way        781-5974
Keys, P. M.              224        163 Armenta St.       348-1233
Kinn, C. J.              242        1117 Maple Ave.       341-
Kreiner, P. F.           268        1007 Hill
Lamia, A.                255        1025 Traid St.
Levine, D. A.            251        19 Irondale Ave.
Mark, I. V.              360        444 Ivy St.
Mason, R. J.             279        411 League
Moore, M. L.             280        33 Frankl
Postley, J. A.           278        412 Cen
Prince, L. C.            255        792 C
Ray, L. R.               251        745
Redekopp, J. A.          276
Smitley, B. L.           274
Stone, R. D.             243
Sunderland, R. S.        276
Taylor, J. R.            276
Utt, C. G.               2
White, R. R.
Zanicchi, J.
```

Figure 9-6. Sample output from MARK IV request

Then, the "next" logical record desired may not be the next physical one. We must create a logical link between the record just accessed and the next desired record. And we must do it for each important dimension of inquiry.

Returning to our invoice illustration, suppose the file sequenced by

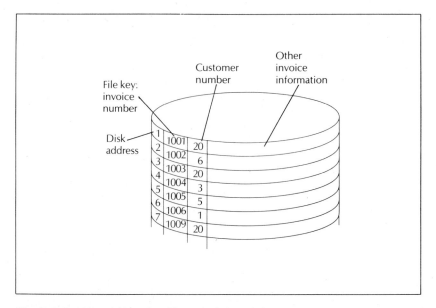

Figure 9-7. Unpaid invoice file stored on a disk

invoice number is now stored on disk as depicted in Figure 9-7. As mentioned, it would be useful to support inquiry not only by invoice number (the key field), but also by customer number (a content field). As stated before, we might want to know the status of all invoices for customer 20. How can exactly these—and only these—records be retrieved *without searching through the whole file?*

Records that are logically related can be linked or tied together by means of **pointers**. A pointer is a reference to another record: its storage address. A data field can be added to a record for the purpose of storing a pointer to the next logical record. Then, the currently accessed record has sufficient information to find the next logical record—*even if it is not the next physical record.* By accessing the storage location indicated by the pointer (called **pointer chasing**), the desired retrieval is accomplished. To do this quickly and economically, direct access storage devices are used. Also, attention must be paid to the structure of logical relationships relative to the actual physical storage.

Our invoice problem requires retrieval of all outstanding invoices for a particular customer from a file sequenced by invoice number. The file is now stored on a disk using storage addresses 1 through 7, as shown in Figure 9-7. To link together the several invoice records all pertaining to customer 20, we could add a **link field**, or pointer, to each record in the file. This would require storage and processing time to set up, but would enhance retrieval capability. The contents of each record's pointer field would be the address of the "next" logical record. That is, the record stored at location 1 (the first record about customer 20) would point to record 3 (the "next" record, since it also deals with customer 20 and no intervening records do). Record 3 would point to the storage address of the next record dealing with customer 20.

A sequence of records related by pointers is called a **chain** or **list**. A **two-way list** has pointers to both the "next" and the "prior" records in the chain. Some schemes also store a pointer back to the master record. This formation, called a **circular list** or **ring**, is shown in Figure 9-8.

You might properly ask how the first record in the chain is found. In our illustration, the file's first physical record *was* the first logical record we wanted. Also, suppose we didn't know the customer number was 20, but remembered that it was ABC Company. After all, that's the way *they* identify themselves. It is only a figment of our system that they are customer 20 to us. We might have to consult a second file—the customer file—to cope with these issues. This is shown in Figure 9-9 and discussed below.

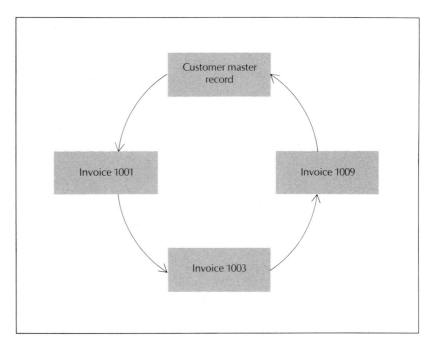

Figure 9-8.   A circular file

Assume that a customer file on another disk is also directly address-able. (The format of this file is illustrated in Figure 9–9.) Its key field is the customer number. It is economical to have such a separate customer file to store the full customer name, address, zip code, credit rating, and so forth without repeating this data for each of several invoices.

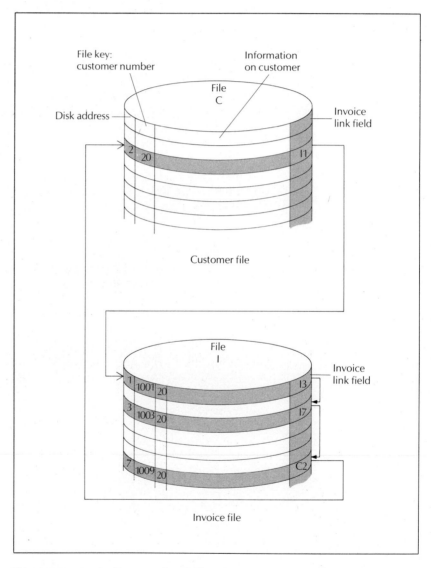

Figure 9–9. Logically interrelated files

Assume that rapid retrieval of a given customer's record is available from an inquiry terminal, preferably by either customer number or customer name. Our data management problem, however, is how to retrieve all the outstanding invoices for customer 20. This can be done by logically tying together all the outstanding invoices for each customer with the customer's master record. Figure 9–8 shows this group of logically related records as a ring through the customer's master record and all his outstanding invoices. This ring was constructed by adding a link field to each record. Each link field contains the address of the next record in the chain. The finished result is shown in Figure 9–9.

Retrieving all the outstanding invoices for customer 20 is now merely a matter of following the chain until the address in the invoice link field equals the starting address—the indication of the chain's end. This is illustrated by the arrows in Figure 9–9. An instruction such as "DISPLAY 'NUMBER' AND 'AMOUNT DUE' FOR ALL INVOICES WITH 'CUSTOMER' EQUALS 20" can be issued from an online terminal. The DBMS should now, with proper retrieval programs and data definitions, be able to respond to this type of managerial inquiry.

Notice that this structure allows the ring to be entered at any point. Either the head of the chain can be accessed via the customer number field in file C or the chain can be entered via an invoice number access to file I. For example, suppose there is a problem with invoice 1003. Then the user might want that customer's credit rating. Moving to the head of invoice 1003's chain provides the full customer record, including the desired credit information. If the user wants to see that customer's other invoices, she can make the full-circle tour through the ring.

List structures differ from other forms of data organization because they use pointers to reorder a logical sequence easily without physically relocating the records. A pointer field contains the address of the next record in *logical* sequence according to one of many possible relationships. Logical relationships may be changed by modifying the pointer field contents. With multiple pointers in each record, several logical relationships can be expressed. Each forms the basis of an inquiry without completely searching the entire file.

Processing data structured as lists allows a record to have any number of keys by associating a pointer field with each key. These pointers form chains through the database, one for each pointer field. This allows records with the same particular attribute to be successively retrieved and processed. Thus, with a table of pointers to the first record in each chain, it is possible to have several access keys and yet have a single physical record arrangement.

In large files, these chains tend to become long. So further techniques must be used to reduce chain length and the associated search time. Also, the pointers must be created, stored, and maintained. (This occurs automatically via the DBMS.) In summary, pointers allow efficient access via multiple keys, reduced redundancy, and complex logical data relationships.

Multiple Index Systems

An **index** is a systematic group of pointers. In an indexed sequential file, records are sequenced by some key and an index shows the addresses of certain records. To retrieve a record, the index can be consulted rather than searching sequentially through the entire file. The file's structure, however, still supports rapid sequential processing of a batch of transactions, as is often desirable.

By using *multiple* indexes, retrieval by more than one dimension of inquiry is possible. For example, the personnel file shown in Figure 9–10 is maintained in alphabetic order by the last-name field. Suppose, however, that we would like to create a file of only the names of males aged 21 through 25. The brute force way is to pass the file sequentially and examine each record. The pointer-chasing solution would require that we add a link field to each record. This would form a chain of all records having the specified attributes.

The third general solution to the problem of content retrieval is to maintain multiple indexes. One commonly used index is called an **inverted index**. It contains the same information that would appear in the link fields of a list. However, the pointers are brought together into a single table. An inverted index for the attributes Sex and Age from our personnel file example appears in Figure 9–11.

With this inverted index, the problem of retrieving all the records of males between the ages of 21 and 25 is now simplified. We need only retrieve the records common to the two pertinent inverted indexes—in this case, records 1 and 9.

Another index scheme used by some DBMS is the **bit index**. Here the presence or absence of a designated attribute is coded in one binary bit. In this illustration, the search would be the logical operator AND between the attributes Sex = male and Age = 21–25. The result again is that only records 1 and 9 exhibit both of these conditions, as shown in Figure 9–12. Thus, the system need only retrieve these records directly—without searching the full file—to provide the requested report.

Let us now compare multiple index systems with the use of pointers for linking records into chains via any of several keys. Any field may be treated as a key, so many lists may pass through a record. Each list has an entry point for searching it. However, extended searches through long chains may be required. List length can be restricted, which in

DASD address	Last name	(Miscellaneous data)	Sex	Age
1	Adams		M	21
2	Baker		F	30
3	Clark		F	32
4	Dodd		F	24
5	Evans		M	39
6	Fara		F	28
7	Gonzalez		M	31
8	Hall		F	36
9	Irwin		M	25
10	Jones		M	40

Figure 9-10. Hypothetical personnel file used for retrieval

Sex = male	Sex = female	Age = 21–25	Age = 26–30	Age = 31–35	Age = 36–40
1	2	1	2	3	5
5	3	4	6	7	8
7	4	9			10
9	6				
10	8				

Figure 9-11. Partial inverted index

	Sex = male	Sex = female	Age = 21–25	Age = 26–30	Age = 31–35	Age = 36–40
Record 1	1	0	1	0	0	0
Record 2	0	1	0	1	0	0
Record 3	0	1	0	0	1	0
Record 4	0	1	1	0	0	0
Record 5	1	0	0	0	0	1
Record 6	0	1	0	1	0	0
Record 7	1	0	0	0	1	0
Record 8	0	1	0	0	0	1
Record 9	1	0	1	0	0	0
Record 10	1	0	0	0	0	1

Figure 9-12. Partial bit index

effect creates sublists with their own entry points. This reduces search time at the expense of an expanded index of entry points.

In the inverted index approach, no pointers appear in the records themselves. Instead, for each key value, a list of the addresses of all records containing that particular value is formed. Thus, each possible value of every field can be the basis of retrieval. Such an approach requires an index, or **dictionary**, of all data values in the system and the addresses of all locations where they occur. This dictionary can be larger than the data file itself. But, it allows access to all data with equal ease. This is especially useful when data retrieval needs are not predictable, as in decision making and planning activities.

DATABASE MANAGEMENT SYSTEMS

Dozens of vendors now offer DBMS packages. On a spectrum of increasing sophistication, the most basic packages, called **report generators**, are not DBMS in the full sense, but they do facilitate the preparation of certain reports. Next are a class of **batch-byproduct systems** that offer users full data management capability as a byproduct of sequential file processing. The most sophisticated DBMS provide online, terminal-oriented access to multiple files by providing one or another method for achieving quick content retrieval.

In addition to their level of sophistication, DBMS can be distinguished by other important criteria. The user who must choose among alternative systems should also consider, for each, the factors of:

- cost—purchase price or monthly rental for the package
- inquiry response time
- interactive data entry—available or not
- types of data structures
- data security features
- impact on throughput of file maintenance requirements
- inquiry terminology and access to other languages
- hardware configuration constraints

Recall the six concepts underlying database systems, as discussed at the beginning of this chapter:

1. Database as a resource
2. Logical versus physical storage
3. Reduced redundancy
4. Data independence
5. Shared data
6. Interfile inquiry

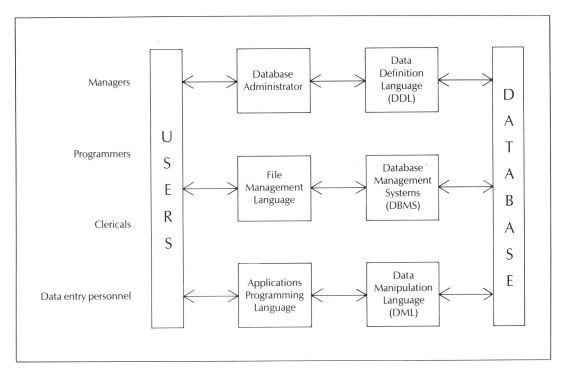

Figure 9–13. Components of a database system

It should be clear that database systems and DBMS packages use a collection of techniques to achieve these concepts. Figure 9–13 diagrams this process. The **data definition language (DDL)** is used to label and state the type of fields, groups, records, and so on; and to specify how data items are logically related. The **data manipulation language (DML)** is used to provide the data as the program wants it, regardless of the way it is actually stored. A file management language lets the manager call for report generation, and an applications programming language lets the programmer specify processing procedures.

Users are insulated from database details, including how data are physically stored. Database administrators oversee data definitions, authority for data access, the DBMS, and the database itself. They must provide for such logical controls as **passwords** that allow access and **audit trails** that monitor changes. Physical security is provided by locks, hazard detectors, personnel identification, and guards and is usually augmented by remotely stored backup copies.

Hierarchical, Network, and Relational Models

One important classification of DBMS is in terms of the overall data structure used to store and relate individual data items. (The smallest data items are sometimes called **data elements**.) Three models, widely discussed in the field, will be briefly introduced here:

- **hierarchical**
- **network**
- **relational**

A hierarchical structure defines relationships between record types called **owners** and **members**. For example, an accounts receivable (A/R) record for a customer may be the owner of many members, which are the individual credit transactions involving that customer. Similarly, the firm's overall accounts receivable record is the owner of all the customer-level records. This forms a hierarchy or tree structure, shown in Figure 9–14. This structure is especially appropriate when records have repeated fields of varying number. Pointers, chains, lists, rings, and indexes are used to establish the logical relationships among data and to support physical retrieval.

A network structure adds complexity in representing logical relationships by allowing references between any records. Thus, links other than an owner-member relationship can be forged. This is diagrammed in Figure 9–15.

A relational database imposes no limits on the relationships

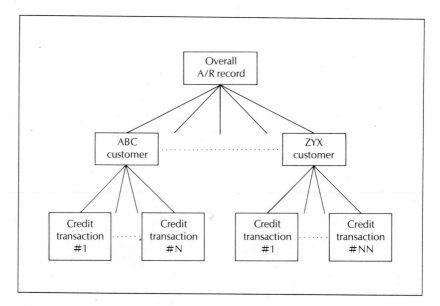

Figure 9–14. A hierarchy of owner and member records

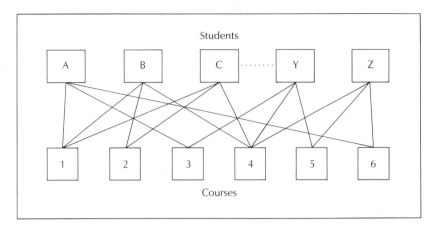

Figure 9-15. A network structure

Faculty	Rank	Spouse Name	Age	Spouse Age	Department
AMOS	PROFESSOR	GEORGE	40	46	MGT
JONES	ASST. PROF.	SUSAN	42	39	MKT
PARKS	ASSOC. PROF.	MARY	29	28	MKT
ANDERSON	PROFESSOR		35		FIN
HICKS	ASST. PROF.	SUSAN	32	26	IS

Figure 9-16. A relation

between records. This concept is illustrated in Figure 9-16. The file appears simple: the column headings are called **attributes** and the rows are called **tuples**, and each must be unique. From this scheme, any complex relationship, including those above, can be specified.

Commercial DBMS Packages As a guide, a few commercially available DBMS, and criteria for their evaluation, are compared in Table 9.2.

TABLE 9.2 DBMS PACKAGES

DBMS Name	Vendor	Remarks	Approximate Price*
ADABAS	Software AG	Batch or online COBOL, FORTRAN, PL/1 English query language Uses inverted indexes passwords and teleprocessing	$100,000
IDMS/ IMS-VS	IBM	Batch or online COBOL or PL/1 Full and partial inverted indexes Passwords and teleprocessing	$1,000/mo.
SYSTEM 2000	MRI Systems	Batch or online COBOL, Fortran English query language Inverted indexes in hierarchy Passwords and teleprocessing	$30,000
TOTAL	Cincom Systems	Batch or online COBOL, Fortran, PL/1 Network or hierarchical teleprocessing	$40,000
IDMS	Cullinane	Batch or online COBOL, PL/1 Linked lists, networks, Passwords and teleprocessing	$50,000
MARK IV	Informatics	Batch COBOL fortran, PL/1 Query coding forms Sequential byproduct	$40,000

*Price depends on features. All systems costs must be gauged relative to total implementation costs and benefits achieved.

S2K *[handwritten annotation next to SYSTEM 2000]*

✳ Most likely to do what it says. *[handwritten annotation next to TOTAL]*

SUMMARY In this chapter we have discussed the need for and concepts underlying database systems. They overcome certain limitations of traditional file organization methods, such as sequential, random, and indexed-sequential access. Database management systems (DBMS) insulate the user from the database's details and relationships while allowing retrieval of requested data items. They balance the benefits of fast data retrieval with economical full-file maintenance.

There are eight levels of increasing interaction with a database: preformatted inquiry, ad hoc inquiry, routine updating, routine additions or deletions, defining database content, defining database structure, managing the logical database, and managing the physical database. Database management systems allow retrieval based on content by using the techniques of sequential byproduct search, chains and pointer chasing, or multiple indexes. In turn, data can be structured by different approaches, such as sequential, random, lists, rings, and various indexes. Finally, we introduced the spectrum of DBMS: hierarchical, network, and relational models, including some commercially available packages and the criteria for their evaluation.

CONCEPTS

database system
management
information system
  (MIS)
database system
resource
logical versus
  physical storage
reduced redundancy
data independence
shared data
interfile inquiry
content retrieval
database
  administrator
  (DBA)
database management
  system (DBMS)

schema
subschema
merge
pointer
pointer chasing
link field
chain
list
two-way list
circular list
ring
index
inverted index
bit index
dictionary
report generator
batch-byproduct
  system

data definition
  language (DDL)
data manipulation
  language (DML)
password
audit trail
data element
hierarchical
  model
network model
relational model
owner
member
attribute
tuple

QUESTIONS

1. What does it mean to say that a DBMS insulates the user from the database?
2. What are the goals of DBMS?
3. Discuss eight levels at which computer users may interact with the database.
4. Explain the evolution of database systems software.
5. A human being can recall by associating content; what techniques do database systems use for content retrieval?
6. What are some alternative approaches for structuring data?
7. Describe an application that seems suited to a hierarchical database structure. To a network structure.
8. Since DBMS are growing in importance, criteria for their evaluation are important. How should such systems be selected?

Chapter Ten

**Distributed
Processing**

10

This is the concluding chapter of Part 3, which covers data processing methods and their comparative economics. This chapter discusses a culminating capability—that of tying separate locations into an integrated information system, each having immediate access to the programs and data it requires. Through distributed processing, the information system can become the central nervous system for an organization. This ultimate system, combining online processing and the database concept together with local access and processing, allows users to retrieve any data, any time, anywhere.

DISTRIBUTED PROCESSING CONCEPT

Distributed processing means *decentralizing* or delegating computing activities and providing the hardware, software, data, and communications to make the pieces part of the whole. It is a technical and organizational issue and is gaining adherents. This represents a reversal of the long-standing trend toward centralized computer activities.

Trend Toward Centralization

Throughout the 1960s and into the early 1970s there was a nearly unanimous trend toward tightly controlled, more centralized, larger scale computer operations. The driving reason was the presumed **economy of scale**. That is, it was felt that largescale operations were more economical per unit of work done.

During this period, it had been shown that large computers did have "more bang for the buck." Despite being more expensive, large systems produced more throughput per dollar. This technological and cost relationship is known as **Grosch's Law**. Herbert Grosch publicized the observation that by paying twice as much for a computer, you could buy one with quadruple the processing power. *(No longer true)*

Thus, organizations tried to centralize computing demands, probably at corporate headquarters, and installed the largest computer possible. It was also asserted that centralized data entry and computer operations could benefit from multishift operations, load balancing, and other efficiencies. Even applications development could become more economical, *if* standardized software could be written to satisfy the needs of many divisions—thereby cutting duplication of effort.

Trend Toward Decentralization

With the emergence of an information systems department and the corporate data center came some loss of touch with the rest of the organization—the users. (The organizational and management aspects of this issue will be explored in Part 5.)

Increasingly, ways had to be sought to keep data processing relevant to users' needs. Also, it became recognized that data entry is best done by someone responsible for the transaction, who knows what the data mean. And answers need to be distributed to users at their worksites, not just printed in a glass-walled computer room at headquarters. This led to an increased desire to distribute to users the I/O function and even processing, programming, and data storage. This is distributed processing—a system with both central *and* local capabilities. It relies on the rapidly improving technology and economics of minicomputers, intelligent terminals, and data communications.

MINICOMPUTERS AND INTELLIGENT TERMINALS

Minicomputers generally sell for under $100,000 and often for under $25,000, or even under $5,000. Traditionally, minicomputers were used mostly for scientific and engineering calculations and for industrial process control. But their capabilities have extended to the business world of transactions processing and MIS applications. Even small-scale systems now have fast processors and a full line of peripherals, such as terminals, card readers, printers, disks, and tapes. Also, minicomputer vendors now offer more support services, such as operating systems, high-level language compilers, business applications packages, and training. In short, minicomputers can be cost effective without being gigantic.

Intelligent terminals are a cross between a minicomputer and a conventional I/O terminal. Their "intelligence" comes from having some memory and processing circuitry built in. They may also have storage using cassette tape cartridges or diskettes. This lets users do some processing and storage at the terminal site.

Typically, data entry and editing might be done during the daytime. Then, at lower nighttime rates, a central computer might call for automatic transmission of the finished results. By morning, processed reports could be communicated back to the remote site and printed. They would then be available for clerical or management attention.

DATA COMMUNICATION

Data communication, also called **telecommunication** or **teleprocessing**, links computers to other computers or to terminals through communication channels. Usually, data communication involves sending electronic signals over ordinary telephone lines. Data communication became commercially feasible with the widespread delivery of third-generation computers in the latter 1960s. (Prior to this, it was used mainly for defense applications and certain leading-edge business uses like airline reservations or experimental time-sharing systems.) After some early difficulties, data communication became increasingly common during the 1970s.

Data communication helps provide quick access to timely data. Also, communicated data is already in electronic form—no further data entry procedures are required. But probably the biggest justification for data communication is that it permits computing demand to be centralized or decentralized. This allows cheaper, better computing. Pooled demand can support a large efficient computer and may make load balancing possible among several smaller computers tied together by communications. Pooled demand may also make specialized applications or integrated databases more feasible.

Communication Alternatives

Several techniques are used to provide the necessary communications. An overview of communication alternatives is presented in Table 10.1. This comparison shows transmission methods, rates, and costs. A transmission rate is often expressed as a **baud** rating, a telegraph communications term. One baud essentially corresponds to one bit

TABLE 10.1   CURRENT DATA TRANSMISSION METHODS
AND CAPABILITIES

Transmission Method	Transmission Rate baud	cps	Transmission* Cost/Month-Mile	Relative Cost at Full Usage
Teletype	100	10	$.50	1
Voice-grade	300	30	1	.6
line	2400	240	1	.08
	9600	960	2	.04
Microwave, infrared, laser	50000+	5000+	5	.02

*Assumes a 1000-mile line.

per second. The characters-per-second rating (cps) reflects the fact that one character involves about ten bits of transmission. The transmission cost figures assume a line reserved for this communications purpose and used at the data rate indicated. Notice that substantial economies of scale are available, especially if an ordinary telephone line, or **voice-grade line**, can be used to full capacity.

The design or evaluation of a data communication system depends on the analysis of the following crucial factors:

1. The volume of data transmission.
2. The distance over which this data volume is transmitted.
3. The configuration of the transmission links.
4. The accuracy requirements and acceptable error rates.
5. The availability of communication lines when needed.
6. The urgency of the data and the profile of its value over time.
7. The code of the transmitted data.
8. The cost of alternative communication techniques.

Communication links provide one of three kinds, or modes, of transmission, as defined below and depicted in Figure 10–1:

- **Simplex:** sends a message in one direction.
- **Half-duplex:** allows transmission in either direction, but not simultaneously. Most United States telephone lines have this type of capability.
- **Full-duplex:** allows simultaneous transmission in both directions. Special-purpose telephone lines provide this capability.

When signals are transmitted along wires (like telephone lines) or through the air (like radio waves), their information-carrying capabilities are due to **modulation** of the underlying signals. Thus, a radio station's carrier signal may either have **amplitude modulation (AM)** or **frequency modulation (FM)**. In addition, some high-speed wire transmissions of data also involve **phase modulation**, or a shifting of the signal's waveform. Signal modulation is illustrated in Figure 10–2.

Modems are devices that interface between a computer device and a communication line. In essence, they produce signals that can be transmitted over phone lines or similar links. A second modem is required at the other end of the line to demodulate the transmitted signal. The term **modem** derives from its function of *modulation-de-modulation*.

Finally, it is useful to distinguish between **asynchronous** and **synchronous** data transmission. In asynchronous systems, the connecting

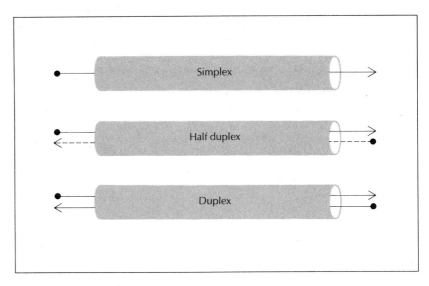

Figure 10-1. Three transmission modes

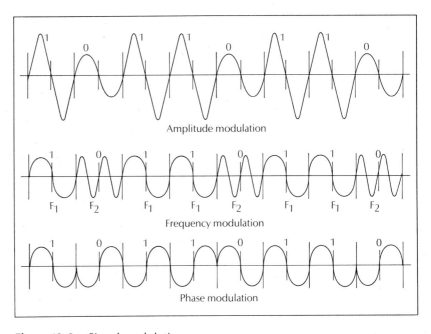

Figure 10-2. Signal modulation

line carries a steady signal corresponding to a binary 1. Each character of transmission is then preceded by a **start bit**—the sending of a binary 0. The receiving terminal then decodes the next several bits as a character. This is followed by a **stop bit** returning the line to the 1 condition. The message is sent character-by-character in this way. The message length depends on the code used—five bits per character for the **Baudot code** and eight bits for a more common code, **ASCII** (American National Standard Code for Information Interchange, also called ANSCII).

Synchronous transmission, in contrast, keeps the sending and receiving modem in proper synchronization throughout an entire message. Thus, the start and stop bits are not needed for each character —only for the message as a whole. This scheme requires elaborate timing circuitry and is more expensive. However, it uses the line capacity more constructively. Most low-speed modems used with phone lines are asynchronous and are called **acoustic couplers**. This name describes their audio connection to a telephone handset. A portable computer terminal and its acoustic coupler are shown in Figure 10–3.

Voice-Grade Lines   Telephone service accounts for the majority of computer-based data communication, just as it does for remote conversations between people. The capacity of a transmission line is called its **bandwidth**. Audible frequencies range from a telephone tone of 300 cycles per second (called 300 **Hertz** or 300 Hz) to 3300 Hz. Thus, the telephone network has a bandwidth of 3000 Hz.

This band of frequencies permits transmission rates in three general speed ranges. These are called low-speed (around 300 bps), medium-speed (around 2400 bps), and high-speed (around 4800 bps up to this line's maximum capacity of 9600 bps). Low-speed transmission of 300 bps is 30 characters per second, the speed of most CRT terminals and of human reading. The high-speed rate, in contrast, is sufficient to drive a fairly fast line printer.

Access to the telephone network can be arranged under various plans, including direct dialing or a **leased line**. The charge, or **tariff** in phone company jargon, depends on the distance called, the time of day, and the type of phone (business or residential). Data communication, however, is often carried on for several hours daily. A leased line may be worthwhile when there is a high volume of data traffic between two specific points. This service involves hiring a dedicated open line between the parties. No dialing is necessary to establish a connection, and telephone switching stations are avoided. Thus, signal quality improves and switching noise or interline "crosstalk" are reduced.

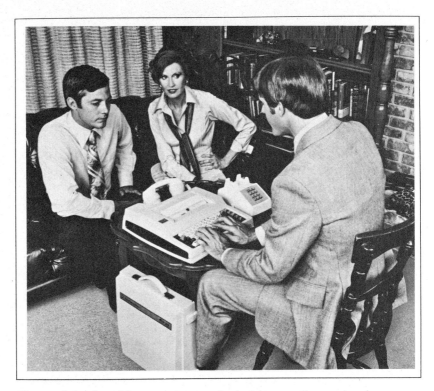

Figure 10-3. Portable computer terminal with acoustic coupler phone connection

High-Speed Data Transmission

High-speed data transmission gives the user very high data rates—typically 50,000 bps and above. The facilities for such communications are becoming widespread. They generally require line-of-sight transmission. That is, microwave transmission requires signal-boosting stations on hilltops or tall buildings every 20 miles or so.

The highest frequency and largest bandwidth of these techniques is the **laser**, or pure-color light beam. Its data carrying capacity equals that of hundreds of phone lines. Also, a light signal can be "bent around corners" when transmitted through a pure glass thread called an **optic fiber**. Thus, existing cable rights-of-way under city streets can be used to string out greatly increased data communications capabilities.

NETWORK INFORMATION SYSTEMS

A **network** is a system of data communication links. There are many possible linkage patterns between multiple endpoints, as shown in Figure 10-4. The objective is generally to reduce line length and there-

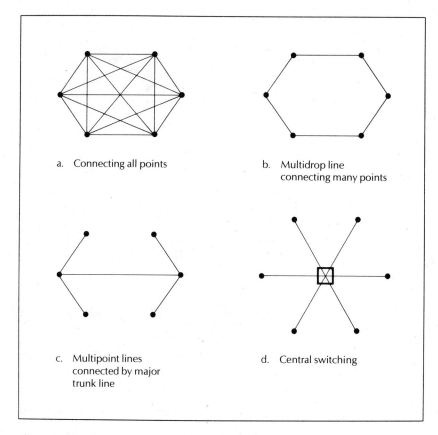

a. Connecting all points

b. Multidrop line connecting many points

c. Multipoint lines connected by major trunk line

d. Central switching

Figure 10-4. Sample network line configurations

by line cost. Usually, however, the information system should not be constrained by lack of communication capacity.

Some network configurations splice many connections onto a leased line called a **multidrop line**. Alternately, a **multipoint line** may be set up to pool data traffic at a central point. These improve line utilization and reduce total line length. Satellite links now provide high-volume capacity and economical communication internationally. Figures 10-5 and 10-6 show the evolution of one particular network—the INFONET system of Computer Sciences Corporation.

Time-Sharing Concept

One major use of data communications networks is for **time sharing**. Time sharing means multiple users can access the same computer while each receives responses quickly. Each user appears to have the use of the machine on command, yet all users appear to get service

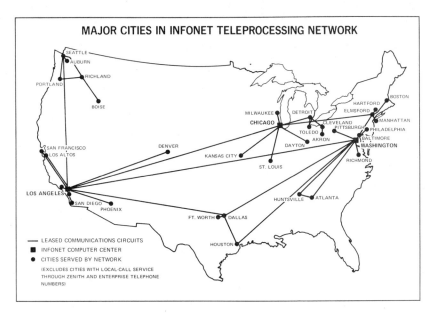

Figure 10-5. Infonet system in 1973

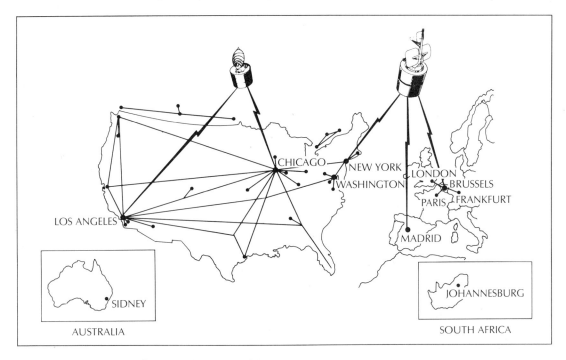

Figure 10-6. Infonet teleprocessing network in 1976

simultaneously. Furthermore, each user can do separate tasks on the shared computer. Time sharing's primary function is to make more computer power available to more individual users by sharing central resources. This makes **interactive computing**—rapid, repeated input and responses—affordable by individual users.

Time sharing was conceived in the late 1950s and was developed experimentally in the early 1960s, notably at M.I.T. in what subsequently became **Project MAC** (*Multiple-Access* Computer or *Machine-Aided* Cognition). Dartmouth has pioneered time-sharing languages, applications, and teaching methods suitable for college students. The widely used time-sharing language called BASIC (reviewed in Chapter 6) was developed principally at Dartmouth with support from General Electric.

The classic commercial example of shared computing is American Airlines' reservations system, called the SABRE system. It was developed and implemented jointly with IBM during the early and mid-1960s.

By some definitions such a single-purpose in-house system is distinguished from time sharing, which usually involves many unrelated users performing separate tasks. Many service companies now sell time-sharing capabilities to thousands of customers, including users who don't wish to have their own computer or who need occasional use of a large computer, or proprietary data or programs. The market for commercial time-shared services amounted to about $800 million by 1978.

Most time sharing involves interactive computing using what are called **conversational programs**. These allow users to interact with the computer in a dialog. Remote users frequently access the computer via terminals and telephone lines; nearby terminals may be **hardwired**, or directly connected to it.

Remote batch processing is a different way users can share computer capability. It involves entering a job into an input queue that is awaiting processing. The jobs are then batch processed and enter an output queue awaiting printer resources. This is suitable when immediate response time can be sacrificed to gain the generally lower costs of batch processing. Also, most remote batch I/O stations use high-speed readers and printers that can accommodate a high volume of I/O. Thus, in batch processing, the computer is shared more on a minute-by-minute or hour-by-hour basis than on a second-by-second or even split-second time frame.

Time-Sharing Configuration Time sharing depends on several technologies that are generally available with third-generation and later computers, but it is a concept distinct from each of them. A time-sharing system, as diagrammed in Figure 10-7, involves most, if not all, of the following features:

- user-oriented terminals
- data communication
- operating system
- multiprogramming
- program interrupts
- in-core compilers or interpretive languages
- large, online direct access storage

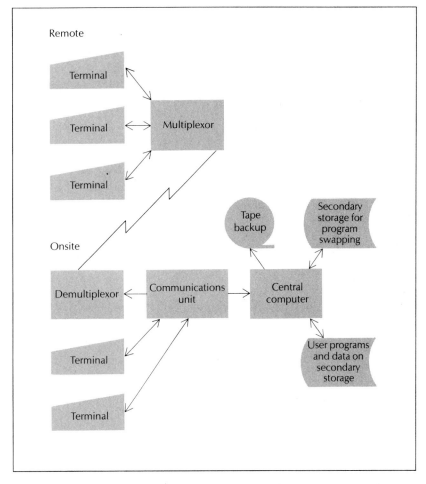

Figure 10-7. Typical time-sharing configuration, showing remote and onsite units

1. *User-oriented terminals* for input and output of data and programs are necessary components of a time-sharing system. Typically, individual users have terminals in the low-speed range (30 characters per second).

2. *Data communication* capability is required for the system to support I/O from remote locations. A short response time provides much of the value of time sharing. Therefore, it is crucial to get data quickly from where it originates, process it, and return it to where it is needed. Ordinary voice-grade telephone lines are used for transmission between terminal and computer, and (usually) back again. A dial-up connection through a switched network is usually sufficient. Higher speed dedicated lines or microwave transmission can accommodate higher volumes.

3. *Operating system* control is needed for the split-second timing of data communication, multiprogramming, and quick access to on-line data storage devices. A time-sharing system's main memory stores a program that allocates and schedules the system's resources.

4. *Multiprogramming* of a time-shared central processor is typical. Multiprogramming involves creating software partitions within main memory. Each can be occupied by a separate program or partial program. The CPU acts on only one at a time. However, since there are many programs available to switch among, the CPU can rapidly rotate its attention. This helps increase system efficiency while maintaining the overall criterion that no user should wait more than a few seconds for a response.

5. *Program interrupts*, issued by the operating system, redirect processing. When one job is completed, has an error, or requests I/O, the processor's attention can then be switched to another user. Interruption is often based on a fixed time increment, or **time slice** (such as 1/10 of a second). This permits many users' jobs to be processed, although perhaps not completed, without any user waiting more than a few seconds. (Conditioned users often become frustrated when heavy use stretches response time to just several seconds, even though they previously coped with turnaround times of hours or days.)

6. *In-core compilers* allow rapid translation of high-level programming statements. This is especially helpful when programs are entered from terminals in the expectation of quick response. (Production programs should be stored in object code, of course, thus eliminating compilation each time they are run.) **Interpretive lan-**

guages, such as APL, are executed on an instruction-by-instruction basis when they are input. They need not be stored in their entirety prior to and during execution. Interpretive languages do not require an in-core compiler as such.

7. *Large, online direct access storage* allows many programs and much data to be quickly accessible for processing. Since many users can be using the system simultaneously, and still others may have stored programs and data in it, time-sharing systems require massive on-line storage, typically disks.

Economics of Interactive Processing

Interactive processing should be evaluated for its benefits and costs. There are several economic justifications for it, but mostly they involve a trade-off of increased hardware cost in favor of added user efficiency, convenience, or computing power. These benefits include:

1. Interactive processing provides prompt response. This in turn aids in solving a variety of problems in management, planning, scheduling, quality control, statistical analysis, engineering, and so forth. Eliminating queues between users and computers can significantly increase user productivity as well as reduce the time needed to complete a particular processing task.

2. Interactive or iterative problems, such as planning decisions of a "what if" nature, are especially aided. In applications such as breakeven analysis, the user applies various forecasting and projecting techniques under different sets of assumptions. Repeated interactive trials allow better approximations of such real-world situations.

3. Users quickly learn the system by actually interacting with it. Programmers are able to create new programs quickly and more efficiently by interacting directly with the computer during debugging. Twenty or more runs of a program can typically be run daily versus only a few with traditional batch operations.

4. Shared systems usually offer a large selection of general-interest applications for the benefit of their subscribers. A typical library might contain a hundred or more programs. Such a library often includes statistical packages, forecasting models, financial and investment packages, special applications for a particular industry and so forth.

5. Access to proprietary data banks, such as marketing, governmental, or financial data is improved. For example, data accessible from remote terminals may describe historical economic trends. Cen-

tralizing the process of assembling and disseminating such data is an obvious benefit. (However, problems arise if inquiries must be formatted to conform with the database structure.)

6. Distributed processing is possible with a network information system. It allows applications to be integrated—for example, throughout the various departments of a hospital or the many warehouses of a nationwide corporation.

7. More economical hardware, including several peripheral devices and a large, fast processor, can be made available to users who might not otherwise have access to such resources. By pooling processing demands into large-scale equipment, lower costs per unit can sometimes be achieved.

8. Access to an interactive system is cheap (under $100 per month) with no capital investment required. Usage costs then vary with actual demand.

9. No geographical restrictions need apply. For example, the IN-FONET system currently receives nationwide inputs as well as satellite-transmitted I/O from Europe and Australia. Because of differing time zones, this allows about 20 hours per day of prime daytime demand.

10. The vendor, not the user, is responsible for equipment service and the costs of reserve and backup capacities.

Interactive processing can also have disadvantages, such as:

1. It can be needlessly expensive for users who do not benefit from quick response or who have a high volume of transactions, such as 1000 entries per day. Most keyboard terminals have limited speeds, which increase communication charges if there is much data transmission. Although remote batch processing reduces these charges, it increases turnaround time to minutes or hours.

2. Sharing resources introduces considerable overhead that users must ultimately pay for. The split-second choreography required for multiple users necessitates a costly operating system. And communications costs aren't required for onsite I/O. Finally, when an outside commercial firm is involved, there are added charges to cover marketing, administration, taxes, and profit. Total charges may exceed $1000 per month per terminal.

3. Usage can be delayed from 5 minutes to a few hours because of telephone line or computer difficulties. In general, interactive sys-

tems are relatively sophisticated with concomitant technical problems. Costly backup may be required.

4. Data privacy and security problems are accentuated by sharing resources. Also, retrieving lost data may be difficult because of the system's dynamic interactions. The user should safeguard all programs and data with paper, tape, or disk backup copies. Similarly, software and I/O procedures should prohibit unauthorized access to others' property.

The typical costs for interactive processing involve all or a combination of the following factors:

1. **Connect time** to the computer: which is the duration of an active transmission link between the user's terminal and the time-sharing system.
2. **CPU time:** which is the period a program occupies the central processing unit.
3. **Storage capacity:** which is required for the user's programs or data files.
4. **Channel time:** which is the duration of channel use, sometimes measured by counting the number of I/O requests.
5. Additional charges: which may be made for file access, languages, applications programs, and terminal and communication equipment.

Total user costs typically range from $3 to $15 per terminal hour; the average is now under $10. This cost has been decreasing rather rapidly and depends, of course, on the size of the computer being shared and the actual amount of processing. Some service firms "bundle" charges into a single fee for use of particular programs. Also, use of less expensive minicomputers has increased dramatically. These machines have adequate capabilities for many applications. Representative costs as of 1978 are shown in Table 10.2.

TABLE 10.2   ECONOMICS OF INTERACTIVE PROCESSING

	Monthly Minimum Charge	Terminal Connect Charge	CPU Time Charge	Storage Charge
Commercial Range	$0–250	$2–12/hr	$1–15/min	$0–250/mo
Typical Large System	$100	$6/hr	$6/min	$100/mo.
In-house Minicomputer	—	$2/hr	10¢/min	$100/mo

Representative Uses   Distributed processing is now widely used. When convenience and quick response are a factor, it pays to keep high-priced programmers, analysts, and managers productive. Also, when an answer to a brief inquiry is sought, a no-fuss technique is helpful. Furthermore, updated inputs and inquiries from many locations can be handled locally and still be pooled into a central current database. Figure 10–8 shows an intelligent terminal with onsite tape cartridge storage capability. This capacity allows both local operations and support of a networked central system.

Figure 10–8.   Intelligent terminal used for distributed processing

Aside from programming activities and quick inquiries to databases, distributed processing can also support computer-aided decision making. Mathematical models of many situations have been created for use with terminals. A representative but not comprehensive list of such applications is shown in Table 10.3.

SUMMARY   Part 3 has described methods of processing. Sequential processing organizes data in order by some key attribute, such as alphabetic by last names or increasing account numbers. Often, new data items are batched and sorted for economical processing against the existing records. Delay in reporting the results to users is an unfortunate by-product of this scheme.

Direct access processing methods require more advanced hardware, software, and data organization schemes. Random and indexed-sequential file organizations permit quick, single-attribute inquiries with varying degrees of capability for economical full-file processing.

Database processing allows content retrieval, possibly via many key attributes of the data. It promotes the creation of a central, single-copy, up-to-the-minute, nonredundant pool of data, with which all authorized users interact.

TABLE 10.3   REPRESENTATIVE APPLICATIONS OF INTERACTIVE PROCESSING

Order entry and billing	Linear programming models
Product pricing analysis	PERT networks
Product cost analysis	Simulation analysis
Monthly sales analysis	Machine utilization
Sales forecasting	Production scheduling
Credit screening	Plant layout analysis
Accounts receivable	Cost estimating
Accounts payable	Job shop simulation
Accounting statements	Production analysis
Fixed asset accounting	Direct labor planning
Cash reconciliation	Purchasing lead time
Cash budgeting and forecasting	Competitive bidding
Project return analysis	Quality control
Risk analysis	Numerical control machine supervision
Inventory control	Critical path network analysis
Facilities location	Ratio analysis
Personnel scheduling	Yield-to-maturity computation
Lease or buy analysis	Discounted cash flow
Distribution system analysis	Bond bidding and pricing
Transportation models	Portfolio analysis
Vehicle scheduling	Economic forecasting
Queuing problem analysis	Real estate investment analysis
Advertising media selection	Merger simulation

Distributed processing extends the user's processing capability by, to some extent, reversing the centralization trend. The increasing availability and decreasing cost of minicomputers, terminals, and data communications, support the creation of network information systems. This makes possible the sharing of resources—processing power, software, and data—and interactive user/computer dialogue. In theory, current, correct, and complete data can be accessed and processed from anywhere in the organization—perhaps the ultimate information systems capability.

CONCEPTS

distributed processing
economy of scale
Grosch's Law
minicomputer
intelligent terminal
data communication
telecommunication
teleprocessing
baud
voice-grade line
simplex
half-duplex
full-duplex
modulation
amplitude modulation
  (AM)

frequency modulation
  (FM)
phase modulation
modem
asynchronous
synchronous
start bit
stop bit
Bandot code
ASCII
acoustic coupler
bandwidth
Hertz
leased line
tariff
laser

optic fiber
network
multidrop line
multipoint line
time sharing
interactive computing
Project MAC
conversational program
hardwired
remote batch
  processing
time slice
interpretive language
connect time
CPU time
storage capacity
channel time

QUESTIONS
1. Define distributed processing.
2. Distributed processing helps local managers regain control over their data and processing requirements. Defend or challenge this statement.
3. The availability of terminals and microprocessors at prices individuals can afford negates the need for large-scale central data processing. Defend or challenge this viewpoint.
4. Discuss the issues to be considered in designing a data communications network.
5. What techniques would you use to minimize costs in a network that has to link the 50 U.S. capitals?
6. Is voice communication fundamentally different from data communication?
7. What components are necessary in a time-sharing system?
8. What economies are achieved with in-house time sharing versus an external commercial service? What benefits can the service provide?
9. What are the potential economic benefits of interactive processing?
10. Describe a distributed processing application you know of personally or have read about.

Part Four

**Applications and
the Development
Cycle**

Chapter 11 **Management Information Systems**

Managers use information for reaching decisions in
all functions and at all levels of organizations.
Tailoring and developing computer systems to
support decision making calls for both management
and technical skills.

Chapter 12 **Systems Analysis**

Crucial to applications development is the first
task systems analysis. Specifications for an effective
and efficient information system are the goal.

Chapter 13 **Systems Design, Programming and
Implementation**

The payoff of computer technology is useful
information from *implemented* systems. We discuss
how to set program design and manage software
development and system implementation.

Chapter 14 **Representative Applications**

Five organizations, as diverse as a small business, a
large national firm, and a university are reviewed and
their computer applications described.

Chapter Eleven

**Management
Information
Systems**

By its nature, management deals primarily with information. Other employees deal more directly with the physical aspects of producing the organization's products and services. The computer is a machine that automates information processing. Its functions include collecting data and transmitting, storing, retrieving, calculating and displaying it. Thus, the computer can be especially helpful in managerial and administrative functions because information processing and decision making are the principal activities.

In this chapter we will discuss a subject generally referred to as **management information systems (MIS)**. The term implies formalized computer-based capability for generating information useful in managing the organization. Frequently, an MIS is built on a collection of transactions-processing applications. However, the term MIS connotes more than this.

THE MIS CONCEPT

An ideal MIS is one that can provide the right information to the right person at the right time. This ideal goal, of course, cannot be reached for all managers and all the decisions they must make. (Such a total system would not be feasible or cost/effective, as we will discuss). An effective MIS is one that *economically* provides appropriately detailed, decision-oriented information quickly. These needs call for an MIS to include:

- decision-oriented reporting
- hierarchical information structure
- decision support systems

Decision-Oriented Reporting

The purpose of an MIS is to provide information that supports management and that, in particular, aids decision making. It is useful to classify the reports an MIS can produce as:

- exception reports
- demand reports
- predictive reports (models)
- scheduled listings

1. **Exception reports** monitor performance and signal those items that require human intervention, such as overdue accounts receivable. Exception reports can be either listed during sequential processing or triggered by an online system. Their essential characteristic is that they provide information only on events presumed to require action. Thus, the MIS calls management's attention to a minority of situations, according to some predetermined standards or policies. Other situations are deemed to be routine and their handling is delegated, possibly to the system itself.

2. **Demand reports** are also part of a true MIS. A demand report is generated only on request. An MIS should be able to provide information that has never been asked for before and that might never be asked for again. (However, if the required data are not available in the organization's database, the request can obviously not be met on demand.) For example, demand reports might deal with products, geographic regions, salespeople, price categories, and so forth. Management might need to compare George Smith's sales of high-priced equipment in the southern region to the average of all other salespeople. Such demand-oriented reporting allows quick answers to historical and statistical questions.

3. **Predictive reports** are used for planning decisions. These reports generally involve decision-aiding techniques, such as statistical analyses or models. The level of complexity in such forecasting models varies widely, but one frequent ingredient is historical data. Thus, the MIS should be designed to allow data to be accessed automatically by predictive models. Reports can then be made to management and the underlying models can be quickly manipulated in response to "what if" inquiries.

4. **Scheduled listings** account for the majority of computer outputs. Such listings are often widely distributed. Because of their general format, they attempt to provide everything to everyone. However, if an MIS provides the needed exception, demand, and predictive reports, there should be little need to distribute scheduled listings. Most scheduled reports are meant to suffice for what is really needed. However, when data items are known to be routinely required, scheduled listings are often the least expensive method

of supplying them. The danger is the tendency to supply an over-abundance of irrelevant data that is neither needed nor used.

Hierarchical Information Structure

An important difference between traditional data processing and an MIS is the focus on providing information to decision makers. The triangle in Figure 11-1 shows that data processing primarily automates operational tasks such as billing, general ledger accounting, payroll, sales analysis, inventory control, and so forth. In contrast, an MIS automates this operational processing and, at the same time, provides information for decision making at higher organizational levels.

The three classic decision levels—*operational*, *tactical*, and *strategic*—are defined by the degree to which their decisions have the following strategic attributes:

- importance
- long time-frame
- cross-functional scope
- qualitativeness
- infrequency

High-level decisions usually require many ensuing subdecisions for implementation. Thus, decisions made at high levels guide and con-

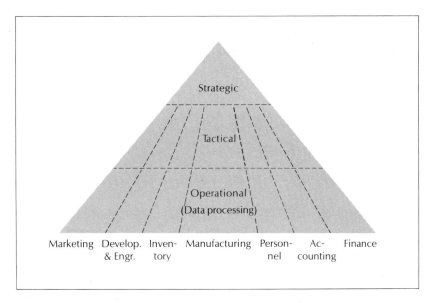

Figure 11-1. Levels of decision making in a functional organization

strain the more numerous ones made at lower levels. For example, a task at the operational level might be to maintain a record of current inventory balances and to reorder under certain conditions. This is a rather straightforward bookkeeping function, easily within the realm of data processing.

An MIS inventory system does more. It provides information for making decisions at both the tactical and the strategic levels. Tactical-level decisions in this case might include determining at which amounts of inventory to reorder the various items and their proper reorder quantities. Strategic-level decisions are much broader. For example, an MIS may provide strategic planners with information used to set inventory policies so that total carrying costs and expected stockouts are tolerable. As shown in Figure 11–2, data fed into the MIS are used for a hierarchy of decision-making levels.

Database Management   The third facet usually characteristic of an MIS is a database. Traditional data processing can be represented by the first diagram of Figure

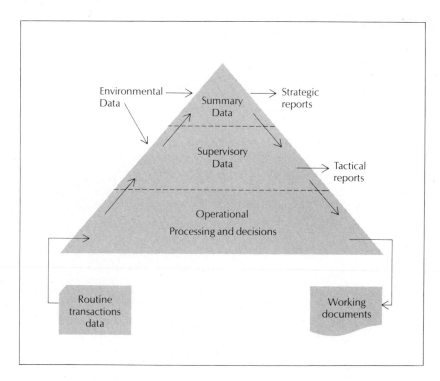

Figure 11-2.   Hierarchy of MIS data and decision levels

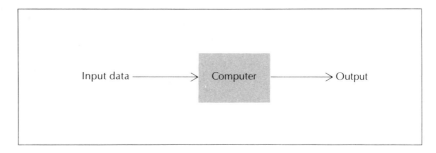

Figure 11-3.   Data processing versus a database MIS

11-3. Here the data are input especially for this run and are processed as a self-contained application.

   An MIS, in contrast, can be conceptualized by the second diagram of Figure 11-3. Here the system has access to a continually updated database. Furthermore, many inputs are inquiries rather than data to be processed or posted to the database. (The means of organizing and managing such databases were discussed in Chapter 9.)

   An MIS is comprehensive and sophisticated. Relatively recent technologies have made MIS feasible and continue to make them more cost/effective. Although no system is or probably ever will be perfect, organizations are increasingly implementing MIS. For instance, on-line inquiry capability helps satisfy the MIS requirement for quick

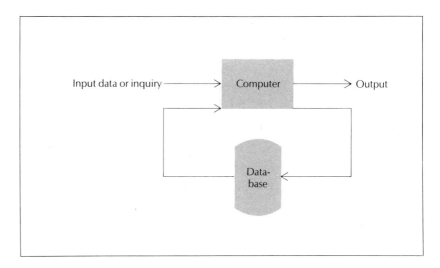

Figure 11-3.   Data processing versus a database MIS (cont'd.)

decision-oriented reporting. Similarly, integrating multiple files into a database tends to allow reports that were previously uneconomical.

Decision Support Systems

Decisions, to be rational, require information. Since the decisions to be made cannot be fully anticipated, the information needed is difficult to predict. Yet, an organization's information system must trap data about relevant events and generate suitable information from them. Increasingly, computer-based systems are used for obtaining, storing, and producing information that can lead to better decisions. This extends computer applications beyond their more traditional realm of transactions processing.

The computer's capability to aid decision making was recognized early. In the 1950s, researchers began to program computers for problem-solving and decision-making behavior. In 1954, A. M. Turing proposed an **imitation game** in which a computer and a person both answer questions. The questioner must then decide which of the unidentified respondents is really the person. This became a classic test of whether computer output could be made indistinguishable from human responses and could therefore be considered "intelligent."

Initial successes at programming decisions led to predictions of further advances in such **artificial intelligence**. For example, it was forecast that a computer would be the chess champion of the world by 1970. This did not happen. However, computer programs were by then able to play at world championship levels in the less complicated games of checkers, dominoes, and three-dimensional tic-tac-toe.

Still others foresaw a **second industrial revolution** stemming from the computer's power for automating human mental (as opposed to mechanical) activities. Frequently, a "new era" of computer-aided decision making was hailed in the literature. Indeed, computer systems have helped human decision makers to decide more accurately and productively than before. And in the future, they are expected to do even more. But progress in aiding decisions has been slower than predicted and some types of decisions have proven less amenable to effective computerization than others.

To understand the computer's role in such **decision support systems (DSS)**, it is useful to formalize a concept of the decision process. A seven-phase description, as diagrammed in Figure 11–4, will be assumed. The initial requirement is that decision making be directed toward some (set of) *objective*(s). A suitable statement of the objective must include an explicit *measure of performance*. Otherwise progress toward the result sought cannot be measured.

Inevitably there will be some gap between actual conditions and

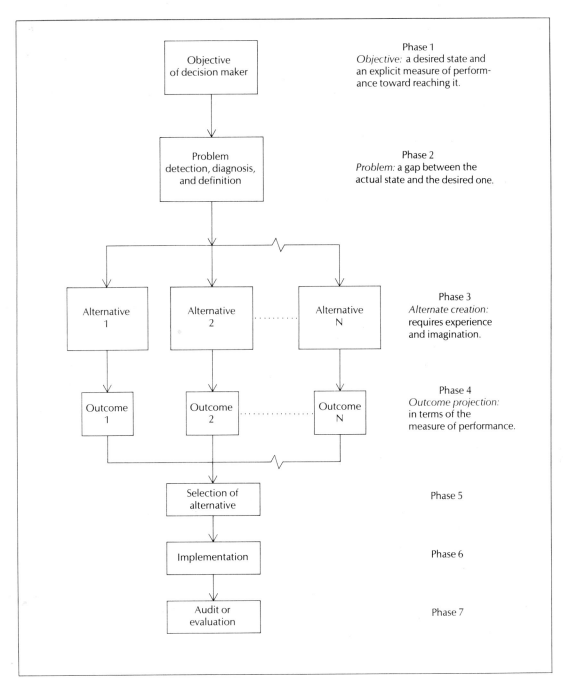

Figure 11-4. The decision process

those sought as the objective. *Detection, diagnosis,* and *definition* of this gap—or problem—is the second phase of decision making. Next, *alternative courses of action* must be conceived. This third phase relies on the decision maker's experience and imagination.

The fourth phase is perhaps the most difficult. It involves *projecting or predicting the outcome of each alternative* as if it were actually decided on. These results should be forecasted in terms of the measure of performance stated as part of the objective. Then the desirability of each projected outcome can be ranked. Phase five *selects* that alternative deemed to yield the most favorable outcome, given the objective.

The sixth phase is *implementation* of the selected alternative. Implementation frequently takes much longer than the other decision phases. In fact, it initiates a sequence of follow-up decisions. It raises such issues as authority, administration, leadership, motivation and control. A projection of alternative outcomes must consider these human relations aspects of systems development and the implementation of change.

Finally, a seventh phase of decision making involves *auditing or evaluating* the preceding process. This phase cannot influence the decision at hand, since it has already been implemented. However, such feedback allows the decision process itself to be controlled and modified. An improved process can then be applied to future decisions.

An example will help illustrate this seven-phase concept of the decision process. Suppose that the government sets an objective of low air pollution from automobiles. The measure of performance toward this objective might be defined as permissible amounts of exhaust emissions of five undesirable compounds. The problem is to close the gap from present emission levels. Then various engine designs are created to meet this objective. Their performance is projected in terms of how well they meet the new emission standards. Decision makers select designs, and they are implemented by the various car manufacturers. Hopefully, audits or evaluations are then made to improve the overall process of subsequent decisions. For example, it might afterward be decided that emission controls alone are an inadequate objective. The new engines' gas consumption must also improve from prior levels. Thus, another cycle of decision making begins trading off pollution and performance.

The point of formalizing a concept of the decision process is to relate decision support systems to it. Indeed, computers can carry out any or all of the decision-making phases defined above—except phase one, setting objectives. Humans and organizations are "will-directed" entities whereas computers are not. (Nonetheless, given an objective and programmed instructions, electricity, and other needed resources, computers have done amazingly well in certain decision-making situations.)

Most decision support systems affect only one phase of the decision process. For example, many management science models attempt to project the outcomes of particular alternative courses of action. For example, a model might be used to calculate an annual percentage interest rate for a loan with various repayment terms. (That is, it might be used to calculate the measure of performance toward the objective of paying low interest.) Other DSS may affect other single phases of the decision process. For example, an exception report of overdue accounts receivable identifies problems. But it says nothing about the courses of possible action, their outcomes, which one to select, and so on.

Single-phase DSS may also aid or accomplish phase three—alternative generation. This step usually requires experience and creativity, and is therefore thought to be outside the forte of computers. However, computers have been used effectively in this phase. Consider a name-generating system used to list alternative product names. Various letters (or numbers) can be assembled rapidly into possible names. This is done without human inhibitions and according to certain objectives such as name length, vowel frequency, initial letter, and phonetic attributes such as hard-sounding (KRUNCH) or soft-sounding (LULLABYE). Such a system attempts to automate only alternative creation. Setting objectives, problem definition (we need a new name), evaluation, selection, implementation, and so on are left to the decision maker. The brand name EXXON was created by such a system and was implemented with a $100 million budget.

Still other DSS have more complete roles in affecting decisions. An example of this type of system is one used by professional football teams for selecting among the available college players. A scouting report on each eligible draftee is entered into the system. A particular team submits its objectives for the ideal candidate for a particular position. The system responds with a short screened list of likely suggestions. Here the DSS handles the decision phases of alternative generation (by retrieving all eligible candidates from its database), projecting all alternatives according to a specified objective, and screening or partially selecting a small group meriting further (nonautomatic) assessment.

The football recruitment system stops short of being a decision-making system. Presumably, some subjective evaluation factors are too difficult or uneconomical to automate. However, this is not always the case. Some systems can actually make a decision rather than merely aid it. **Process control**—automated operation—is increasingly done by computers. Such systems gather inputs on temperature, pressure, flow rate, and so forth. In turn, they "decide" on appropriate actions, such as "set valve 6 to position 3," and implement them. Chess and checker playing models, mentioned above, are further examples. And some brave souls have even computerized stock market investment decision making.

Total Systems Myth

The MIS literature, and many managers, speak to the concept of a **total system**. This term implies an all-functions, all-levels, online, immediate response, decision support system. In some cases, "support" is too mild a word, as nothing less than automated decision *making* is sought. Such a goal is unattainable and systems so described are myths.

Recall the decision process and its seven phases, pictured in Figure 11–4. Decisions begin with some objective of the decision maker. Problems are gaps between the actual and desired states of affairs. Any total system would have to generate complete and accurate information on all relevant events. It would then have to include superior prediction models and the means for selecting from among self-generated alternatives. Even then, some decision maker would have to provide the system with objectives, resources, and the authority to decide.

For complex, managerial-level responsibilities, such capability is far beyond current know-how. In fact, if it were not, organizations and managers would raise their objectives—creating fresh gaps, or problems. If these could be solved by already programmed computers, then it is likely that the problems were not of managerial level in the first place. In short, people can remain in control of computers and will need to be.

MIS SUBSYSTEMS

It should be clear that developing an MIS is a major undertaking. Its success depends on the competence and dedication of the development team as well as on the support and cooperation of top management and users. Although its overall goals and design should be planned in advance, its creation and implementation should be modular.

Modularity is a design concept that focuses on one part while never losing sight of its interactions or relationships with the other parts. A modular approach to an MIS permits interim progress, feedback, and acceptance. The alternate approach of "wait 3 years until we throw the switch and everything will work" seldom does. The comprehensiveness of an MIS and its modular subsystems are depicted in Figure 11-5.

Functional Subsystems An MIS is composed of major subsystems that affect the firm's significant functions. In turn, these major subsystems each have several major components. Many share data or common processing procedures with other applications. Most subsystem components themselves consist of separate programs. And even these may be implemented in a modular way by using software written as short programs or subroutines.

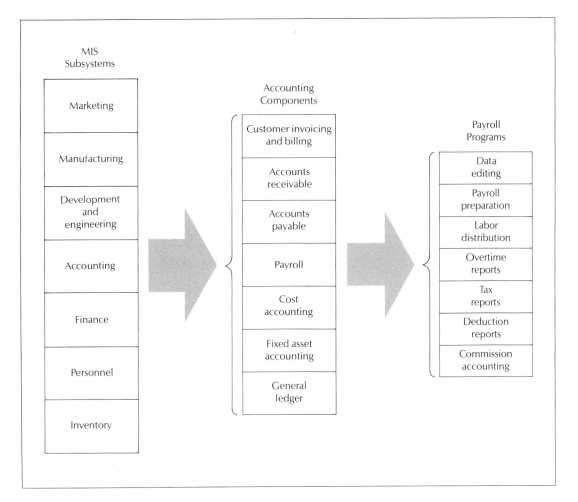

Figure 11-5. MIS subsystems for a typical manufacturing firm

As an MIS matures within an organization, its parts tend to become progressively more integrated. Also, it begins to include subsystems that reach higher and wider in the organization. For example, initial transactions processing applications may become the base for modeling and simulation applications that aid decision making. Also, functional subsystems begin to spread across all activities of the firm. These can be grouped as:

- administrative subsystems
- line subsystems

The initial applications in most organizations are what we can call **administrative subsystems**. Referring to Figure 11–5, such systems generally span the accounting, finance, and personnel functions. These initial applications typically involve transactions processing for file updating and paperwork handling. Invoicing, collection, payments, and payroll are examples. Such voluminous, routine, quantitative activities should be recorded and processed with speed and accuracy.

After its introduction into such bread-and-butter applications, the computer generally attracts other devotees within the firm. Other applications become economical once transactions data are available in machine-processable form. For example, a payroll file containing name, address, job title, department, salary, and similar data can also support applications such as personnel planning, newsletter mailings, job-and-skills matching, overtime analysis, turnover by department, and so on.

As computer applications penetrate other functions of the firm, the proportion of accounting, finance, and personnel applications declines. However, many organizations spend one-half or more of their computer-related resources in this administrative area. Even large firms with long histories of computer use still devote over one-third of their computer resources to these functions. But increased integration blurs the distinction between such applications and those affecting line operations, such as marketing or manufacturing. Also, the dividing line between transactions processing and decision support applications fades in importance.

Line subsystems are those directly involved with the organization's reason for being—for a business, profitably selling and supplying its products and services. Of the areas shown in Figure 11–5, the following can be considered line operations functions: marketing, manufacturing, inventory, and development and engineering. Information systems that affect these functions usually seek to increase the firm's profitability via increased sales, improved operational efficiency, better resource allocations, and the like.

An example of a highly integrated system that spans several line functions is a "sales tracking-inventory control-production scheduling-purchasing" system. Transactions in these areas are clearly interrelated. They have traditionally been separated only to make each task manageable in size and complexity.

Computer-based information processing makes it feasible to couple these activities more closely together. Thus, sales and current inventory data are input to derive a production plan. This, in turn, drives a purchasing application that orders the proper amount and type of raw materials and components. Furthermore, the sales data may improve forecasting. For instance, historical data can be tested for any seasonality effects and can be correlated with national economic statistics.

Modeling and Simulation   Models, usually mathematical in nature, have surged in popularity due to the computer's accurate computational powers. New professional and academic disciplines have been created by this thrust—operations research, management science, and decision sciences, for example. New techniques like large-scale linear programming and simulation of complex queuing problems, are now in the analyst's arsenal.

Analytical models are mathematical means of developing solutions or "optimum" answers. **Simulation** supports decisions in a somewhat different way. Simulation essentially imitates the situation that requires a decision. This permits the decision maker to experiment with various choices. The simulated system's behavior over time can then be observed. The advantage, of course, is that if the decision's results are poor, there are no actual hardships—simulated history can be cancelled!

Often, a problem solver will not have the knowledge or time to determine a solution analytically. Simulation may be helpful here because several trials of the model may be sufficient to provide a satisfactory, if not perfect, decision.

The acceptability of a mathematical optimum or of a decision analyzed via simulation depends, among other things, on the accuracy and precision designed into the model. Computation is getting cheaper with technological progress, but building an accurate and precise model requires skilled analyst and management time, which is increasingly expensive. Special-purpose computer languages—including **GPSS** (General Purpose Systems Simulator) and **SIMSCRIPT**—have been developed to help in the creation of simulation models. FORTRAN, BASIC, or APL are especially useful for algebraic models or matrix manipulation.

Modeling is a flexible problem-solving tool that enables many situations to be analyzed in detail. It has, in fact, been successfully applied to studying computer operations themselves. For example, the dynamic interactions of a time-sharing system can be simulated, producing such performance measures as average response time versus number of users and utilization rates for key system components. Bottlenecks may thereby be discovered and removed.

ADMINISTRATIVE SUBSYSTEMS

As discussed, administrative areas of a business firm include accounting, finance, and personnel functions. Computers are often initially applied in this area, and such applications persist over time. In this section we will review typical MIS subsystems for these functions. Then, in the next major section of this chaper, we will look also at line operations systems. These include marketing, manufacturing, inventory, and development and engineering.

Accounting

The objectives of the accounting function are to record the movement of cash and other valuables and to report periodically on the organization's financial condition. Thus, accounting has interactions with every other function in the business. And while physical goods (or services) move from suppliers to the firm, and then to its customers, there is an accompanying chain of paperwork. This is also the province of accounting—payments and receipts. These interactions are diagrammed in Figure 11–6.

The accounting subsystem ties together the company's operations. Periodically, usually monthly, formal financial statements are produced. To do this, the separate types of transactions illustrated in Figure 11–6 are drawn up in a **general ledger**. This is the firm's master account book or **chart of accounts**. In the quill-pen–armband-and-eyeshade days of accounting, each transaction was initially posted to a **general journal**, which listed all activity in chronological order. Today this step is not needed; computers can post transactions directly to the accounts affected. A typical component of the accounting subsystem—the processing of accounts receivable and related transactions—is shown in Figure 11–7.

Finance

The objective of finance is capital management—cash raised and cash raising. This cycle is shown in Figure 11–8. Of course, finance and accounting are closely linked, with the latter usually reporting to the former. In addition to the controller's accounting activities, other responsibilities of finance are:

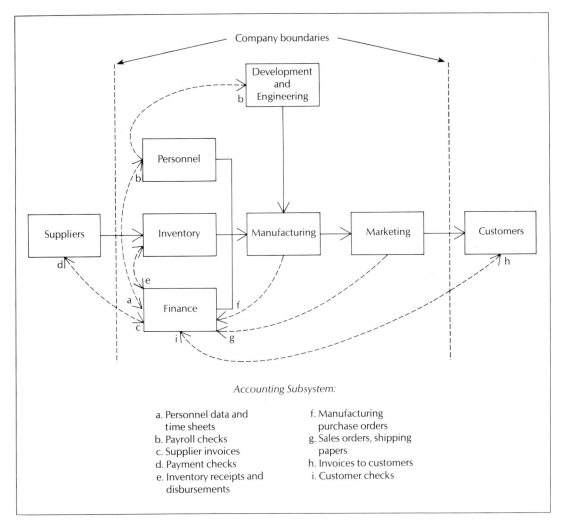

Figure 11-6.   Interactions between the accounting subsystem and other subsystems

1. *Cash management:* collecting, disbursing, and short-term investing and borrowing.
2. *Capital structure:* equity, dividends, and long-term debt
3. *Financial analysis:* asset justifications, return on investment, purchasing and pricing analyses
4. *Forecasting:* budgeting, planning, pro-forma statements, and contingencies
5. *External relations:* shareholder communications, and bondholder, banker, creditor, and IRS interactions

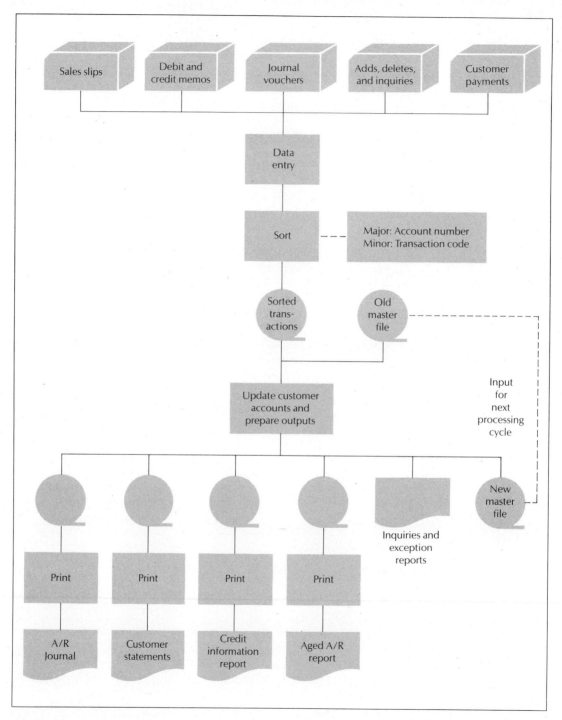

Figure 11-7. The accounts receivable component of the accounting subsystem

Personnel This functional area has grown in both its management importance and its dependence on information systems. Originally, payroll was the largest application in this area. Weekly checks, complex tax withholding, other deductions, and the need for absolute promptness and accuracy posed formidable problems. Now many proprietary software packages are available for handling payroll. Also, service bureaus and banks will frequently perform this service—some even specialize in it.

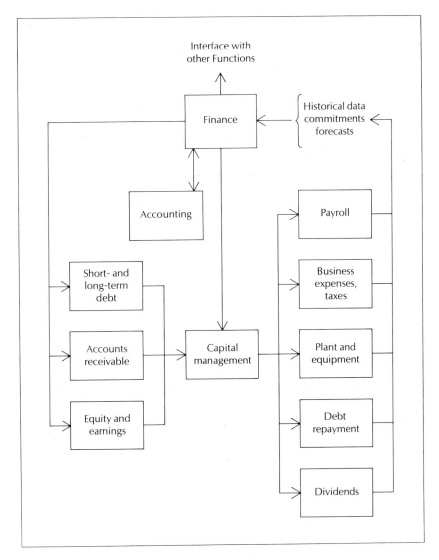

Figure 11-8. Financial management subsystem

Human resource management is an enlarged, enlightened view of the personnel function. For most firms, especially service firms, people really are the most important asset. (However, they are not listed on the balance sheet.) And legislated reporting requirements, such as Social Security payments (FICA), Equal Employment Opportunity (EEOC), Occupational Safety and Health (OSHA), and Employee Retirement Security (ERISA), have multiplied the complexity of personnel information systems.

LINE SUBSYSTEMS Line operations functions include marketing, manufacturing, inventory, and development and engineering. As seen from Figure 11-6, these functions have a direct impact on the firm's product and profitability. But only in the past decade have most firms placed major attention on these information subsystems. These subsystems are a vital part of an MIS, although they are usually more difficult to develop than administrative applications. After all, computers are good at repetitive paperwork processing that requires tireless accuracy. But, more so than mere administrative tasks, line operations functions *are the business itself.* Therefore, applications in this area directly relate to decision, the essence of the managerial job.

Cost of goods sold (COGS) is the accounting term for the sum of costs embedded in the items sold. It is the major expense item offsetting sales revenues. Typically, half to three-quarters of sales goes for COGS. In some industries, such as auto manufacturing or supermarket retailing, COGS is about 80 percent of sales. This shows that the major cost—and the major opportunity for savings—lies in the product itself. To this cost, selling expenses must be added. Obviously, line operations are the key to profitability. Why not have computers support these functions, as well as the administrative ones?

The example MIS, discussed in detail below, shows the kind of decisions required in a manufacturing firm, and the supporting information required. The context is from a computerized management game (or simulation, if you prefer) developed by the author to illustrate "the top management experience." In a sense, it represents the extreme of the MIS movement—there is no real company at all in such a simulation, it is all MIS.

MIS EXAMPLE Management means decision making, which requires information. An MIS is nothing more than a system for providing information to management. In a real firm, a total system is not technically or economically feasible and probably not organizationally desirable either. But as a simulation for learning about management, and for illustrating the role of information and an MIS, we present below a management game called *The Top Management Experience*. Actually, an entire industry of competing firms is simulated. The report received by each firm, produced by its MIS, is shown in the following pages.

To appreciate the structure and content of these reports, note that the five pages follow the outline:

- decisions
- internal information
- external information

Decisions Page 1 lists 40 top management decisions, grouped by function. The firms compete for sale of "regular" and "deluxe" products in each of three geographic zones. "Alpha" and "beta" raw materials are required to manufacture these products. Alternately, regular units may be ordered from subcontractors. The firm's decisions for each of the past three 6-month periods are shown.

Internal Information Page 2 presents the firm's income statement and balance sheet for the simulated 6-month period. Important context information is also computed. That is, percent-of-sales or percent-of-assets and percent-change analyses are displayed.

Page 3 shows more detailed internal operating data. Cost and materials flows and personnel can be tracked. The financial analysis section shows liquidity and management performance, as reflected by certain ratios, and the funds available to the firm, should it care to raise capital.

External Information Page 4 helps management gauge the impact of the external environment—specifically, the response of the regular-deluxe marketplace and the actions of competitors. Unit sales for each product in each zone are shown. This is vital knowledge for short-run inventory and distribution decisions. And it is key for determining the overall size of the firm in the longer run. The marketing information runs from accurate (prices), to incomplete (ranks), to estimates (market share, promotion budgets, personnel and compensation). The more you spend for marketing information (decision 1), the more accurate these estimates tend to become, including the forecasts for real economic growth and the consumer price index.

Page 5 shows each firm's audited financial statements. While the first four pages are confidential to each firm, this page is standard, public information. A simulation has the advantage of letting all firms start evenly. Then, after several periods of decision making, all can see which firms succeed—and by what measures of performance. The experience is one of pure information analysis and decision making —and the report makes a good example MIS.

SUMMARY   Management information systems (MIS) involve four characteristics transcending mere data processing: decision-oriented reporting, hierarchical information structure, database management, and decision support systems. Because MIS are aimed at managerial needs for information and decisions, they need to provide differing types of reports: exception, demand, and predictive (models), in addition to the traditional scheduled reports of data processing.

High-level strategic decisions need support from the MIS as well as the lower-level, more frequent, operating decisions. Inquiry and exception report needs dictate a database of history and standards. Predictive reports call for decision support systems, such as analytical and simulation models. But it is a myth that an MIS can comprehensively meet the organization's need for information, decisions, and management.

MIS subsystems usually evolve along functional organization lines, such as marketing, manufacturing, and finance. Both administrative and line operations can benefit from computerized support. An example MIS, drawn from a management game, shows that decisions, internal information, and external information are all part of an MIS.

```
INDUSTRY A   FIRM 1   PERIOD  3    YOUR COMPANY'S NAME GOES HERE         PAGE 1

••• M A R K E T I N G •••                         PER 1      PER 2      PER 3

    1 MARKETING INFORMATION      $1000            25         25         30
    2 PRODUCT DEVELOPMENT        $1000           250        250        300
    3 PRICE OF REGULAR           CENTS           650        675        675
    4 PRICE OF DELUXE            CENTS           875        899        899
    5 CREDIT SALES ALLOWED       PERCENT          50         50         55

    6 PROMOTION--REGULAR-- NORTH $1000            80        100        100
    7                      WEST  $1000           100        100        120
    8                      SOUTH $1000            50         50         70
    9 PROMOTION--DELUXE--- NORTH $1000            50         50         50
   10                      WEST  $1000            40         50         50
   11                      SOUTH $1000            25         25         25

••• P E R S O N N E L •••

   12 SALES FORCE SIZE---- NORTH PERSONS          14         16         16
   13                      WEST  PERSONS          14         16         16
   14                      SOUTH PERSONS           7          8          8
   15 SALES FORCE BASE SALARY    $/WEEK          115        115        115
   16 SALES FORCE COMMISSION     PERCENT           3          3          3

   17 LABOR FORCE HIRES          PERSONS          20         15         25
   18 LABOR FORCE FIRES          PERSONS           0          0          0
   19 LABOR WAGE RATE            $/WEEK          220        232        240

••• M A N U F A C T U R I N G •••

   20 REGULAR PRODUCTION PLANNED THOU.           500        600        600
   21 DELUXE PRODUCTION PLANNED  THOU.           300        300        300
   22 PLANT EXPANSION IN UNITS   THOU.             0          0         50
   23 PRODUCTION ENGINEERING     $1000           150        150        200
   24 PLANT MAINTENANCE          $1000           250        200        200

••• I N V E N T O R Y •••

   25 REGULAR UNITS ORDERED      THOU.            50         50         50
   26 ALPHA PARTS PURCHASED      THOU.           700        750        800
   27 BETA PARTS ORDERED         THOU.           900       1100       1350
   28 AVER, FIFO OR LIFO (0,1,2) CODE              0          0          0

   29 REGULAR SHIPMENT-- WEST    THOU.           200        250        250
   30                    SOUTH   THOU.           100        150        100
   31 DELUXE SHIPMENT--- WEST    THOU.           100        115        150
   32                    SOUTH   THOU.            60         80         50

••• F I N A N C E •••

   33 CASH INVESTED IN MKT SEC   $1000             0          0          0
   34 PAYABLES--DAYS OUTSTANDING DAYS             40         40         45
   35 SHORT TERM LOAN REQUESTED  $1000           250        100        300
   36 INSURANCE COVERAGE         $1000          2000       2000       2000

   37 BONDS SOLD (-BUY)          $1000          1500          0          0
   38 PREFERRED SHARES SOLD (-BUY) SHARES       2300          0          0
   39 COMMON SHARES SOLD (-BUY)  SHARES            0          0          0
   40 DIVIDENDS PER COMMON SHARE CENTS           120        140        160
```

Figure 11-9. Sample MIS report from computer simulation called *The Top Management Experience*

```
INDUSTRY A    FIRM 1    PERIOD  3     YOUR COMPANY'S NAME GOES HERE          PAGE 2
••• I N C O M E   S T A T E M E N T •••                    % SALES    % CHANGE

SALES   (REGULAR = 70%)              $ 6469827              100          -4
COST OF GOODS SOLD                     3992681               62          -3
                                      --------              ---         ---
GROSS MARGIN                           2477146               38          -4
SELLING, GENERAL AND ADMIN EXPENSES:
     PRODUCT DEVELOPMENT       300000                         5          20
     COLLECTION EXPENSE        109313                         2          17
     PROMOTION--TOTAL          415000                         6          10
     SALES FORCE COMPENSATION  313695                         5          -3
     PRODUCTION ENGINEERING    200000                         3          33
     DISTRIBUTION              377884                         6          -3
     ADMINISTRATION            397632                         6          18
TOTAL SELLING, GEN AND ADMIN   -------  2113524              33          10
DEPRECIATION                            140000               2           0
                                      --------              ---         ---
OPERATING INCOME                        223622               3         -58
OTHER INCOME   (C.D. INTEREST        0)      0               0           0
OTHER EXPENSE  (LOAN INTEREST    11250)  71250               1          12
               (BOND INTEREST    60000)--------             ---         ---
INCOME BEFORE TAXES                     152372               2         -68
INCOME TAXES                             76186               1         -68
NET INCOME                               76186               1         -68
                                      ========


••• B A L A N C E   S H E E T •••
                                                           % ASSETS    % CHANGE
ASSETS
     CASH                               242741               4         -50
     MARKETABLE SECURITIES                   0               0           0
     ACCOUNTS RECEIVABLE                948864              16           8
     INVENTORIES                       1656359              28           4
                                      --------             ---         ---
     TOTAL CURRENT ASSETS              2847964              48          -4
     NET PLANT                         3120000              52          17
                                      --------             ---         ---
TOTAL ASSETS                           5967964             100           6
                                      ========

LIABILITIES
     ACCOUNTS PAYABLE                   437500               7          29
     ACCRUED LIABILITIES               480637               8          18
     SHORT TERM DEBT                    300000               5         200
                                      --------             ---         ---
     TOTAL CURRENT LIABILITIES         1218137              20          44
     LONG TERM DEBT                    1500000              25           0
                                      --------             ---         ---
TOTAL LIABILITIES                      2718137              46          15

OWNERS EQUITY
     PREFERRED STOCK ($100 PAR)        230000               4           0
     COMMON STOCK ($1 PAR)              50000               1           0
     CAPITAL IN EXCESS OF PAR          2450000              41           0
     RETAINED EARNINGS                  519827               8          -3
                                      --------             ---         ---
TOTAL OWNERS EQUITY                    3249827              54           0
```

Figure 11-9. Sample MIS report from computer simulation called *The Top Management Experience* (cont'd.)

```
INDUSTRY A   FIRM 1   PERIOD  3    YOUR COMPANY'S NAME GOES HERE          PAGE 3

••• S O U R C E S   A N D   U S E S   O F   W O R K I N G   C A P I T A L •••

SOURCES:                              USES: PLANT INVESTMENT        600000
    NET INCOME           76186            PURCHASE OF BONDS              0
    DEPRECIATION        140000            PURCHASE OF PREFERRED          0
    SALE OF BONDS            0            PURCHASE OF COMMON             0
    SALE OF PREFERRED       0            PREFERRED DIVIDEND ($4.00)  9200
    SALE OF COMMON          0            COMMON DIVIDEND   ($ 1.60) 80000
                        --------                                    --------
TOTAL SOURCES           216186        TOTAL USES                  689200
                        ========                                    ========
WORKING CAPITAL CHANGE  -473014


ANALYSIS OF WORKING CAPITAL CHANGE    STATEMENT OF OWNERS EQUITY CHANGE

    INCR IN CASH+MKT SEC  -242479     BEGINNING BALANCE        3262841
    INCR IN ACCTS REC       75980         NET INCOME             76186
    INCR IN INVENTORIES     66865         STOCK TRANSACTIONS         0
    DECR IN ACCTS PAYABLE  -98612         LESS: DIVIDENDS        89200
    DECR IN ACCRD LIAB     -74768     ENDING BALANCE           3249827
    DECR IN S-T DEBT      -200000                               --------
                          --------     OWNERS EQUITY CHANGE      -13014
WORKING CAPITAL CHANGE    -473014                               ========


••• A C C O U N T I N G   F O R   C O S T   O F   G O O D S   S O L D •••

--RAW MATERIALS INVENTORY--    --MANUFACTURING COSTS--    --FINISHED  GOODS--
   ALPHA              BETA
       0  BEG INVEN       0    ALPHA COST     400000    BEGIN BAL    1589494
  400000  PURCHASES 1100000    BETA COST     1000000    PURCHASES     250000
  400000  LESS:USED 1000000    DIRECT LABOR  1539245    MFG COST     3709546
       0  END INVEN  100000    OVERHEAD       770301    LESS:COGS    3992681
       0  END PARTS  100000    TOTAL MFG COST 3709546    END BAL     1556359


••• P E R S O N N E L   A N D   M A N U F A C T U R I N G   A N A L Y S I S •••

--SALES FORCE FACTS--          --MANUFACTURING LABOR--    --MFG PRODUCTIVITY-

SALES/PERSON    161746         BEGIN LABOR FORCE    232   UNITS MADE   800000
AVERAGE PAY        301         LESS: FIRES    0     232   PLANT SIZE   391392
RESIGNED             4         LESS: QUITS   10     222   SHIFT RATIO    2.04
FIRED                0         AVER. LABOR FORCE    227   AVER. LABOR     227
HIRED                4         PLUS: HIRES   25     247   MAX/WORK/SHIFT 4000


••• F I N A N C I A L   A N A L Y S I S •••

--LIQUIDITY RATIOS--      --MANAGEMENT  PERFORMANCE INDEX--   --AVAILABLE  FUNDS--
                                                              PRIME RATE= 7.5 $000
QUICK RATIO     1.0     EARNINGS/SALES(%)    = ROS = 1.2      ST LOAN   @ 9.3 1700
CURRENT RATIO   2.3     X SALES/ASSET(YR)(2.2)= ROA = 2.6     LT BONDS  @ 8.7 1300
RECEIVABLE DAYS  48     X ASSET/EQUITY ( 2.0)= ROE = 5.0      PFD: YIELD@ 8.8  600
INVENTORY DAYS   70     X PRICE/EARNINGS(26.6)= MPI = 134     COMMON:YLD@ 4.0  600
```

Figure 11-9. Sample MIS report from computer simulation called *The Top Management Experience* (cont'd.)

••• U N I T   S A L E S   A N D   I N V E N T O R Y   R E P O R T •••

		BEGINNING INVENTORY	UNITS RECEIVED	AVAILABLE FOR SALE	UNIT SALES	ENDING INVENTORY
REGULAR-----	NORTH	139782	300000	439782	266223	173559
	WEST	15215	250000	265215	265215	0
	SOUTH	64072	100000	164072	143979	20093
	AT FACTORY	100000	------	------	------	100000
	TOTALS	319069	650000	869069	675417	293652
DELUXE------	NORTH	0	8333	8333	8333	0
	WEST	0	150000	150000	136114	13886
	SOUTH	19275	50000	69275	68096	1179
	AT FACTORY	41667	------	------	------	33334
	TOTALS	60942	208333	227608	212543	48399

••• M A R K E T I N G   I N F O R M A T I O N   A N D   E S T I M A T E S •••

FIRM	REGULAR PRICE	DELUXE PRICE	EST REGULAR MARKET SHARE NORTH	WEST	SOUTH	EST DELUXE MARKET SHARE NORTH	WEST	SOUTH
1	6.75	8.99	20	20	19	21	20	21
2	6.75	8.99	21	19	20	16	16	19
3	6.75	9.99	19	21	17	18	23	20
4	6.75	8.99	20	22	23	21	17	21
5	6.75	8.99	20	18	21	24	24	19

FIRM	PROD DEV (RANK)	ENGR RANK	EST REG PROMOTION--$1000 NORTH	WEST	SOUTH	EST DLX PROMOTION--$1000 NORTH	WEST	SOUTH
1	1	1	84	107	78	51	58	21
2	2	2	98	123	84	60	60	24
3	3	3	120	117	62	53	53	28
4	4	4	107	96	59	44	47	29
5	5	5	93	112	56	49	44	23

FIRM	SHIFTS WORKED	OVERTIME (1 =YES)	EST LABOR AND SALES PAY WAGE	$ BASE	% COMM	EST SALES FORCE SIZE NORTH	WEST	SOUTH
1	2	1	220	120	3	14	17	7
2	2	1	240	130	3	16	17	8
3	2	1	220	130	3	17	16	9
4	2	1	240	120	4	15	18	7
5	2	1	230	110	2	16	19	10

--WHOLESALE PRICES-- ALPHA PART	BETA PART	REGULAR UNIT	--REAL ECONOMIC GROWTH-- PER 3 ACTUAL	PER 4 APPROX	PER 5 APPROX	--CONSUMER PRICE INDEX-- PER 3 ACTUAL	PER 4 APPROX	PER 5 APPROX
0.50	1.00	5.00	100	104	107	100	102	104

MESSAGE: PLEASE PREPARE A WRITTEN GOALS AND STRATEGY STATEMENT
         TO GUIDE YOUR FIRM

Figure 11-9. Sample MIS report from computer simulation called *The Top Management Experience* (cont'd.)

```
INDUSTRY A    FIRM 1    PERIOD  3     YOUR COMPANY'S NAME GOES HERE           PAGE 5

••• C O M P A R A T I V E   I N C O M E   S T A T E M E N T S •••
        (IN THOUSANDS OF DOLLARS EXCEPT PER SHARE )
                                                        --SECURITY PRICES--
                                                        BOND   PFD  COMMON
FIRM   SALES   COGS    SGA   DEPR   TAX   INC   EPS    DIV  YIELD  STOCK  STOCK

 1     6470    3993   2114   140     76    76   1.34   1.60   8.7    91     81

 2     6470    3993   2114   140     76    76   1.34   1.60   8.7    91     81

 3     6470    3993   2114   140     76    76   1.34   1.60   8.7    91     81

 4     6470    3993   2114   140     76    76   1.34   1.60   8.7    91     81

 5     6470    3993   2114   140     76    76   1.34   1.60   8.7    91     81

AVER   6470    3993   2114   140     76    76   1.34   1.60   8.7    91     81

                --PERCENT CHANGE IN ITEMS ABOVE--

 1      -4      -3     10      0    -68   -68   -70     14     9     -9    -19
 2      -4      -3     10      0    -68   -68   -70     14     9     -9    -19
 3      -4      -3     10      0    -68   -68   -70     14     9     -9    -19
 4      -4      -3     10      0    -68   -68   -70     14     9     -9    -19
 5      -4      -3     10      0    -68   -68   -70     14     9     -9    -19

••• C O M P A R A T I V E   B A L A N C E   S H E E T S •••
        (IN THOUSANDS OF DOLLARS)

       CASH +          TOTAL   NET  ASSETS=                S-T  BOND   PFD COMMON
FIRM   MKT SEC   A/R   INVEN  PLANT LIAB+OE   A/P   A/L    DEBT  DEBT EQUITY EQUITY

 1      243     949    1656   3120   5968    438   481    300   1500   230   3020

 2      243     949    1656   3120   5968    438   481    300   1500   230   3020

 3      243     949    1656   3120   5968    438   481    300   1500   230   3020

 4      243     949    1656   3120   5968    438   481    300   1500   230   3020

 5      243     949    1656   3120   5968    438   481    300   1500   230   3020

AVER    243     949    1656   3120   5968    438   481    300   1500   230   3020

                --PERCENT CHANGE IN ITEMS ABOVE--

 1     -50       8      4      17      6     29    18    200      0     0      0
 2     -50       8      4      17      6     29    18    200      0     0      0
 3     -50       8      4      17      6     29    18    200      0     0      0
 4     -50       8      4      17      6     29    18    200      0     0      0
 5     -50       8      4      17      6     29    18    200      0     0      0

FOOTNOTE: INVENTORY ACCOUNTING METHODS:          INDEPENDENT AUDITOR OPINION:
          FIRM 1: AVER                           FIRM 1: UNQUALIFIED OPINION
          FIRM 2: AVER                           FIRM 2: UNQUALIFIED OPINION
          FIRM 3: AVER                           FIRM 3: UNQUALIFIED OPINION
          FIRM 4: AVER                           FIRM 4: UNQUALIFIED OPINION
          FIRM 5: AVER                           FIRM 5: UNQUALIFIED OPINION
```

Figure 11-9. Sample MIS report from computer simulation called *The Top Management Experience* (cont'd.)

CONCEPTS

management information system (MIS)
exception report
demand report
predictive report
scheduled listing
imitation game
artificial intelligence

second industrial revolution
decision support system (DSS)
process control
total system
administrative subsystem
line subsystem

analytical model
simulation
GPSS
SIMSCRIPT
general ledger
chart of accounts
general journal
cost of goods sold (COGS)

QUESTIONS

1. What differentiates an MIS from mere transactions processing?
2. What computer technologies, in particular, make MIS more feasible now than a dozen years ago?
3. Users often complain of being inundated with computer printouts that they seldom use. Why is this so?
4. Different managers have varying styles. Winston Churchill is said to have required that reports be summarized in the middle of one typed sheet of paper. Relate this to the concept of an MIS.
5. Why is it unlikely that total systems will ever be developed for large organizations?
6. Choose a particular administrative job that usually exists in a college or university and state the types of demand reports you think such a manager might need.
7. Interview such a university administrator to find out the types of decisions actually made and the various reports really needed.
8. Accounting, finance, and administrative applications often provide the basic payoff of computers. Why?
9. Explain why line subsystems are justifiable after transactions processing and some administrative tasks have been implemented.
10. Discuss the strengths and weaknesses of a *simulation* of top management decision making versus the real experience itself.

Chapter Twelve

Systems
Analysis

By discussing MIS at the outset of Part 4, an overall, top-level perspective on computer usage was presented. In this and the next chapter we will discuss how to develop the applications that make up or enhance an organization's overall MIS. Then, Chapter 14 describes representative uses of computers in six different sample organizations.

This chapter discusses the systems approach, the systems development cycle, and the systems analysis phase of development, in particular. This phase concludes with a specific systems analysis report, which we will outline. Since cost/benefit analysis is a crucial tool in this phase, we will then discuss the benefits and costs of information and consider whether to make or buy the software. Any proposed project should be subjected to such an economic appraisal and guidelines for it are developed. To assist understanding and application of these ideas, the chapter includes a case that poses a significant systems analysis problem.

THE SYSTEMS APPROACH The **systems approach** is a procedure for solving problems. It views a **system** as a set of interrelated parts, with its boundaries defined to serve some purpose. Hence, the earth is a system; so is the world economy, or that of the United States, or a particular industry or specific firm. An **information system** may include a computer and all of its uses in some organization. Or the term *information system* may refer to a single application, including only those data items, programs, and hardware resources devoted to it.

After taking a comprehensive, systems-level view of the problem, the systems approach proceeds through four distinct phases:

1. Systems analysis
2. Systems design
3. Systems implementation
4. Systems evaluation

Thus, the systems approach, like a system itself, is composed of sub-parts. Each of these four phases can be pursued using the systems approach. For example, doing a thorough systems analysis involves, as we will see, defining the "best" system for the purpose. This means that during systems analysis, potential systems must be analyzed, designed, implemented, and evaluated, at least preliminarily or analytically, if not actually. Thus, the first phase—systems analysis—involves the full systems approach, as does each phase.

The full systems development cycle is discussed in the next section. Then, the systems analysis phase is detailed. We look at its three component steps, its concluding report, the supporting analytical tools and procedures, and a case example for discussing and applying these ideas. The next chapter then details the latter three phases of development—systems design, implementation, and evaluation. Remember, however, that the systems approach to problem solving pervades the entire four-phase process, and each of their steps, as well as systems problems in fields other than information systems.

THE SYSTEMS DEVELOPMENT CYCLE

Developing new information systems is a creative, stimulating activity. The information system produced can and should be a source of new economic benefits to the organization. Or it can be a "disaster"—people time, computer time, and dollars expended with no payoff except some hard-won experience. In practice, the systems development effort has often gone either way. But a full understanding of the systems development cycle, shown in Figure 12-1, should help you produce a positive result more consistently.

The systems development cycle can be viewed in four phases, as diagrammed in Figure 12-1. For each phase, Table 12.1 describes the task to be achieved, the types of human skills involved, and the approximate portion of the total effort and cost expended on each component step of each phase.

The *systems analysis phase* has three component steps (see Figure 12-1 and Table 12.1). These are:

1. Define system objectives
2. Create and analyze alternative systems
3. Specify information requirements

Then, the *systems design phase* picks up from the specification of information requirements—now that these system outputs are known to be suitable, feasible, and economical to produce. Systems design is

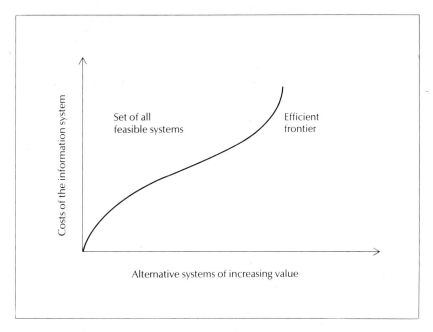

Figure 12-2. The set of all feasible systems and its efficient frontier

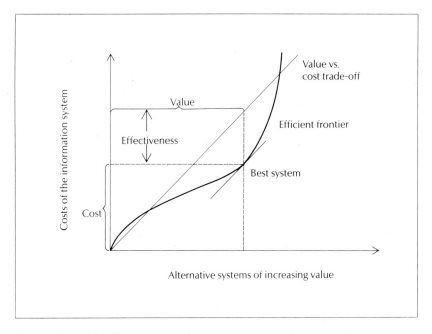

Figure 12-3. The "best" alternative system is both effective and efficient

sen to meet those requirements can produce a more favorable balance of value and cost.

Information Requirements   As discussed, the ultimate task of systems analysis is to define outputs able to meet user needs acceptably. This involves both users and systems analysts. It is often wise to prepare an interview outline in preparation for such discussions. This assures that the agenda will be organized and that the right questions will be satisfactorily answered. Then, the meeting's results should be documented. Four general lines of inquiry should be covered during one or more such user-analyst exchanges:

- the *objectives* the user has, based on the *decisions* he or she has to make, and the *information* needed to make them.
- the nature of the *present system*, including its capabilities and limitations and any constraints it imposes.
- the nature of the desired *processing*, including developing data on transaction volume, number of accounts, and so forth, by which the analyst can determine the application's activity, volatility, response time, file size and growth, integration, and security and backup criteria
- the *value versus cost* trade-offs that the user is willing to make, culminating in a specific systems proposal and its budget

1. **Objectives, Decisions, and Information:** The user's need for an information system stems from the decisions she or he must make. A system is not necessarily effective just because it gives users more information, faster information, or information they say they want. Computer users may already receive an overabundance of printouts, but not necessarily the ones they need for decision making. Furthermore, better information does not automatically lead to better decisions. Also, grievous results can befall users who know how to use their information system but don't know how it derives the information presented. The recommended systems analysis phase (Figure 12-1) begins with this crucial issue—defining system objectives—and concludes with the information requirements specified.

2. **Present System:** The nature of the present system should be investigated. Decisions are currently being made in some way, even if they are being left to chance. More likely, a manual of procedures or a computerized system already exists. Its attributes and problems should be noted as well as any salvageable features or constraints

on some new system. For instance, imagine computerizing an accounting system based on codes that employees already understand. You would probably choose to retain those codes, even at some extra computer processing expense.

3. **Processing:** The user and systems analyst must develop the overall processing steps deemed appropriate. This means choosing the hardware, I/O techniques, organization methods, and so forth needed for an efficient system. Parts 2 and 3 of this book explained the options available to the systems analyst in the areas of hardware and software technology and in methods of processing. The next chapter discusses systems design—the process for transforming these processing options into the details suitable for a particular system.

4. **Value versus Cost:** The value of information and its costs must be properly balanced if the system is to be more effective than any other. The analyst should suggest various information possibilities. Often these can be easily provided once the underlying data are in the system. For example, sales analysis by customer, product, or district may be worthwhile if the underlying transactions are already computer processed. In turn, the analyst should elicit from the user an estimate of the value of such information. Then, to judge whether value exceeds cost, an estimate of an efficient system's cost is necessary.

THE SYSTEMS ANALYSIS REPORT

The difficult, challenging first phase in the systems development cycle should end with a **systems analysis report**. This document is the basis for the systems design phase that follows. Both the user and the technical staff, primarily the systems analyst, should agree on the report's contents. A traditional administrative procedure is to have each party "sign off" on its conclusions.

The report should include:

1. A statement of system objectives
2. A review of the alternative systems considered, including extending the present system's life
3. An information requirements specification based on a definition of the decisions and processing activities to be affected by the system
4. A schedule and table of resources needed for development of the defined system

5. An investment valuation of the system, including a discussion of its benefits, costs, and risks and key checkpoints during development and operation

6. User and systems analyst approval, including the criteria for system acceptance by the user

The information requirements specification should be detailed and precise. This takes considerable effort. But the understanding and agreement developed during this step will probably result in less effort and change to the system during the later phases of its development.

One useful format for specifying the proposed system's outputs is to prepare an **I/P/O notebook**. In it, one page is used for each possible report or type of inquiry that the system should handle. Each page lists three things:

- *inputs:* the data items needed to produce the intended results
- *processing:* a general statement of the algorithm or procedure for transforming inputs into the intended results
- *outputs:* the intended results, which will satisfactorily meet the user's transactions processing or decision-making needs

The systems analysis phase, and its concluding report, may require 25 to 40 percent of the entire systems development effort. This phase is the most uncertain and involves the highest paid people (user management, users, and systems analysts). In fact, substantial interviewing, brainstorming, preliminary design work, cost/benefit estimation, assessment of the present system, and review of alternative systems must be done just to decide intelligently if the systems analysis phase and the whole project should move ahead further. Thus, it is pertinent to review a vital tool of systems analysis—cost/benefit analysis.

COST/BENEFIT ANALYSIS

The need for information systems begins with some user who has a problem. The systems approach helps us understand, dissect, analyze, and synthesize a "best" solution to the problem, given some defined objectives. But problems do not usually come in neat, identifiable packages, and the user's information needs are often vague. The analyst must help crystalize these needs as either a desire for current information at less cost or as a desire for better or faster information.

The benefit of getting currently available information at less cost equals the cost saving. However, the economic benefit of better or faster information is more complex to derive. Part of successful systems analysis involves balancing the costs of supplying information against the benefits realized by the user.

Benefits stem from the **quality of information**, or the extent of its usefulness. These benefits generally increase with:

- **accuracy:** the correctness of information in reflecting reality
- **timeliness:** the degree to which information is up to date
- **reliability:** the certainty that sought information is available
- **response time:** the speed of retrieving sought information
- **completeness:** the thoroughness of information in relation to that sought
- **relevance:** the ability to provide that information, and only that information, which is desired

The task of systems analysis is to determine the best information system for the user. For a system to yield benefits it must help the user solve problems. It must also, of course, be technologically and organizationally feasible, since its economic benefits can only be attained through systems implementation. These benefits, whether from lowered costs or improved information, should be measured against the total costs of providing the information system.

Benefits of Information Systems

The benefits, costs, and risks of information systems are often hard to define and harder still to quantify. But this is true of many investment decisions and future plans. The difficulty of such assessments makes them all the more necessary. Besides, the information systems development cycle is a process that must be *managed*. An understanding of the benefits, costs, and risks of the project can help management "make it happen" the way it is supposed to.

Benefits are often categorized as:

- reduced costs for information of current quality
- improved quality of information
- "intangible" benefits

The first category is often called **hard benefits**, whereas the latter two are called **soft benefits**. Cuts in costs already being incurred provide identified, "hard dollar" savings. Consider, for example, the administrative and clerical costs incurred in clearing bank checks. Costs per check processed have been lowered dramatically with the introduction and subsequent improvement of computers.

Check processing is also now more accurate. This improves the quality of information for the bank and its customers. How much is this benefit worth? It is certainly worth the cost previously incurred to correct manual errors. Also, better service and quicker response with fewer errors yields other marketing benefits.

Because quantifying soft benefits is difficult, some firms insist that information systems be economically justified by considering only the hard benefits. If other benefits result, that is said to be "so much the better." There are flaws, however, in this reasoning. First, we would want to know "how much the better." Second, as information systems continue to evolve from the more mundane transactions processing type into the more sophisticated decision support type, the majority of the payoff is in soft benefits. In the sections below we will present a way to quantify and judge the extent of these increasingly important categories of benefits.

Value of Information   Information derives value by its impact on some user's productivity or decision making. For example, a computer-based system often increases clerical productivity, especially for repetitive processing of transactions. Cost displacement is the usual objective of such routine data processing. Traditional work measurement procedures can determine the system's economic payoff, which equals the overall cost saving.

By contrast, information systems that improve the quality of information and affect decisions are harder to appraise. If, for example, added information does not change your decisions, you might as well not have the information. There is no economic payoff in such a case. Thus, when information does not affect decisions, the decision maker seems as well off without it as with it.

In addition, a message or item of information that is always the same or can be predicted is not helpful. Such "news" would not alter a decision that could have been made without it. The eminent turn of the century banker, J. P. Morgan, was once asked what the stock market would do. He replied, "It will fluctuate." Such a "no-surprise" message given as free advice has a value equal to its cost. A popular restatement of this conclusion is that valuable information must have some element of surprise. For example, a clinical lab test gets ordered when a doctor is not sure what the result may be and when some decision may depend on it.

Information must also be relevant as well as somewhat surprising if it is to have value. People have both entertainment and economic motives. For example, knowing yesterday's sports scores is interesting and entertaining, perhaps, but it affects few economic decisions. Valuable information should tend to change decisions, and the changed decisions should tend to produce better results. Thus, valuable information must be expected to:

- have some element of surprise
- affect some decision that depends on it
- produce improved outcomes

We are almost continually making decisions. One of the most frequent ones is the choice *not to decide now*, thereby extending the decision process of information search and analysis. Even if a message has little surprise or confirms what one already thought, it may precipitate the decision to decide now. As such, even confirming information may be valuable since it may reduce uncertainty and shorten the decision process.

Quantifying the value of information is necessary in order to evaluate the system providing it. The value of information can be succinctly defined as the **incremental expected payoff** derived by using it to affect decisions. A *payoff* is the benefit received from a particular decision. The notion of *expected* payoff reflects the fact that using the information precedes the decision making that alters payoffs. Finally, only the *incremental* portion of a changed decision's payoff can be attributed to having the information.

An example will help illustrate these concepts. The methods and terminology used are drawn from **decision theory**—a way of analyzing situations involving choice. Suppose a product costs $10 and sells for $15. Ten percent of the items produced are defective. A defective item is defined as one returned during the 30-day warranty period. A full refund is made for the defective item, which must be discarded. The processing costs and lost goodwill average $8 per return. Thus the sale of a good item yields $15 in revenue and $5 in (pretax) profit. A defective item causes an overall loss of $18, including the return costs. If an item is scrapped rather than sold, no revenue results to offset its costs, but no customer return is possible. The profit outcomes of these two possible actions, for both good and bad items, are summarized in Table 12.2

Thus, the company encounters a decision situation as an item rolls

TABLE 12.2   PROFIT OUTCOMES OF TWO POSSIBLE ACTIONS

Actions	State of Item	
	S_1 = good (90%)	S_2 = defective (10%)
A_1 = sell	$5	−$18
A_2 = scrap	−$10	−$10

off its manufacturing line. Ninety percent of the items are capable of service during the warranty period. But the rest are defective and will be returned. Given these two states of nature describing an actual item, the company must decide whether to ship each item or to scrap it on the spot. This prevents the possibility of its return. Table 12.2 is called the company's **payoff matrix**, or tabulation of outcomes for each state of nature and each possible action.

Suppose the decision maker's objective is to maximize expected profit. Then, the "best" decision, in the absence of additional information, is to sell all items. If so, the company makes $5 on each good item. It loses $18 all together on each defective item. Expected profit per unit, E, is then:

$$E = (.90)\,(\$5) + (.10)\,(-\$18) = \$2.70$$

Perfect information about the state of each item would change decisions. The revised decision pattern would become "sell the good and scrap the bad." The expected unit profit of this revised decision rule based on perfect information is:

$$E = (.90)\,(\$5) + (.10)\,(-\$10) = \$3.50$$

Thus, the incremental expected payoff of perfect information about each item is $3.50 − $2.70 = $.80 per unit. But, the information's cost, and the cost of deciding which units to scrap, would partially offset this benefit.

Information is usually not perfect. For example, suppose an information system is devised to report on the state of each item. In this case, a red light that signals each defective item might suffice. Suppose that this information system has the accuracy characteristics shown in Table 12.3.

The reported information accurately identifies 94 percent of the good items. But it falsely classifies 6 percent of them as defective. It properly classifies all of the defective items. Thus, the overall quality of

TABLE 12.3 ACCURACY CHARACTERISTICS OF AN IMPERFECT INFORMATION SYSTEM

Reported Information	States of Nature	
	S_1 = good (90%)	S_2 = defective (10%)
I_1 = good	.94	0
I_2 = defective	.06	1

this information is less than perfect, as is typical. Suppose the decision maker acts on the basis that the reported information is accurate (that is, he or she rejects all items reported as defective). Then the expected unit profit is:

$$E = (.9)[(.94)(\$5) + (.06)(-\$10)]$$
$$E = + (.1)[(0)(-\$18) + (1)(-\$10)] = \$2.69$$

This profit expectation is *less* than the sell-all decision made with no information. Thus, this information system is useless, regardless of its cost. Furthermore, it is harmful since it sways decisions even though the information should be ignored. This information system must provide greater accuracy if it is to improve decision making.

Suppose the false defective reports could be cut in half, from .06 to .03 of all good items. Then, items shown as good would be sold and the remaining scrapped immediately. This improved information/decision system provides an expected unit profit of $3.095. This is well above the $2.70 profit expected with no information.

Other types of information can also be shown to have value. Suppose that improved manufacturing knowledge increases the production yield of good items from 90 percent to 92 percent. Then, the expected unit profit would be raised from 2.70 to $3.16 without any further information, just by selling all items. Table 12.4 summarizes this situation.

Thus, using low-quality information to affect decisions may cause a lower payoff than having no information at all, as with the 6 percent defectives system. However, this negative value is not a property of the information, but rather of its use. When ignored, as it should be, this "information" has zero value (excluding its cost).

The value of information is its incremental expected payoff—how

TABLE 12.4 SUMMARY OF PAYOFF WITH DIFFERENT INFORMATION SYSTEMS

		Level of Manufacturing Knowledge	
		90% good	92% good
Quality of Information on Items	No item information	$2.70	$3.16
	6 % false defectives	$2.69	$2.972
	3 % false defectives	$3.095	$3.386
	Perfect information	$3.50	$3.80

much it beats the payoff of not having the information. Thus, when manufacturing makes 90 percent good items, an information system reporting only 3 percent false defectives is worth $3.095 minus $2.70, or $.395 per unit. When manufacturing knowledge improves to 92 percent good items, this same information system produces an expected item profit of $3.386. This is only $.226 better than with no information about which units are the 92 percent of good items. Thus, as manufacturing knowledge improves, an information system of given accuracy declines in value because it yields fewer surprises—not as many items are bad ones.

As seen from Table 12.4, two types of information can have value. First, information about individual items improves decisions if it has sufficient quality. Second, improved knowledge about how to make the units also provides a source of improved payoff.

These two types of information can be called **news** and **knowledge**. News tells you what's happening now. Knowledge tells you what to decide based on this news. Most transactions processing systems are designed to report the news—what is occurring in the business now. Management information systems are designed to build knowledge—based on these facts, how might the business be run better?

It is worth noting other qualities of the information in the above example. The information was timely—the defective-or-not message came in time to affect the sell or scrap decision. Also, the information was up-to-date, perfectly relevant and reliably issued for each item. Thus, this information was perfectly matched to the decision maker's needs. Usually, however, this cannot be achieved.

In conclusion, the value of information depends on a decision's alternatives, their payoffs, trade-offs between types of information, and the quality aspects of the information. Of course, information's value can only be approximated. Nonetheless, good systems analysis requires that the value of information be estimated carefully. For example, it is easy to overvalue an information system. Assuming that a system produces perfect information, or that a model perfectly represents reality, leads to overestimating the system's value in improving decisions.

Costs of Information   The costs of an information system can be categorized as **capital costs** and **operating costs**.

The capital costs of a system are the first three phases of the systems development cycle, incurred before the system becomes operational:

- systems analysis
- systems design
- systems implementation

The operating costs of an information system are those needed to keep it functioning:

- data gathering and output usage (users typically perform these tasks)
- computer hardware
- computer operations
- maintenance of hardware and software

Data entry and output display alternatives and costs for I/O were reviewed in Chapter 5. The operating cost category called computer hardware is the expense of renting or leasing equipment or, if owned, an appropriate charge for depreciation. Computer operations costs, discussed in Chapter 15, consist of personnel and supplies costs for running the computer installation. Finally, maintenance of both hardware and existing programs is a normal, ongoing item. It is properly allocated as an operating expense. **Software maintenance** includes only those modifications needed for the program's continued operation. True program enhancements are better classified as capital costs.

Return on Systems Investment

Proposed information systems should be analyzed in the same way that other investments are. Too often this does not happen. Information systems are not tangible or physical as are traditional brick and mortar assets. Computer hardware is tangible enough, but the content of programs, forms, procedures, employee training, and other resources of an information system are often intangible. Although the costs of information systems may be measured, the benefits of better, faster, and more accurate processing and decision making are difficult to quantify. Nonetheless, a return on investment procedure can and should be applied to selecting among proposed information systems.

Three methods are widely used for gauging the investment merit of a particular project. In order of increasing complexity, they are computing the proposed asset's:

- payback
- internal rate of return
- risk-return distribution

Payback measures the number of years required for an asset's returns to recover (or pay back) its original cost. Suppose an asset has an initial capital cost of $1,000,000. If it nets $200,000 per year, its payback period is 5 years. Alternately, this same result can be expressed as a 20 percent average annual return of the original investment during the payback period.

Calculating an asset's **internal rate of return** is more complicated, but it overcomes some simplifications of the payback method. This method measures the *timing* as well as the *amounts* of investment outflows and inflows. Thus, a $1,000,000 investment that returns $200,000 per year for only 5 years, and nothing thereafter, has a zero percent internal rate of return. The initial capital is recovered but nothing more is returned. If this same asset were to return $200,000 per year for 10 years, its internal rate of return would be about 15 percent. Only if the asset returned $200,000 per year forever would its internal rate of return be 20 percent. This method automatically adjusts for the time that capital is tied up by discounting future inflows at the computed internal rate of return.

The third method involves computing a **risk-return distribution**. This recognizes variations in future outflows and inflows. The investment evaluation considers the range of results as well as their timing. Since information systems are evaluated and selected before they are implemented, their exact costs and benefits can only be estimated. Various levels of risk, or variations in the rate of return, accompany such projects. By analyzing risks as well as returns, management can select projects more knowledgeably and can focus efforts on controlling the largest sources of risk.

Taxpaying organizations must also consider the tax aspects of their investments. When corporations apply any of the analyses cited above—payback, internal rate of return, or risk-return distribution—they are usually interested in after tax results. Curiously, software development acts as a tax shelter. Most development costs are for salaries and can be immediately expensed for income tax purposes. However, the purchase of existing software must currently be capitalized for tax purposes. Depreciation is then allowed over its useful life, which is usually assumed to be 5 years in the absence of evidence to the contrary. Property taxes on software are equally curious. Currently, a program's appraised tax value is the cost of the punched cards, tape, or disk storing it—not its development cost. Some state legislatures have considered amending this definition to the much higher development-cost basis.

In addition to estimating value, costs, risks, and any tax effects, an evaluation should also judge the system's **economic life** This is the estimated period of usefulness of the proposed information system. Tangible assets usually have observable physical obsolescence rates. This serves to guide estimates of their useful life. However, the economic life of information systems has often been shortened by rapid technological transitions—such as incompatible generations of hardware, evolving computer languages, and expanded operating systems.

In fact, the estimate of a system's economic life is one of the major sources of its risk. A system that is abandoned soon after implementation is usually a poor investment, unless it has a significant salvage value toward a revised system.

The four asset valuation variables are: benefits, costs, risks, and life. They help answer the question: Is the proposed project economically worthwhile? The criteria for answering this should be the same as that required for approving other investments of similar capital cost and risk. An estimate of each project's probable outflows and inflows over its lifetime needs to be made. Such an analysis is presented in Figure 12–4.

The graph in Figure 12–5 shows a range of possible outcomes from developing and implementing a proposed information system. The optimistic and pessimistic projections should reflect specific probability levels. Most results should fall between these outcomes. The median outcome (or, alternately, the expected outcome) is also shown.

Historically, information systems are rather high-risk investments. In the example in Figure 12–5, the time before net benefits are achieved ranges from about 15 months to over 2 years. Clearly, there is also some possibility that the system will be abandoned and will never achieve any net benefits.

System output: A monthly production schedule
System inputs: 1. Forecasted demand by product
               2. Initial inventories
               3. Production capacity
               4. Labor, capital, and raw materials constraints
System value and costs:
   Capital cost = $200,000 over 1 year of development
   Decisions per year = 12 monthly schedules
   Incremental expected payoff per decision = $8000
   Operating cost per decision = $2000
   Estimated useful life = 4 years
System rate of return:

$$\$200,000 = \sum_{i=1}^{4} \frac{12 \text{ times } [\$8000 - \$2000]}{(1 + r)^i}$$

Where r is the information system's internal rate of return on both a before- and aftertax basis because of the immediate tax deductability of system development outlays
System risk: If life = 4 years, then r = 20%, but for life = 3 years, then r = 4%.

Figure 12–4. Sample economic analysis of an information system

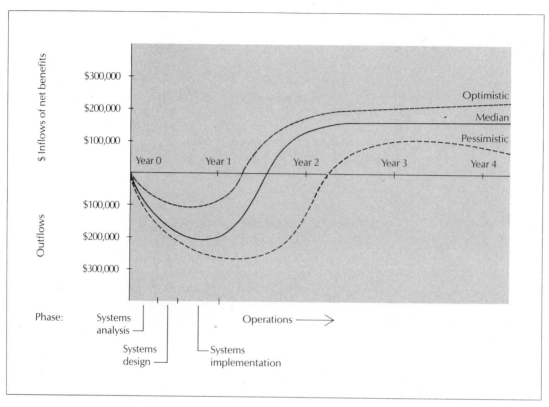

Figure 12-5. Projected cash outflows and inflows due to an information system

Estimates of the total capital costs, operating benefits and costs, and system lifetime are necessary for an internal rate of return calculation. Then, varying these estimates sheds light on the system's risk. A calculation of how the rate of return varies for differing system lifetimes is included in Figure 12-4. While benefits and costs of information systems are often discussed, the system's longevity is a crucial key to its success—yet it is often overlooked.

THE MAKE OR BUY DECISION A user's information needs can be satisfied with a proper hardware-software-data-people-system. The user can choose to acquire the software by making it or by buying it from an outside supplier. In seeking outside help, users may choose to contract for a tailored program or to obtain an existing program, if a suitable one is available.

The make or buy decision is a traditional business problem. Its importance in the development of information systems is fairly recent, but rapidly growing. Externally prepared software now approximates a $1 billion per year market.

The discussion of systems analysis in this chapter is aimed at creating new programs. However, the user and analyst should always be aware of other sources for software. Existing software is usually well proven and documented. Either purchase or lease terms are often available. Typically, when a developed program is suitable, acquiring it is less expensive and almost certainly quicker and less risky than creating it in-house. But the systems analysis phase is still necessary to know what is suitable and cost/beneficial. Buying existing software tends to reduce systems design and implementation effort more than systems analysis. (Software and consulting services will be discussed further in Chapter 16.)

KOLACO, INC., CASE

Since its founding 50 years ago, Kolaco, Inc., has become a leading beverage marketer and manufacturer with worldwide sales of $1 billion annually. Products include Kool-Kola soft drink and snack foods. The corporation is organized into three distinct companies: Kool-Kola in New York City, Foods in Atlanta, and international operations. All divisions are permitted a high degree of autonomy.

The Kool-Kola division is of particular interest as a case context for discussing systems analysis. It accounts for nearly half of the company's sales and pretax profit and is divided into two facets:

1. Syrup, which makes the soda concentrate sold to 200 franchised bottlers throughout the United States, and
2. Bottco, which operates bottling and distribution organizations in six regions of strong demand. These are essentially company-owned "franchises" that buy concentrate from the syrup division, the same as other franchises do.

The Bottco Division

Total revenues of Bottco operations are about $200 million per year, somewhat less than half of the Kool-Kola division revenues. The major costs in making the product are for packaging and distribution, rather than for the ingredients.

Bottco is organized along functional lines, with vice-presidents for marketing, operations, and finance. This represents a change from a few years ago. Previously, the general managers for each of the six area bottlers made almost all decisions about marketing, production, and accounting. Now policy decisions are made at higher levels in the overall Bottco organization. This permits greater coordination of efforts and the development of management talent. It is also designed to increase the bottom-line contribution of the various Bottco units, since the individual area managers did not previously have incentives tied to profit performance.

Sales at the local level occur in two ways:

1. "Store-door" sales occur when the truck driver/salesperson pulls the truck up to the store and writes and fills the order immediately from stock carried on the truck.
2. "Presell" orders are taken by a salesperson and communicated to the warehouse for later delivery.

With "store-door" sales, a truck is loaded at night. In the morning, the load is checked by the driver and a checker and signed out. At the end of the day, the driver turns in receipts and invoices, the remainder of the load, and the difference in cash. With the presell method, trucks are loaded at night and a route schedule is printed for the driver, who then merely drops off each order. Some optimization of truck routing and loading can be performed, since the shipments for the day are known with certainty.

The operations function is also structured around the geographic regions. Because of economies of scale and large changeover costs, soft drinks in particular package sizes are typically made in long production runs. In fact, in some regions, canning and bottling are done in separate facilities. Production is mostly a one-shift operation, except in the late spring and summer when inventory building and high sales typically require two shifts.

After products are produced, they are stored at the plant and some additional warehouses. The Bottco operations vice-president is responsible for inventory levels at all plants, and has to pay for the working capital tied up in inventory. Usually, production runs are decided on at the regional level, based on inputs from marketing and operations.

Plants report production and costs on a weekly basis. These are accounted for against a standard costing system, with the standards set yearly. Adjustments are made for variances at the end of each year.

Bottco Finance, Accounting, and EDP

The organization of the Finance department is shown in Figure 12–6. All cash coming into Bottco is immediately deposited to the Kolaco, Inc., lockbox system. Thus, none of the operating units handle cash beyond local cash sales collections. Cash management and certain

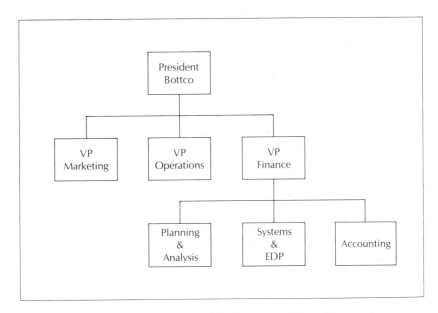

Figure 12-6. Finance department of the Bottco division of Kolaco, Inc.

other administrative services are the province of the central corporate staff.

The six regions use various outside data processing firms to handle their payrolls, each one using a different system. Similarly, there are currently six accounting systems, and different methods are used to control receivables and payables in each of the regions. The different systems exist for historical reasons. Since the functional reorganization, there has been an attempt to bring more standardization to these accounting systems by imposing a single chart of accounts. However, interpretation of some of the accounts still varies locally.

At the New York headquarters of Kolaco, there is an IBM 370/158 with one million bytes of core, ten 3330 disk drives, a 3350 drum, and six 3420 tape drives. These devices are attached to three block multiplexors and one byte multiplexor channel. The CPU runs under OS/VS, the virtual machine operating system. About 40 percent of the machine time is used to provide remote batch services to Bottco, for accounting and general ledger purposes. Currently, the regions collect accounting data on local data entry terminals, store this data on floppy disks, and transmit it at night for batch processing in New York.

Some of the transaction volumes are as follows: There are about 14,000 active customer accounts on file. These represent 40 percent of the total customers, and about 60 percent of the revenues. The rest of the customers pay cash for store-door deliveries. About 9,000 accounts payable invoices are handled per month. Bottco has an overall employee roster of about 2,000 people, with about 20 percent per year turnover. Bottco also owns and maintains records on about 12,000 vending machines. There are about 15,000 truck settlements per month—that is, a loaded truck leaving the plant and coming back after the day's sales, after which the driver "settles" the accounts.

These figures are for all six regions. Of course, there is some skewness in region size—the largest has five times the sales volume of the smallest and twice the sales volume of the median. In terms of seasonality, the four calendar quarters usually have 20, 27, 33, 20 percent, respectively, of the annual sales volume.

Over the years only two of the six regional operations have developed any in-house EDP operations. The Illinois region, the largest in sales volume, has sophisticated online computing. It utilizes the presell system. Clerks sitting at CRT terminals enter telephoned orders. A nightly batch run performs truck loading and route optimization, and prints a route ticket for the driver to follow during the next day's deliveries.

Accounting and inventory control functions are also performed on the region's computer, an IBM System 3/15. Since this Illinois group is the most sophisticated, it "became" the corporate EDP group when the recent functional reorganization took place. To date, however, its expertise has not been called upon outside of the Illinois region.

The second region using internal EDP is Connecticut. It uses remote batch processing for performing general ledger accounting and inventory control using the Corporate 370/158.

The Problem   Tom Lipton, the new vice-president for Finance at Bottco, is trying to put together an information system that will, in his words, "give every manager the information he or she needs to make decisions, and feedback on the effectiveness of decisions already made." The information system should help in solving the following problems:

1. Providing timely and accurate information that can be used by the various levels of management in the Bottco chain of command.

2. Interfacing data flow among different functional areas. Sales and operations must get together to decide how much to produce. Normally, sales are forecast and production schedules are set monthly by product and package. The first 2 weeks are "locked" and the following weeks are for planning purposes. However, at the current time, there are two sets of estimates being produced.

3. Making the credit-granting decision. This decision is at the marketing/finance interface. Marketing wishes to maximize sales, and often wants to extend credit to marginal risks, while accounting tends to be more conservative.

4. Providing feedback to managers. There is currently no useful feedback to the managers after they have made decisions. The proposed system should provide not only the right information for making decisions, but also feedback on the outcomes of those decisions.

Mr. Lipton sees a need for the following types of reports, at the associated managerial levels:

- general management: summary reports of statistics, efficiency of production, standard costs, variances, forecasts
- middle management: sales reports, production reports, promotional cost analyses, and so on
- operations level: accounting, general ledger, fixed asset management, and so on

In view of this information, you are asked to provide a systems analysis report proposing an information system meeting Tom Lipton's concerns and objectives. Discuss:

1. How to get the functional areas to interface.
2. Should Bottco EDP be centralized or decentralized, or some combination? If the latter, what combination?
3. What potential saving might accrue from the better use of information? Mr. Lipton believes some areas might be in production scheduling, measurement of promotional effectiveness, control of shrinkage, distribution routing, and extension of presell capability.

Second, prepare an overall EDP plan for the next 3 years for Bottco. This plan should include the applications description just requested and then discuss:

1. The organizational structure and staffing levels of the Bottco EDP group.
2. An overall systems plan with phasing of the various applications, including a Gantt or similar chart showing the tasks, timing, and interrelationships among tasks.
3. A hardware plan and configuration chart.
4. A budget including the estimated costs and presumed benefits.

SUMMARY The systems approach to problem solving can be thought of as consisting of four phases: systems analysis, design, implementation, and evaluation. Each of these phases can itself be subjected to the systems approach. In this chapter, we defined the systems development cycle and the task of systems analysis, in particular.

Systems analysis consists of three steps: define systems objectives, create and analyze alternative systems, and specify information requirements. In total, this phase can comprise 25 to 40 percent of the total systems development effort. It ends with a specific systems analysis report, acceptable to both users and technical staff, and detailing system outputs and economics.

A necessary tool in this phase is cost/benefit analysis, including the estimation of a proposed system's benefits, costs, risks, and life. A system's benefits stem from lowering the cost of, or improving the quality of, information available to users. The value of information is the incremental expected payoff of a changed decision.

An investment analysis illustration was cited as well as the need to consider acquiring existing software, if suitable. The system selected should be both effective and efficient for meeting user objectives. The Kolaco, Inc., case was cited as a context for discussing systems analysis.

CONCEPTS

systems approach	timeliness	news
system	reliability	knowledge
information system	response time	capital cost
cost/benefit analysis	completeness	operating cost
effectiveness	relevance	software maintenance
efficiency	hard benefit	payback
systems analysis report	soft benefit	internal rate of return
I/P/O notebook	incremental expected payoff	risk-return distribution
quality of information	decision theory	economic life
accuracy	payoff matrix	

QUESTIONS

1. The systems approach involves four phases. Define each phase.
2. When applying the systems approach to the development of information systems, each phase has a specific conclusion. Describe the end point of each phase of the systems development cycle.
3. Should systems development always proceed *sequentially* through the four phases?
4. It usually takes 5 to 10 percent of the total effort just to define systems objectives and 25 to 40 percent to complete the systems analysis phase. Justify the need for this heavy investment.
5. Why is the systems analyst's job said to be the most crucial one in information systems? What skill mix is required for effective performance?
6. Construct a sample page from a possible I/P/O notebook for an employee pension accounting system that you feel a large corporation might wish to develop.
7. Cite some hard and some soft benefits that such a system might achieve.
8. Using cost/benefit analysis, compare reading the daily newspaper with watching the TV nightly news as alternate information systems.
9. Cite an actual corporate information system and estimate its return on systems investment.
10. Explain the growing tendency to purchase software.
11. Using systems analysis, and assuming reasonable responses from users to any questions you would pose, write a systems analysis report for the Bottco division of Kolaco, Inc.

Chapter Thirteen

**Systems Design,
Programming,
and Implementation**

Systems development spans three phases: systems design; systems implementation, including computer programming and testing, and then organizational installation and usage; and systems evaluation. These phases of the information systems development cycle follow logically from the systems analysis phase discussed in the previous chapter, and shown in Figure 12-1.

An overview of each phase is useful before we look at the detailed guidelines for systems development presented in this chapter. We saw that systems analysis concludes with definitive specifications for the system's outputs. In support of that, the needed inputs and overall processing scheme are also identified. And the need for the proposed system, and its value, are verified by both user and analyst. This often takes the form of a systems analysis report, which includes a feasibility study and development schedule and is signed by the responsible parties.

Systems design means setting the specifications for an efficient information system, given a statement of its desired outputs. Thus, systems design picks up where systems analysis leaves off. In fact, some of the same personnel usually remain involved—analysts, programmers, or similarly titled systems specialists.

Producing the desired outputs efficiently means minimizing the resources consumed. These costs include programming, data entry, and computer operations over the life cycle of the application. The most efficient design is probably *not* the one that uses the least computer resources. Since people's time is getting more expensive, while the cost of hardware is declining, it is more and more necessary to use people time wisely. Systems design should call for programming and operating methods that conserve and balance these various resources.

Computer implementation involves those tasks needed to transform the systems design specifications into operable, tested, and documented software running on suitable and available hardware. Usually, this means doing the programming and testing in-house and on an already available computer. However, as part of systems analysis, a make or buy decision should be made, as discussed. If it is decided to make the software, outside specialists are still sometimes used (**contract programming**), but over 90 percent of newly created software costs are spent in-house.

Implementation has another aspect—getting the operable hardware/software system adopted by users. Without this vital step, all is in vain. **Organizational implementation** is surprisingly expensive—often 30 percent of the overall effort. It deserves special planning and control, including a desired schedule and budget. Installing the system involves documentation, training, conversion, and usually running it in parallel with its predecessor system.

System evaluation is the final phase of systems development. But it is crucial to the ongoing attempt to create effective and efficient information systems. As we saw in the decision process (Figure 11–4), this last step involves auditing or assessing results against projections or plans. It is too late to reanalyze, design, program, or install this particular system, of course. But it's not too late to modify it, hold its developers responsible for results—good or bad—and to learn from the development process.

SYSTEMS DESIGN Systems design is the linking phase between systems analysis and the programming and testing needed for computer implementation. We will discuss systems design in terms of four areas of concern:

- data collection and entry
- forms design for input and output
- system flowcharting
- database design

Remember, the guiding criterion of systems design is efficiency of total resources over the system's life cycle. Therefore, for each area of concern we will seek to imbed techniques that aid productivity, reduce errors, and lower costs. This means:

- using high-level languages
- seeking simplicity in design
- employing recent but reliable technology
- specifying modular programs
- emphasizing control and security

Data Collection and Entry The design of data collection and entry should reflect its purpose. In particular, the goals of data entry include reducing costs, errors, and delays. The following design guidelines frequently help to achieve these goals:

1. Collect and convert only those data items that have an expected value greater than their cost. If data aren't used, don't capture and store them.
2. Reduce data entry volume via sampling, coding, or prerecording fixed data items. A computer-prepared punched card is frequently used as a **turnaround document**, which accompanies a transaction and contains most or all of the pertinent data. The punched card accompanying your telephone bill is an example. When returned with your check, it reduces subsequent manual data entry.
3. Diagnose alternative procedures according to their steps of *sense*, *record*, or *convert* and according to each step's fixed and variable costs.
4. Avoid data conversions by capturing data in a machine-readable form near their source. Point-of-scale terminals and programmer-operated time-sharing terminals help achieve this.
5. Validate data, when justified, by redundant entry, visual verification, check digits, format validation, and range checks. Credit card transactions usually involve these accuracy-boosting techniques.
6. Control source documents with labels, routing slips, transmittal logs and similar orderly procedures. Bank checks are routinely processed in bundles, for example, with a validating total computed for each bundle.
7. Analyze the likely types of errors and their consequences and design the system to report automatically on error types and rates. Prevention requires detection.
8. Assign responsibility for errors and establish procedures for their correction. When people know errors are traceable, they make fewer and correct more.
9. Design forms, procedures, and working conditions that foster speed and accuracy. Income tax forms have long suffered on this point!
10. Consider a lower-cost, higher speed technology when high data volumes and standardized input forms warrant one. Thus, machine scoring of the millions of college aptitude tests has been feasible for two decades now.

Data collection and entry procedures deserve scrutiny because input is often the weak link in an information system. Data entry is costly, time consuming, repetitive, and often inadequately evaluated. It is the largest source of errors. Data entry performance can be measured by its costs per unit, error rate, and elapsed time delay. In general, do not treat data collection, entry, and error control as the unglamorous segment of an information system. Like humans, computers are what they eat.

Forms Design

"Good" I/O formats were defined to be useful program attributes during our discussion in Chapter 6. Now it is time to design such data collection forms and output report layouts. In designing any presentation or communication format, it is appropriate to ask, "What is the objective of this communication?"

On the data entry side it may be desirable to avoid forms altogether. Data are often best entered directly at their source by the person responsible, for whom the data have meaning. This shortcuts costs, errors, and delays. When intermediate recording steps are necessary, forms should be simple, clear, the smallest standard size, color coded, and spaced to allow for handwritten or typed entry. Fixed data such as firm name and address or data labels should be preprinted. Multicopy forms should be used, but only to the extent necessary for aiding subsequent processing or for backup. Physical characteristics should include:

- address positioning for easy mailing (say, with window envelopes)
- perforations
- paper grade and weight
- legibility of copies
- business reply or turnaround document requirements

On the output side, report formats are constrained by the hardware's printing, spacing, and forms-handling capabilities. Some terminals use thermal printing elements that sensitize special paper. Thus, preprinted forms are impractical or expensive. Normal computer printouts (11 ×14⅞ inch) are sometimes too large for convenient storage or photocopying. But 80-column formats (8½ inch with small margins) may be too confining. Also, the programming logic may limit sequence or layout alternatives.

Some design criteria to consider include:

1. *Data labels:* numbers are meaningless without identification, preferably concise but unambiguous
2. *Context information:* even labeled numbers are irrelevant without context, such as the percent change from last period or the percent of this period's total

3. *Information density:* the more compact the presentation, the better for repeat users; but fully described, noncoded, well-spaced formats are better for one-time users
4. *Printing technology:* equipment such as the IBM 3850 uses plain paper and overlays an image of the desired graphics; the Xerox 1200 produces 8½ by 11 inch copies with 132 print position capacity; computer-driven typesetting equipment can produce high-quality, fully justified text with variable character spacing, as in a book

The format of input data must coordinate with the data collection and entry procedures and with any preexisting forms, records, files, or database layouts. Also, output forms should be specified and possibly mocked up using dummy data. Review by the user is then essential. A sample output report is shown in Figure 13-1.

System Flowcharting With I/O particulars determined, the systems designer is ready to flowchart the overall processing system. The choice of an appropriate programming language involves considering available skills, program standardization policies, the nature of the data and processing, hardware and compiler availability and constraints, programmer productivity, and documentation. Then the processing needed to transform inputs into outputs must be specified in sufficient detail to guide programming.

The overall programming task should usually be subdivided or made modular. As we will see, initial programming is generally more productive—and maintenance programming substantially easier—for small programs. Thus, large processing tasks should be designed as separate, but precisely interfaced, modules. Hopefully, any change during development or later will then affect only one module. This step concludes with a system flowchart or block diagram of modules, their defined interfaces, and system inputs and outputs. A sample is shown in Figure 13-2.

Database Design Chapter 9 discussed database systems. Processing design necessarily interacts with data format and storage issues. However, the database concept seeks to limit the designer's concern to the *logical* aspects of data. The database management system (DBMS) then handles *physical* storage and retrieval aspects, hopefully efficiently. This greatly aids designers and programmers, who previously had to construct such data handling methods themselves. Also, the comprehensive, centralized, secure database may already have the required data in it. If so, an authorized subschema definition is sufficient to solve the whole input part of the problem. Output items being returned to storage are similarly easy to handle.

Tailored To Your Organization

☐ Sequence defined by you through the Profile
☐ Variable grouping of accounts to match your business office structure

Accurate Third Party Control

☐ Coordination of benefits for accurate third party billing
☐ Automatic allowance calculation eliminates manual effort
☐ Prorated insurance balances for simultaneous billing to patients and third parties

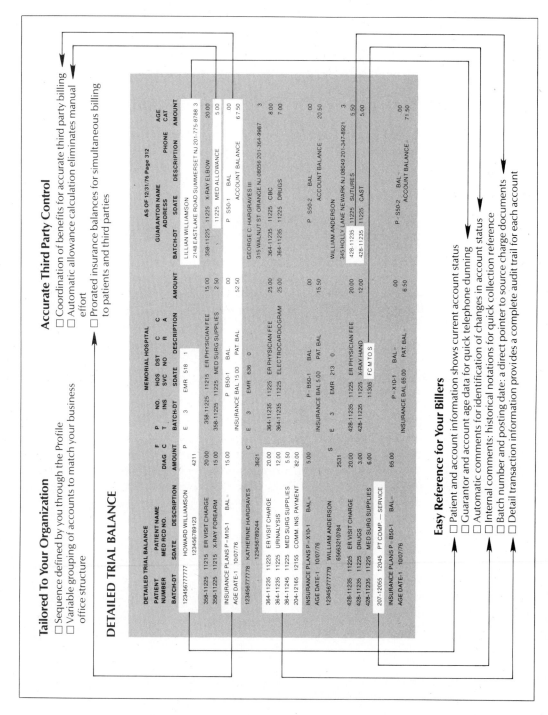

Easy Reference for Your Billers

☐ Patient and account information shows current account status
☐ Guarantor and account age data for quick telephone dunning
☐ Automatic comments for identification of changes in account status
☐ Internal comments: historical notations for quick collection reference
☐ Batch number and posting date: a direct pointer to source charge documents
☐ Detail transaction information provides a complete audit trail for each account

Figure 13-1. Sample computer output report

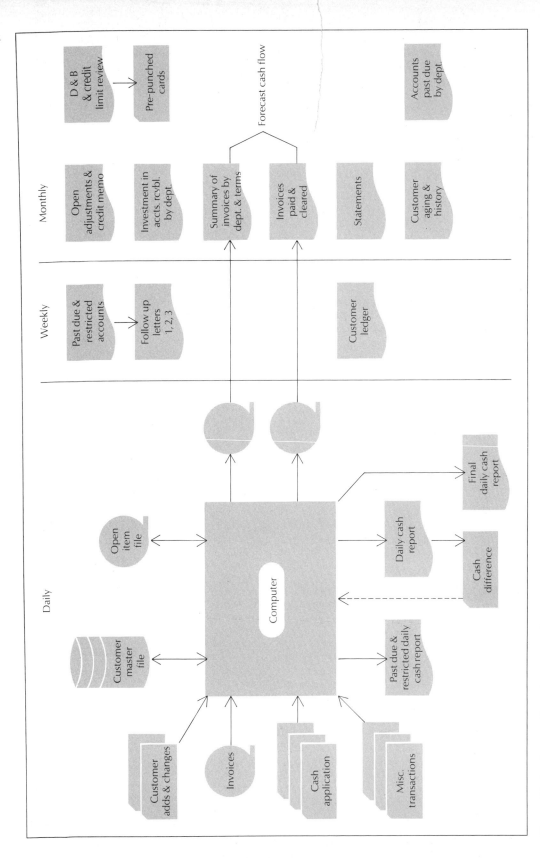

Figure 13-2. System flowchart example

In the absence of a DBMS, more traditional techniques of file organization and processing should probably be employed. Thus, the designer must decide issues such as setting the key field, record sequencing, field lengths, any indexes, storage codes, storage media, and so forth.

PROGRAMMING AND TESTING

This step in systems development is the most unique to, and the most associated with, computer-based systems. After all, other steps in the systems approach can be applied to the whole range of systems problems, not just to information systems. For example, providing transportation across a river might be the objective. By considering alternatives, perhaps a suspension bridge would be chosen over a ferry or conventional bridge options. Then, design details and construction implementation follow. But with a computer system, "construction" means programming.

It is wrong to assume, as many users or managers do at first, that programming is *all*, or even *most*, of what is involved in developing information systems. Some managers facing a computer-information problem say, "Get me a programmer." But, because of the extensive and expensive people involvement in systems analysis and in organizational implementation, programming is only a small part of the total task.

Still, the program is the end product of the systems development effort. It, together with the specified hardware, generates the desired information outputs—if provided with suitably organized and accurate input data. So, programming is a vital link in the chain of development. Also, most people's introduction to computing involves doing some programming, and most computer specialists were once (or still are) programmers.

While hardware technology has advanced dramatically, programming has remained something of an art. Productivity varies widely among programmers, and most aptitude tests designed to predict programming skills have low reliability. The first few years of programming experience have been definitely shown to increase skill and productivity levels. Beyond that, further professional growth is uneven or doubtful. So, the programmer and the programming project are evidently difficult to predict and manage. (The attributes of a good program were listed in Chapter 6, and the management aspects of programming are discussed in Chapter 15.)

In the following sections, we will discuss methods for doing the programming and testing work itself. Two techniques have come to the fore: modular design and structured programming. Then we will discuss testing from two perspectives: the programmer debugging his or her own work and the user doing acceptance testing.

Module Design

In designing the overall system, a **modular** concept was encouraged. This means breaking the task into logical pieces, yet being explicit about their interrelationships. The advantages of breaking up a programming task into smaller pieces are straightforward and verifiable:

1. Small programs can usually be written more productively per line of code than large ones.
2. Hardware compile and execute time is shorter when only a part, rather than all, of the program needs to be compiled and executed, as often occurs during debugging or revision.
3. Errors in small programs are easier to isolate and correct.
4. Program maintenance (that is, its correction and revision over time) is easier with small programs.
5. Separable modules allow more than one programmer to work easily on the same overall project.
6. Any repeated functions can be programmed once and used throughout the system.
7. Progress can be made and measured more quickly, permitting better management of systems development.

The disadvantages of designing and writing an information system in a modular fashion are:

1. Statements that define the specific data available to each particular module must be coded.
2. Statements that define the logical relationships between modules must be coded.
3. Testing of the separate modules as a system is necessary.

Most experts feel that the advantages of modular designs exceed their disadvantages, especially for medium-sized or larger tasks. (The small program is already small enough to be tackled all together and by a single programmer.) Often, an overall program is divided into modules, each comprised of 50 to 100 or so lines of code. Each module should have a single entry point and exit point. This tends to assure that the logic is correct and that the required task is always completed.

Module design concludes with a set of program flowcharts—one for each module. These expand on the overall systems flowchart developed at the design stage. This progressive development of hierarchy and ever-more detailed programming specifications is known as **top-down design**. It tends to produce a clear structure, program logic that is easy to follow, fewer interface and integration difficulties, and programs that fully meet the user's specified requirements.

Like a book, top-down design proceeds from a concept of objectives and content. Identifiable and separable portions are defined, such as parts or chapters in a book, and a linkage or sequence among them is specified. Even within modules, the overall function is broken down into simpler and simpler functions, like sections and subsections in a book chapter. So, just as outlining is useful to a writer, top-down design and modularization are useful to a designer/programmer.

Structured Programming

One method for developing the logic needed in a program module is called **structured programming**. Normally, programming uses four main types of logic flow:

SEQUENCE
IF-THEN-ELSE
DO-WHILE
GO TO

Simply put, structured programming gets along without the last type—the unconditional GO TO statement. This leaves the logic flow more linear, or at least organized into logical blocks. These blocks are executed, skipped, or repeated, but are not detoured over, around, and back again as is the case with overuse of GO TOs.

These concepts are illustrated in Figure 13–3. Notice that each of the three permitted logic flow patterns has a single entry point and, later in the sequence, a single exit point. When GO TOs are permitted, this desirable simplicity is often lost, complicating the logic sequence, making errors hard to trace, and even causing them.

The main benefits of structured programming show up in the productivity of large projects, in testing, and in ongoing maintenance. Whether structured or not, the design and coding of the system usually take just as long, because the defined logic flow of each module must still be coded. However, when many people work on the same system, clear and standard structure is a big advantage. Also, as with any program, variables should be named, using mnemonics or abbreviations for clarity and conciseness of expression. Adequate comments or remarks should be embedded in the program itself, explaining and documenting its logic.

Debugging and Testing

Errors in programs are to be expected. Humans are sometimes forgetful, fallible, or falsely informed. Computers are never forgiving. Thus

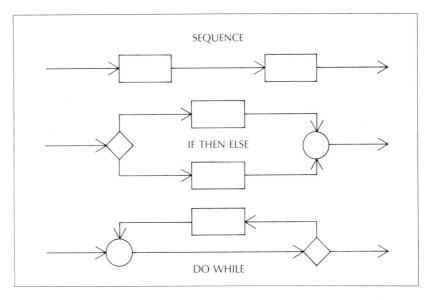

Figure 13-3. Structured programming logic flows

when a module has been coded according to its design, it should be debugged and tested. When every module has been debugged and tested separately, a series of system tests, including acceptance testing, should begin.

Programming errors can be classified into three types:

- **syntax**
- **code logic**
- **problem logic**

Syntax errors include omitted parentheses, miscounted character lengths, unallowed data codes, misspelled (and therefore unrecognized) variable names, and so on. Compilers detect these errors easily. In fact, sometimes it is wise to let the computer be the one to find errors of this type—it doesn't have human fallibility in working with such details.

Code logic errors are more difficult to find. They include operable statements that produce wrong results. Some such bugs are obvious—a misspelled word or misaligned title on an output report, for example. Other errors are difficult to discern, such as transferring control incorrectly after an IF statement and bypassing some intended instructions. Still others are insidious—for example, errantly substituting one variable name for another in an equation. The results may seem undecipherably random.

When the syntax and code logic are correct, *problem logic errors* may still exist because the program doesn't properly address the user's problem. For example, if range checks on input data are omitted, the system may let data entry errors go unnoticed, and therefore the user's output will be wrong. The user may or may not recognize the error and confidence in the system may erode. Also, a correct program, for payroll, for example, might be rendered wrong by a tax law change, or by a user's or analyst's misunderstanding of the existing law.

Debugging and testing can be a lengthy step. The user should, and sometimes must, be involved in testing in order to design suitable tests and know when results are valid. What is the range of input data that must be accommodated? How is an inaccurate result to be noticed? What sets of module interactions must be anticipated and simulated during testing?

Acceptance Testing

System acceptance criteria should be set *in advance, and by the user.* The criteria are to be addressed in the systems analysis report, as discussed in the preceding chapter. Details of acceptance testing should be specified, and agreed upon, during that phase. Typical performance criteria include:

- hardware reliability
- data accuracy
- turnaround time of processing
- response time for inquiries
- operating cost per transaction

Time and money must be allowed for acceptance testing before proceeding to installation and usage.

INSTALLATION AND USAGE

Organizational usage is the goal of the systems development cycle, as portrayed in Figure 12-1. It encompasses documentation, training, conversion (of data, forms, methods, and procedures), operation of the system, and, usually, maintenance to keep it ongoing and updated. Thereafter, the evaluation phase closes the loop by reporting back to users, analysts, and managers on the system's usage and degree of success.

Documentation

The need for, and types of, program documentation were discussed briefly in Chapter 6. But in the systems development context, **documentation** has a wider scope than just during programming. The system's objectives and the agreed upon output specifications are key milestones in the system's evolution. The systems analysis report documents them. The system flowchart, together with data collection and entry methods, designed forms, and data structures, and revisions to manual procedures document the conclusions of the systems design phase. Program documentation includes a commented listing, a dictionary defining variable names, and a logic flowchart for each module. Installation requires a users' manual and examples of input procedures and output reports.

How is documentation gathered and preserved? Reluctantly. Both users and systems specialists have a natural tendency to want to get on with development—not to write down what has already been decided on or done. However, to have the information system be an asset of the organization, it should not be dependent on any one user or specialist. Thus, the need for documentation becomes clear. It should be gathered *throughout* system development, not just at the end when final listings are available. A project librarian or systems standards person should be given responsibility for soliciting, storing, and maintaining documentation materials.

Training Installing information systems is really a matter of managing change. And, in any fast changing field, the need for training and ongoing education is great. Training systems staff and managing them will be discussed in Chapter 15. Here we are concerned with training the new system's users, and to some extent its supporting data entry and computer operations personnel.

Training in support of system installation can take several forms—literature, briefing meetings, demonstrations, simulated usage, and on-the-job training (OJT). These methods are progressively more involving and effective. However, cost increases in this same sequence and OJT may be unfeasible.

Usually, a multimedia training effort should be launched. Literature can explain the system's availability, capability, and general usage to those partially or indirectly involved (management, other departments, and perhaps customers). But briefings should be held for those directly involved. Briefings provide in-depth explanation, interaction, and question answering. An actual demonstration, illustrating input and output procedures, and a hands-on simulation provide extra learning by seeing and doing.

Conversion **Conversion** means change, which most people resist. Employees may feel that new bosses, forms, methods, and measures of performance have been imposed on them—and that the "new system" is to blame.

Hopefully, user involvement in the systems analysis phase, coupled with skillful training and professional communications during installation, will preempt this problem. Substantial technical support should be devoted to detecting and correcting any emerging difficulties. Gaining and keeping users' confidence and support is vital.

Conversion may involve change in one or several of the following areas:

1. People—new skills, organization, work methods, pay and promotion opportunities.
2. Facilities—new computer, I/O equipment, location, machine room
3. Data—new data collection, conversion to machine-readable format, existing data restructured
4. Procedures—new forms, workflows, output reports, policies, and responsibilities
5. Operations—new job tasks, programs, deadlines, backup methods

Conversion to a new information system involves transition and requires displacing some old activities—manual or computerized. For example, consider a small wholesaler converting from a manual to a minicomputer-based invoicing and receivables system. Assume hardware and software have been selected, obtained, installed, and tested. Conversion from the manual system requires special programs to build the necessary customer files; data collection and entry (perhaps during operation, if current records are incomplete); and pilot operation. After data and system validation in an operational setting, staffed by trained users, the old system can be abandoned, giving appropriate attention to any backup requirements.

Conversion requires some form of cutover or duplication in the processing operation. **Immediate cutover** is risky, but sometimes warranted for incompatible or minor changes. **Parallel operation** is expensive—it involves running both systems for a while, until validation of the new one. These two methods, and a third one, are compared in Figure 13-4.

Phased conversion is helpful when feasible. Like test marketing a new product, it helps to refine decisions and lower risk, with the sacrifice of some cost and delay. The phasing can be based around:

1. Elements of the system: for example, first the data entry; next, programs to build files; third, normal reporting; fourth, inquiries and exception reporting; and last, year-end reporting.
2. Elements of the organization: for example, first region 1 is converted; then region 2, and so on.

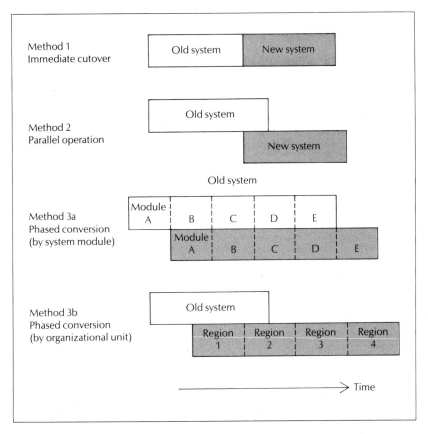

Figure 13-4. Three methods of conversion and pilot operation when a new information system replaces the old system

Operations   The goal of systems development is usage or ongoing operations, as specified in the systems analysis report. As diagrammed in Figure 12-1, **operations** include data collection and entry, operation of the hardware/software processing system, and report distribution. As Chapter 15 will discuss, the operation of existing applications consumes some 60 percent of the computer-related budget. Development, conversion, and maintenance of systems consumes about one-third. The remaining 7 percent or so is spent for supplies. Clearly, smooth operation is not only the goal, it is also the major activity of the computer department.

Maintenance   Hardware maintenance is a familiar and expected activity. But, perhaps surprisingly, information systems also require substantial **software maintenance**—ongoing repair and modification of programs. Some maintenance is in response to emergencies, for example, a nonfunctioning program or a changed requirement, as from withholding tax legislation.

Operating systems are probably the most complex programs around. Such systems programs may take millions of dollars to develop and may be used to manage computers at thousands of separate user sites. Typically, some "bugs" remain in such systems when released. So periodically, in response to testing and operations discoveries, a new version is released. It patches the uncovered problems and usually includes enhancements. The maintenance concept also applies to applications software.

Theoretically, system enhancements are really new development. In practice, any modification to an existing system meant to keep it in existence and up-to-date is considered maintenance. Many proposed system changes are postponable and should be done, if at all, on a **scheduled maintenance** basis. Perhaps every 6 months or so, a programmer/analyst might review the collected suggested changes, become familiar with the system, make the modifications, test them, document the new release, and install it. Then, subsequent changes, of a nonurgent nature, could await the next scheduled maintenance cycle.

SYSTEMS EVALUATION

Evaluating the ongoing system follows its design, programming, testing, installation, and usage. Naturally, evaluation of each activity should go on while it is in progress. Sometimes, unfortunately, a final evaluation never occurs at all. Yet the process of future systems development, as well as personnel performance measurement and system maintenance, can benefit from a rigorous systems evaluation. We will first discuss auditing the system and then the criteria for terminating it.

Auditing

Postinstallation follow-up usually involves two types of audit: a **performance audit** and an **external audit**. The performance audit is performed by a systems analyst, preferably not the one who developed the system. (Many large firms have an internal audit staff for this function.) An objective appraisal of results versus plans is the goal. Are the information requirements being provided? Are information quality and system performance specifications being met? Have vestiges of the old system been displaced as planned? Is the new system paying off? Is documentation on file? Are security and backup controls implemented? What modifications are recommended?

An external audit, by an independent certified public accountant (CPA), is an annual requirement for all publicly owned companies and for many private ones, too. Increasingly, these audits necessarily involve scrutiny of the firm's computer-based information systems. And since the large Equity Funding fraud in the early 1970s, auditors—and managements—have been more concerned and cautious in relying on ever-more-vital computer operations. Auditors must now verify that the firm's internal procedures and controls are adequate. (Management has always had this responsibility.)

Auditors have their time-honored methods: inspection, sampling, validation, and inquiry. Among other things, they seek to verify the "fairness" and "consistency" of the firm's financial statements and their conformance with "generally accepted accounting principles."

In the past, paper records could be inspected in support of an audit. When computers first became prominent, auditors requested certain information from the firm's computer department—called **auditing around the computer**. Now there may be no human-readable records at all for some transactions. So direct operation of the computer and verification of the accounting programs are desirable in checking for misuse or errors. This is called **auditing through the computer**. It requires CPAs with computer knowledge.

Another technique uses a preset group of transactions that are processed as a test. If the existing programs don't produce the known correct answers, they can be inspected line by line, if necessary. Statistical tests are also run to search for atypical transactions or for unusual account activity. This focuses attention on the unusual—and possibly suspect. For example, the Internal Revenue Service (IRS) selects the tax returns it chooses to audit, in part, by comparing transaction amounts to established norms.

Terminating Periodically, it is advisable to reaffirm the system's continued usefulness. The economic test is: do system benefits cover operating costs. (The development investment is a sunk cost at this point.) If not, the system should be terminated or a new one created from this base, but only if the new system's benefits would exceed both its investment and its operating costs. This concept is like **zero base budgeting**, which calls for a periodic rejustification of all expenditures, rather than their blind continuance merely from inertia. Terminating every system, at some point in time, will be the best decision.

However, more than economic criteria must be considered before terminating a system. For example, alternate methods of processing must be arranged or agreement reached that processing is dispensable.

Also, user relations require consultation on this issue and adequate notice of any termination decision.

Universal Insurance is a hypothetical but typical life and casualty insurance company. We shall discuss the firm's information systems, how they have evolved over time, and current plans for change. As you read about Universal's past, present, and planned systems, you will find this case summarizes the issues covered so far in Part 4: MIS, systems analysis, and systems development. It will also provide an introduction to Chapter 14 on representative applications and insight into the issues in Part 5: managing information systems and computer impact—present and future.

Universal's premium revenue in 1970 came from the lines of business shown in Table 13.1. The revenue profile estimated for 1980 is also shown. The firm's organization chart is shown in Figure 13-5.

The company sells primarily through 1500 independent insurance agents and brokers located throughout the United States and Canada. It normally does not have an exclusive arrangement with an agent. That is, each agent handles the policies of an average of four other insurance companies in addition to Universal. When a transaction occurs, such as an application for a new policy, change of an existing policy, premium payment, or a claim, the information is sent to the agent by the policyholder. Universal's system then interacts with these agents.

TABLE 13.1   UNIVERSAL INSURANCE PREMIUM REVENUES

Type	Annual Premiums (in millions) 1970	1980 (est.)
Individual life	$150	$500
Group life	60	300
General liability	175	400
Automobile (commercial and personal)	90	200
Homeowners	60	200
Workmen's compensation	30	100
Reinsurance (syndicates)	35	100
	$600	$1800
Other financial data:		
Stockholders' equity	$420	$1000
Total assets	1200	3000
Net income (including investments)	35	100
Annual growth in premiums	10 percent	10 percent

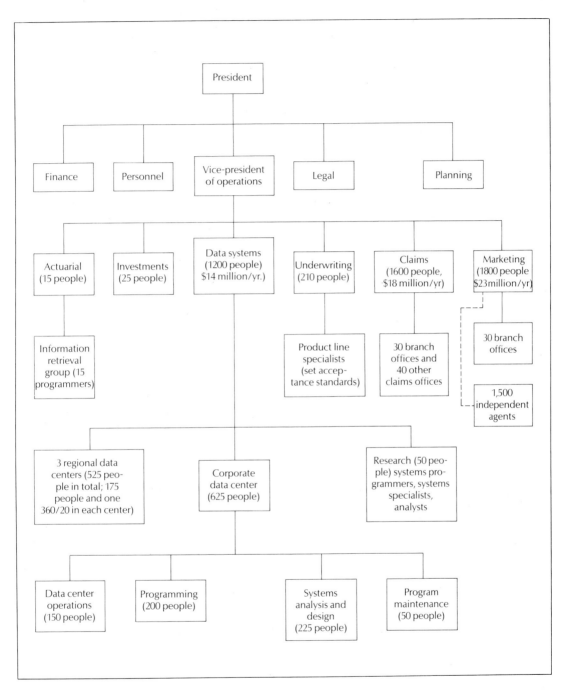

Figure 13-5. Universal Insurance—organization chart as of 1970

In the sections below, we will describe the company's information system as of 1970; then its systems analysis, design, and development during the 1970s; and finally the changes planned for its "system for the 1980s."

1970 System   As of 1970, the data systems department was responsible for data conversion, storage, retrieval, and processing. It consisted of the corporate data center in Chicago and three regional data centers, plus a research group.

The corporate data center operated three IBM 360/65s and two IBM 7080s. In support of these were two 360/30s and three 360/20s used for printing, card-to-tape conversion, and small jobs. Overall utilization of capacity was about 55 percent, based on three shifts and seven days per week. Most of the capacity of the 360/65s was devoted to the emulation of old 7080 programs written specifically for the 65s). Corporate hardware rental and amortization amounted to about $3 million annually. The 7080s were owned; the other equipment was leased from a third party or rented from IBM.

The average branch office (shown in Figure 13–5) had 60 employees—25 underwriters, who decided whether an application should be accepted; 25 administrative and clerical personnel; and 10 marketing representatives. The offices ranged in size from 20 to 160 people.

One of the major functions of the branch office—then and now—is to screen applications for coverage and accordance with company standards. It also verifies that all required information from agents is complete. The offices typically reject only about 5 percent of the applications for life, homeowners, and personal auto insurance. The acceptance criteria are rather well defined for personal lines. So the agents themselves screen out prospects who do not meet the standards. In the case of commercial insurance, however, the reject rate varies from 25 to 35 percent. Commercial accounts involve several kinds of coverage, possibly at several locations, and require close underwriting review at the branch office.

Each of the 30 branch offices used to mail transactions data to the nearest of the three regional data centers or to the corporate data center. A typical regional data center had 175 employees—10 administrative, 125 clerical, 18 keypunch, 10 accounting, and 12 in EDP operations.

At each data center, transactions were coded for further processing. The coding procedure was performed by clerks who earned approximately $100 to $120 per week. Coding entailed preparing a handwritten summary sheet from the source documents received from branch offices. The coding sheets summarized such data as state, tax authority, agent, type and amount of coverage, and so forth.

One difficult aspect of coding that still persists is breaking down comprehensive policies into geographical areas and lines of business. For example, Hilton Hotels might purchase a comprehensive policy that covers their risks throughout the country. The various state statutes require that Universal report the amount of insurance covered in each jurisdiction. These reports must classify the policies by line of business (for example, workmen's compensation, general liability, and so forth). County or other tax districts require similar reports. The purpose of the coding is to provide the basic data for preparing these statutory reports.

Once the transactions data were coded and keypunched from the summary sheet, the data were filed in standard-sized file cabinets. The average file storage space at a regional data center was a 50 × 70 foot room of cabinets. An average of 35 clerks performed the filing at each center. Altogether, about 400,000 policy folders were stored (the exact number was unknown). The originating branch office and the independent agent also kept copies or equivalent summary documents.

The keypunched transactions data were transferred to magnetic tape by the 360/20 at each regional data center. These tapes were then mailed to the Chicago corporate data center once a month. The monthly processing of these tapes constituted the largest single processing task, consuming 216 hours of computer time.

Three types of reports were then and still are prepared. The first is an analysis of lines of business broken down by state, as legally required. This report gives premium income, claims paid, and expenses as derived by accepted allocation procedures. The second report breaks states into tax districts for reporting, as required, by lines of business. It contains much the same information as the first report, except that it is sorted in a different order. The third report is a summary of each independent agent's activity. These reports go to the 50 states, 2400 tax districts, and the 1500 agents.

The run procedure for producing these reports required 28 full-time schedulers. Runs were never exactly the same. Programs had to be changed continually to accommodate revised rate structures, local legislation, expense allocation rules, and so forth. Many programs were written in AUTOCODER assembly language. Modification was difficult and error-prone. Due to program changes, documentation was not consistent. Figure 13-6 shows the flow of transactions data through the system.

There were no reports especially tailored for management. Universal had developed a special information retrieval program permitting re-

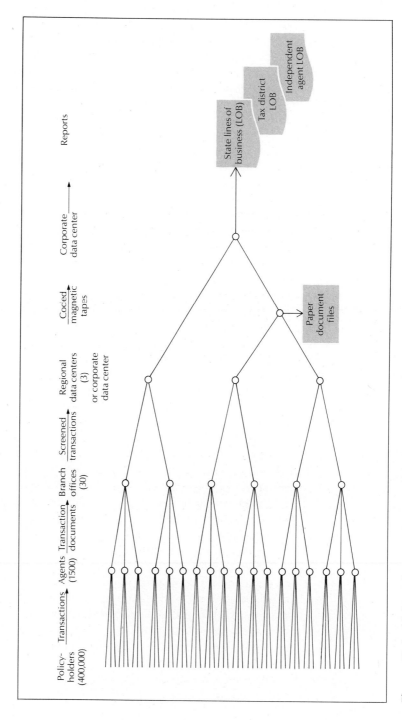

Figure 13-6. Universal Insurance–transactions data flow previous to the "system for the seventies"

quested information to be extracted from the transaction files. Because of the huge size of these files and the complexity of the retrieval system, it normally took about 6 weeks to prepare a special report. Little other use was made of transactions data. For example, planning and forecasting did not rely on these files.

The 1970 information systems described above had evolved from those designed in the early 1950s based on the punched-card tabulating equipment then available. Some of the regulatory reports dated back to the 1920s. There had been several abortive attempts to modernize the system. For example, in 1968, Universal invested 40 labor-years and over $1 million in developing an information retrieval system for their personal auto insurance. After management expressed dissatisfaction with the lack of progress on the project, the three people in charge quit, leaving inadequate documentation. There was no alternative but to abandon the project. An earlier data processing disaster ended after 3 years and $2.3 million. This project was to provide comprehensive data on losses by line of business. It was aborted with no salvageable results.

In 1970, the director of the data systems department had been in the position for 6 years. He came to the job after serving as sales manager of the life insurance group. His background in data processing and systems was relatively limited. But the company felt it was compensated for by his knowledge of company operations and his "boardroom rapport." He had been described as the best speechwriter in the organization.

Management and the planning department became increasingly concerned with the effectiveness of the organization's use of computers. A steering committee of top managers (including the president) was appointed to review the situation. As a result of their efforts, a full-time systems planning team was appointed and asked to develop a plan for making long-range improvements. Among the problems that motivated this assignment were the following:

1. Lack of management information. For example, it was impossible to find out such basic information as the number of outstanding policies. Any serious attempt to relate losses to individual policies was also out of the question.
2. Data about an individual policy were not consolidated. Instead, the information was embedded in paper files and the magnetic tape archives of monthly transactions.
3. Errors and delays resulted in poor service to policyholders and independent agents.

4. The cost of data processing was growing at about the same rate as premium income, showing that little had been done to exploit possible technological economies.

System for the Seventies

In 1970, the systems planning team began its work. This six-member group included two users, two systems analysts, an outside consultant, and the planning director (the chairperson). After 8 months, and based on a corporate 10-year forecast, the team completed a preliminary systems analysis report, or **systems master plan**. The master plan proposed a comprehensive redesign and fresh implementation of the transactions processing system. On top of this, extensive decision support systems were envisioned for later—such as, underwriting refinement, line of business profitability analysis, and agent performance measurement.

The crux of the plan was a large central computer facility communicating nationwide with every branch office, and eventually with an additional 40 offices that would just handle claims. This meant that the regional processing centers would be bypassed and discontinued. The central database would include a policyholder master file. All transactions would be posted to this file and online inquiries would be supported from any authorized location. The design would be modular, having three dimensions: systems functions, transaction types, and lines of business. This concept is illustrated as a cube in Figure 13–7.

Systems implementation was to be modular also. First, detailed analysis of each module was required. Then, design followed, including data, forms, and flowchart details. Programming, debugging, and a rigorous philosophy on testing and user acceptance criteria were spelled out. Implementation included documentation, training at a simulated branch office, and file conversion. After building the hardware and systems software capability, all of this was to proceed on a step-by-step plan through a sequence of transaction types by line of business.

For example, the simpler "personal lines" like individual life insurance, homeowners, and auto insurance would be first. They were small now, but slated for greater corporate emphasis and rapid growth. Within each line, transactions would include application review, policy issuance, premium billing, receivables posting, claims processing, inquiry, and update. The more complex business lines, such as general liability and workmen's compensation would be left for the last half of the 5-year development plan.

Throughout the early and mid-1970s, Universal's systems development generally went as planned. The total investment (above the

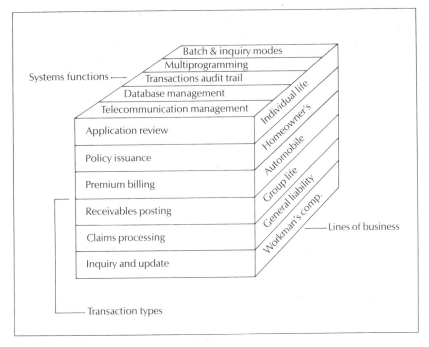

Figure 13-7. Universal Insurance's modular systems design, showing three dimensions: systems functions, transaction types, and lines of business

normal operating budget) swelled from a projected $9 million to $11 million. But user satisfaction and customer service levels were dramatically improved, as predicted. Also, costs under the old system would, by then, have equalled current levels, without service improvements. By 1976, a systems evaluation team was able to document results of the initially installed modules, as cited in Figure 13-8. Equally important, management decisions were now being based on more accurate, timely data.

System for the Eighties   By 1978, the last modules of the planned system were approaching acceptance testing. Meanwhile, top management and the systems planning group had already staked out the next round of computer-related applications: *word processing* and *office automation*. While continued enhancement and tuning of the current system was expected, large leaps forward were envisioned by increasing clerical productivity and cutting paperwork.

Word processing is a concept that views words as products and the

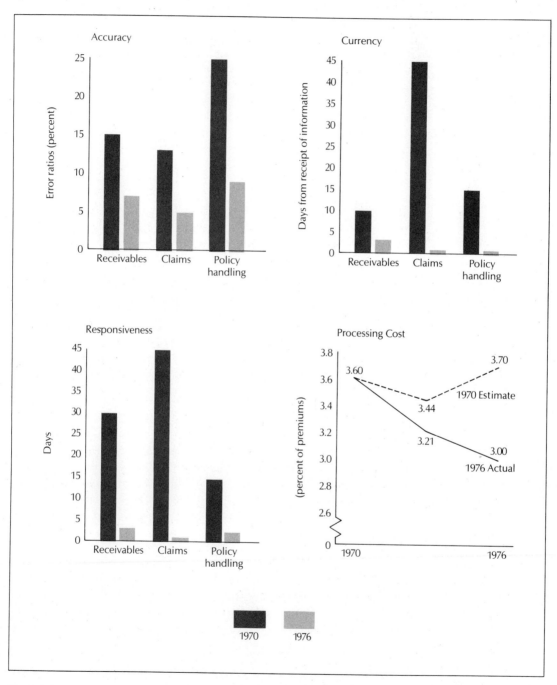

Figure 13-8. Universal Insurance's documented information system improvements

office as a production facility for words. Equipment has been developed to help transcribe, replay, power type, edit, reproduce, store, and transmit such words as comprise standard letters, legal paragraphs, and corporate memos. **Office automation** extends this idea. It encompasses communication, scheduling, planning, electronic mail delivery, document storage, maintenance of personal files, and a host of further applications of computers, communications, and terminals.

An insurance company, in particular, is saddled with paperwork. After all, paper is the firm's product—applications and premium checks come in and policies and claims checks go out. The organization mirrors this paper flow. The marketing department generates the applications and premiums; the actuarial group and underwriters set the premium size in view of the risks; the claims department verifies losses and authorizes payments; the investment group manages the float; and the computer department processes the resulting paper! In this environment, it is hoped, the potential from improving paperwork processing efficiency is great. What do you think? How would you plan Universal Insurance's "System for the Eighties"?

SUMMARY   Systems development spans three phases: systems design, systems implementation (programming, testing, installation, and usage), and systems evaluation. Systems design picks up where systems analysis leaves off—with the output requirements specified. Design then seeks the most efficient system, over its life cycle and considering all resources: people as well as hardware. Information systems design includes conceiving data collection and entry procedures, and doing forms design, system flowcharting, and database layout.

Programming and testing are but a portion of the overall development cycle, although some users naively assume programming is all that is required. The logic and structure of each program module must be defined, coded, debugged, and tested. A final step, along guidelines agreed to in advance, is acceptance testing by the user.

Installation and usage requires that good documentation be maintained throughout development and prepared for user understanding. Training, conversion to the new system, and ongoing operations are additional steps. Software maintenance is a surprisingly large activity, especially if not controlled, scheduled, and analyzed for suitable benefits compared to costs.

Systems evaluation means an objective assessment of results versus plans. Two types of audits are internal, carried out by the firm's own staff, and external, usually carried out by the firm's CPAs. A procedure and criteria for terminating systems were also discussed.

To illustrate the issues discussed in Part 4 and to prelude Part 5, the Universal Insurance case was presented. It traced a large firm's information systems activity from where it was in 1970, through changes made during the seventies, to proposals for a "system for the eighties."

CONCEPTS

systems development
systems design
computer
   implementation
contact programming
organizational
   implementation
systems evaluation
turnaround document
modular
top-down design

structured
   programming
syntax
code logic
problem logic
documentation
conversion
immediate cutover
parallel operation
phased conversion
operations

software maintenance
scheduled maintenance
performance audit
external audit
auditing around the
   computer
auditing through the
   computer
zero base budgeting
systems master plan
word processing
office automation

QUESTIONS

1. What prerequisites and skills should be present for systems design?

2. Describe three techniques for improving data entry productivity.

3. Flowcharting creates a visual image of tasks and sequence. Why does this display mode aid understanding?

4. Why is "modular" program design encouraged? What are its drawbacks?

5. Interview an experienced programmer to find out and report on three difficult program bugs he or she has encountered, and how they were discovered and corrected.

6. All money spent before system operation should be considered as an investment and the installed system as an asset. Discuss this statement.

7. Cite a recent example of computer-aided crime and the security and audit steps meant to prevent and detect it.

8. Why should the temptation to "fine tune" or maintain programs be resisted? When should it be encouraged?

9. Why are information systems crucial to the performance of financial services firms, such as Universal Insurance?

10. What do you recommend as Universal Unsurance's "System for the Eighties?"

Chapter Fourteen

**Representative
Applications**

14

Over time, computer vendors have provided an increasing array of CPUs and devices for I/O, storage, and communication. In addition, advanced operating systems, file organization methods, and database management systems provide processing opportunities that were not practical a dozen years ago. These improved capabilities have made hardware and systems decisions tougher by increasing both the available alternatives and the level of sophistication required to analyze them. On the other hand, today's systems are often easier to use and cheaper than before. This lets even the uninitiated gain the benefits of computer information systems.

This chapter illustrates this broad spectrum of systems and applications. Five representative organizations are presented each with its own particular applications environment. Although some names will be fictional, the situations all reflect actual organizations. These systems can be classified as follows:

- minicomputer business system
- medium-sized business sytem
- large business system
- online database system
- large university system

MINICOMPUTER BUSINESS SYSTEM

Mom's Truck Parts, Inc., is a wholesaler/distributor of supplies needed by transportation firms. Mom's business now does $5 million a year in sales and employs 60 people. In a mid-semester letter requesting money, Mom's son suggested installing a business minicomputer, considering the size of the operation:

- 3000 customers, averaging $1 million in total accounts receivable
- 5000 inventory items, averaging $1 million of total cost
- 200 orders per day, averaging three items each

- $1 million of other assets
- $1.5 million of liabilities
- $200,000 annual aftertax income, excluding Mom's salary and perks.

Typical Applications

Initial applications would be confined to traditional areas of accounting and operations, such as:

- order entry
- invoicing
- accounts receivable
- inventory control
- sales analysis
- accounts payable

An outside service bureau already does the payroll for under 50¢ per check. Since Mom pays every other Friday, this is not a large cost, and payroll rules and tax rates seem to be forever changing. The firm's controller, often bolstered by an outside accountant, draws up monthly financial statements. Depreciation calculations are made using a calculator. And inventory accounting is on average-cost basis to simplify record keeping. Of course, the real essence of the business is stocking the items that sell well, coupled with credit and collection activities. Even efficient operations would be unprofitable if wrong decisions were made in these areas.

Alternate Configurations

Small organizations with modest data processing budgets (say, from $500 to $5000 per month) traditionally had two systems alternatives for satisfying their needs. One was access to the shared computing facilities offered by **service bureaus**. Most such firms provided batch processing on their computer, including operating staff, programmers and programs.

Traditionally, firms also used various combinations of accounting/invoicing machines or sorting and totaling machines. Such devices are often called **unit record equipment**. They have a limited logical capability and deal with a single record at a time in a basically mechanical way.

During the 1970s, small users have increasingly accepted two additional systems alternatives. The first is online use of remote computers. This allows in-house I/O with access to large-scale processing and storage capacity. Reliable backup capability, a network for nationwide access, and proprietary programs are other possible advantages.

The second is in-house use of a small-scale, general-purpose computer. Such business systems initially included IBM's System/3, NCR's

Century 50 and 101, Honeywell's 2020, Univac's 9200, DEC's PDP 11, and Burroughs' B700 and B1700. More recently, other small business computers have been introduced: IBM's System 32 and 34, Sperry Univac's BC/7, DEC's 324, and the Basic/Four computer from MAI.

Competition and service demands are causing more and more wholesaler/distributors to adopt computerized systems. Therefore, to gain experienced advice, Mom called on a friend who owned a similar, but larger, firm in a noncompeting location—Uncle's Truck Parts, Inc. This firm had started using an IBM System/3 several years earlier and willingly provided Mom with a description of their system, shown in Figure 14-1.

Their System/3 processor has 32K bytes of storage. The multifunction card unit for I/O is capable of 300 cards-per-minute reading and 200 cards-per-minute punching. In addition, the system has a 200 lines-per-minute printer, and may be accessed for interactive use via the operator console. A data recorder unit stands nearby to punch or verify cards. This device allows keystroke correction by backspacing and rekeying, which electronically erases the erroneous data from buffer storage before punching. The cards themselves are small—only

Figure 14-1. Uncle's IBM System 3

about 40 percent as large as the more common punched-card size. However, since they use a round hold in a compact binary pattern, they can store up to 96 punched characters and 32 additional printed characters.

Uncle's system supports both inquiries and batch processing by using indexed-sequential file organization on disk. System/3 is programmed in a simple report-oriented language called RPG II (discussed in Chapter 6). Six key business programs were tailored by the hardware vendor to the firm's specifications. These major applications are order entry, general ledger, payroll, accounts receivable, accounts payable, and inventory control. Other specialized programs were developed in-house and two were purchased from an outside specialist. These include programs for sales analysis, product profitability, distribution planning, and customer analysis.

Uncle's systems staff consists of two RPG programmer/operators and four data entry operators, scheduled on two shifts. The computer runs either one or two shifts, depending on the particular day and week of the month. The system does not require a special environment; the computer and its associated equipment are housed and operated in an 18 × 15 foot room next to the administrative department.

In the face of this experience, Mom is willing to consider an in-house minicomputer. A suitable configuration should rent for about $1000 per month or less or cost under $50,000. Staff and software would

TABLE 14.1   INDUSTRIES SERVED BY MINICOMPUTER APPLICATIONS PACKAGES

Appliance Distribution	Manufacturing
Automotive Industry Supplies	Membership Associations
Candy and Tobacco Distribution	Paint and Chemical Distribution
Contracting	Paper Products and Office Supplies
Electrical and Electronics Distribution	Plumbing, Heating, and Air Conditioning Distribution
Food Processing and Distribution	Public Accounting
Group Medical Practice	Service Supplies Distribution
Hardware Distribution	School Administration
Hospitals	Tire Distribution
Industrial Distribution	Toys, Sporting Goods, and Recreational Supplies Distribution
Legal Firms	Wine and Distilled Beverage Distribution
Lumber and Building Materials	Wholesale Food Distribution

be extra, but packages exist to serve the special needs of many industries, such as those listed in Table 14.1.

Wishing an early return on the investment in her son's tuition, Mom writes back that the minicomputer suggestion sounds interesting but that she will await an early reply to the following questions:

1. Do you think a computerized system is worthwhile for a business of our size?
2. Do you think it is better to get a business minicomputer or to employ an outside service?
3. Which two systems would you suggest we study?
4. Which system would you choose?
5. How would you finance it?

MEDIUM-SIZED BUSINESS SYSTEM   XYZ is a manufacturer and marketer of various industrial and consumer products, parts, and supplies. After growing at about 10 percent per year, it now has annual sales of over $200 million. In 1966, the company leased two System/360 Model 30s and installed them at corporate headquarters. Each system had the features listed below, and appeared as shown in Figure 14-2.

Figure 14-2.   XYZ's earlier computer, an IBM 360/30

65K bytes of core storage
2 disk drives (6 megabyte packs)
5 tape drives (9 track)
1 1100 lines-per-minute printer
1 600 cards-per-minute reader/punch

Each computer was leased at $9800 per month from a third-party financial firm for a 7-year term ending in 1973. Maintenance was contracted for with an independent supplier at $1000 per month. The leasing and maintenance agreements allowed unlimited usage. There were usually two shift operations five days a week and one on Saturday. Staff consisted of six computer operators, eight data entry personnel, and six analyst/programmers.

Current Configuration In 1973, a System/370 Model 135 was obtained on a 5-year lease; maintenance and some software were obtained as additional, separately priced services. This system is described below and its configuration is diagrammed in Figure 14–3.

The 370/135 mainframe has 500K bytes of main memory and three channels connected to various families of I/O and storage devices. The disks are used for storing the operating system, most of which is not normally resident in main memory. They also hold object code copies of all programs. Backup disk copies of these object programs are kept in the computer library. Tape and card copies of the source listings of these programs are stored away from the computer center. Certain data files that are accessed continuously are also stored on disks. Others are mounted on a disk drive unit as required. Some disk capacity provides a **scratch pad**, or working space, as needed. XYZ also stores many files on magnetic tape. Two distant locations have had remote batch terminals attached for medium speed I/O. This setup is shown in Figure 14–4.

Applications The processing time on XYZ's headquarter's computer is devoted to:

- 60 percent for file updating of accounting or clerical programs
- 30 percent to production runs of decision support systems
- 10 percent to new program development, including the creation of new files

The accounting and clerical applications produce the information necessary for company activities, such as sales orders, invoices received, employee time reports, cash disbursements, inventory withdrawals, and so forth. **Decision support systems** produce infor-

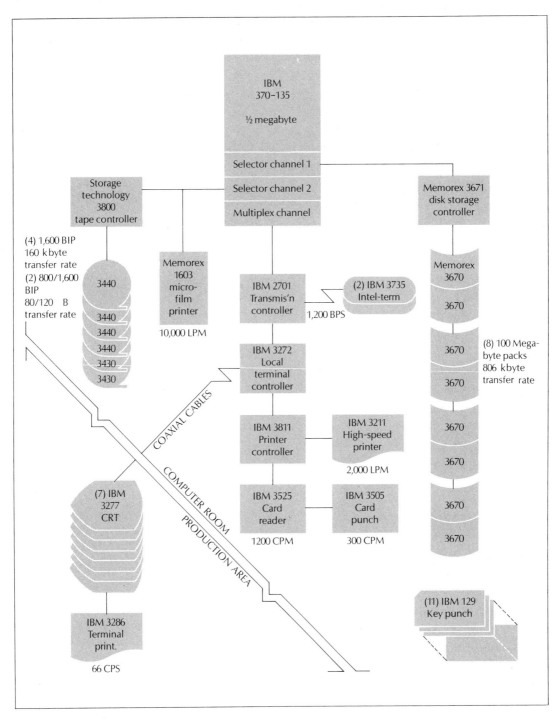

Figure 14-3. Current configuration of XYZ's System 370/135

Figure 14-4. XYZ's remote batch terminal, an IBM 3780

mation specifically to guide management in production scheduling, materials requirements planning, cash management, and sales tracking.

The computer time used for new program development is principally aimed at additional accounting or clerical-replacement programs, including the redesign, integration, or reprogramming of existing applications. Increasingly, it is also used for new decision support and management science applications. A partial list of applications is shown in Table 14.2. This information constitutes a **run book**—the list of applications and the resources involved in processing each one.

Systems Staff The systems analyst, programming, and operations staff includes five systems analysts (who are not active programmers), a dozen pro-

TABLE 14.2 XYZ'S RUN BOOK (LIST OF APPLICATIONS AND RESOURCES USED)

Application	Master File Medium: Key	File Size: Rec'd-Chars. ea.	Processing Frequency	Transaction per Run	Average Run Time (hr.)
Order entry	Tape-sales order no.	40,000–200	Daily	700	1/4
Product specification	Disk-sales order no.	10,000–200	Daily	1,200	1-1/2
Sales tracking	Tape-sales order no.	25,000–200	Weekly	2,000	2
Purchasing	Disk-purchase no.	10,000–100	Daily	400	1/2
Master production schedule	Tape-part no.	200,000–70	Biweekly	15,000	2
Inventory	Disk-part no.	100,000–400	Daily	5,000	3
Material require- ments planning	Disk-part no.	100,000–1200	Biweekly	20,000	4-1/2
Payroll	Disk-employ. no.	3000–500	Weekly	1,500	1
Accounts receivable	Disk-custom. no.	25,000–500	Weekly	1,000	2
Accounts payable	Tape-vendor no.	5000–200	Weekly	200	1/2
Product costing	Disk-part no.	100,000–400	Monthly	30,000	1
Bill of material control	Disk-part no.	225,000–100	Daily	500	1/2
Mathematical program	Disk-sales no.	—	Daily	Variable	—

grammers (most of whom are skilled in COBOL), a three-shift operating staff, and personnel skilled in management science and systems standards. Their organization is shown in Figure 14–5.

About half of analyst/programmer time is devoted to developing new applications. Decision support systems tend to demand more time than do routine clerical/accounting jobs. The remainder of analyst/programmer effort goes toward software maintenance. For example, maintenance is required to reflect changes in hardware operating systems, tax laws, reporting requirements, and so forth.

XYZ attempts little systems programming and no reprogramming of the operating system. The vendor is relied on for operating system maintenance, language translators (compilers), utility programs, and hardware component interfacing.

The program library includes 250 separate application programs that are run at least once a month. In addition, 70 other programs are run in-house from time to time. Copies of all such software are documented in XYZ's program library. Some special programs or reports are generated using outside time-sharing computers when access to certain programs or databases is required.

In 1978, XYZ's lease on the System/370 expired and it considered upgrading to an IBM 3033. What configuration of this computer would be needed to meet current applications requirements? What new applications might be added? Under what conditions would you recommend purchase, rather than lease, if you were to upgrade?

LARGE BUSINESS SYSTEM

Nationwide Manufacturing Company is one of the 200 largest companies in the United States with annual sales of over $2 billion. Nationwide makes a wide range of metal industrial products and consumer items. It has an annual computer-related budget exceeding $10 million, including management, analyst, programming, and operation staff salaries and overhead. (Representative organization structures and budgets will be discussed in Chapter 15.)

Nationwide's computers are located in 12 different computer centers around the country. Since it is a multidivision, decentralized organization, the different product divisions have each developed computer operations. However, some of them are connected by direct high-speed communication links. In all, some 130 plants span the United States and Canada, although computers are located only at divisional and regional headquarters. Many of the remaining plants, warehouses, and sales offices have direct data communication capability to

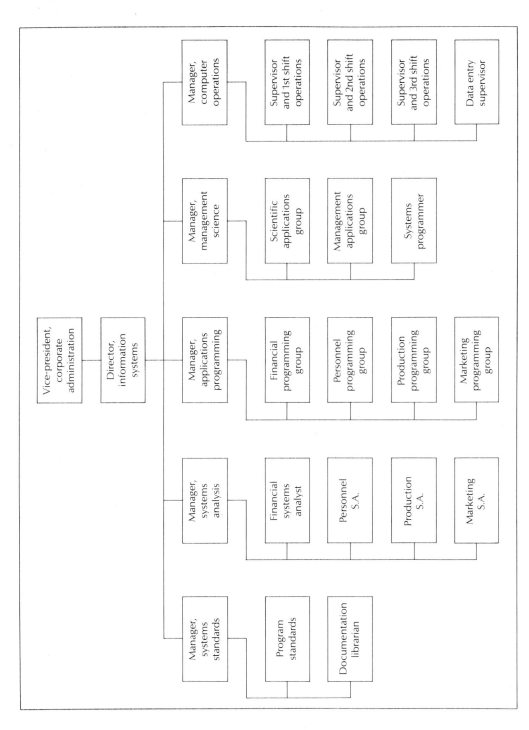

Figure 14-5. Organization chart for XYZ's systems staff

the headquarters' computers. Still, much information is phoned in and most paperwork is mailed or delivered via in-company routing. The 12 computer operations have the hardware and staff shown in Table 14.3.

Nationwide's applications vary from center to center. Certain functions are centralized, others are done at the divisional or regional level. For instance, payroll for nearby work locations is generated at each computer center, and the required input and output is then delivered to the appropriate plants. In contrast, all accounts receivable are mailed by customers either to New York, Chicago, or San Francisco,

TABLE 14.3   COMPUTER HARDWARE AND STAFF OF NATIONWIDE MANUFACTURING COMPANY

Location	Computer Configuration	Staff Categories		
		Analyst/ Programmers	Operations Staff	Data Preparation
New York	IBM System 370/158 (owned) 2000K memory 3330 disk units (3 of 8 spindles each)	40	18	25
Chicago	IBM System 370/158 (on a 7-year lease until 1980) 2000K; 3330 disk unit	22	14	15
San Francisco	IBM System 360/40 (owned) 128K memory 2314 disk unit	12	9	13
Houston	Burroughs B2700 (acquired lease with division)	4	5	8
Minneapolis	Honeywell 2060	5	5	7
Atlanta	Remote batch telecommunication with NY and Chicago	3	4	10
Philadelphia	IBM System 370/135 256K memory Tape- and disk-oriented	6	6	8
St. Louis	Univac 9300 32K memory Tape-oriented	4	5	6
Each of: Hartford Columbus Oklahoma City Seattle	IBM System 32 I/O and disk-oriented	3	3	6

TABLE 14.4 NATIONWIDE COMPUTER APPLICATIONS

Centralized	At All (or Most) Centers
Accounts receivable	Salaried payroll
Fixed asset accounting	Hourly payroll
Profit budgeting	Billing
Engineering cost standards	Accounts payable
Product pricing model	Cost accounting
Purchasing analysis	Inventory control
Plant operating simulation model	Sales forecasting
Invoice profitability	Budgeting
Distribution analysis	Sales analysis
New facility location model	Manufacturing scheduling
Industrial relations system	Capital equipment schedule

whichever is closest. Therefore, only those centers process incoming checks and post the results to accounts receivable files. A partial list of computer applications showing where they are performed is summarized in Table 14.4

ONLINE DATABASE SYSTEM

NASDAQ (National Association of Securities Dealers Automated Quotations) is a pioneering nationwide, computer-based stock quotation and transaction recording system. It became operational on February 8, 1971, and was originally confined to stocks not listed on national stock exchanges. (Such transactions are said to be made in the "over-the-counter" market.)

The system acts as a centralized marketplace within which competing stock dealers provide ready markets. It includes over 3000 securities. The 2 to 30 participating dealers in each security continually post their current buy and sell prices. The system handles nearly 10,000,000 shares daily in approximately 25,000 separate transactions.

The computer hardware, shown in Figure 14-6, is operated by Bunker Ramo Corporation under contract to NASDAQ. In all, it is a $25 million electronic processing and communications system. Computer facilities are in rural Trumbull, Connecticut, in a secure, guarded, stand-alone central operations center. Hardware consists of twin Univac 1108 computers with online drum and disk storage used for direct-access storage and retrieval. Vital components are fully backed up to increase reliability. Batteries and an auxiliary generator stand by in case of public power failure. Smaller supplemental computers are located in several cities around the country to support the flow of data communications.

Figure 14-6. NASDAQ computer center

The system works in the following way. Each stock in the system has a unique four-character alphabetic key, or stock symbol. A user can request the current bid and ask for prices for a particular stock. To do so, she or he merely uses any of 20,000 standard desk-top quotation units that are ubiquitous in stock brokerage offices. When the proper sequence of alphabetic input buttons and a button requesting a quotation are pressed, data about that stock are retrieved in less than a second and are displayed on a small screen. This is shown in Figure 14-7.

A second level of service—beyond requesting a representative bid-ask quotation—is used for executing a transaction. This involves one of over 1000 Level II terminals with specially designed keys and a TV-type screen. A securities broker or dealer can display the current bid-ask prices of all market-makers in a particular stock, ranked in order of the best quotations. This can be seen in Figure 14-8.

The particular market-maker currently offering the best price is easily determined. A phone call can trigger a 100-share transaction at the firm price he or she has displayed through NASDAQ. Larger orders may still involve price negotiation. But before NASDAQ, it was standard procedure to phone at least three market-makers for their current quotes if any transactions were contemplated. Most of this calling is now eliminated.

Over 400 market-making dealers are equipped with Level III terminals. These have additional special-purpose keys that allow stock dealers to enter or change their own quotations. Within 5 seconds,

Figure 14-7. A stock-quotation terminal

Figure 14-8. NASDAQ Level II terminal for market-maker quotations

such updated bids and asks are displayed on all Level II terminals requesting quotes on that stock and market-maker. Also, each updated quote affects the computation of the single representative quote supplied to Level I terminals.

LARGE UNIVERSITY SYSTEM

COLLEGE (*COLLection of Easterners Giving Education*) is a group of eastern colleges and universities that share a central computer. This facility serves two large universities, five medium-sized colleges, and three community colleges.

The heart of COLLEGE is an IBM System/370 Model 168 with 3

Figure 14-9. COLLEGE's central computing facility, an IBM 370/168

million bytes of main storage, as shown in Figure 14-9. In addition, it has 16 spindles of 3330 double-density disks, organized as two units of eight spindles each. Each pack stores 200,000,000 characters. Seven tape drives (2 seven-track and 5 nine-track) are also available. Card readers, printers, remote batch, and CRT terminals provide I/O.

The central facility is augmented by remote reader printer units located on the two university campuses. The smaller colleges, which are up to 30 miles away, also have equipment connected via leased lines to the main center. These colleges do a little independent processing, but transmit most work to the central facility because of its favorable economics, greater hardware resources, in-memory compilers, and other available programs. The central facility is also time-shared by many keyboard-type terminals at each campus.

The hardware configuration of the COLLEGE computing network is diagrammed in Figure 14-10. A typical month of operating data is shown in Table 14.5. Notice that nearly 57,000 jobs—separate program executions—were processed during the month. Notice also that Table 14.5 lists the workload by **job class**. These are different run categories denoting priority, maximum execution time, maximum lines of printer output, charging rate, and so forth.

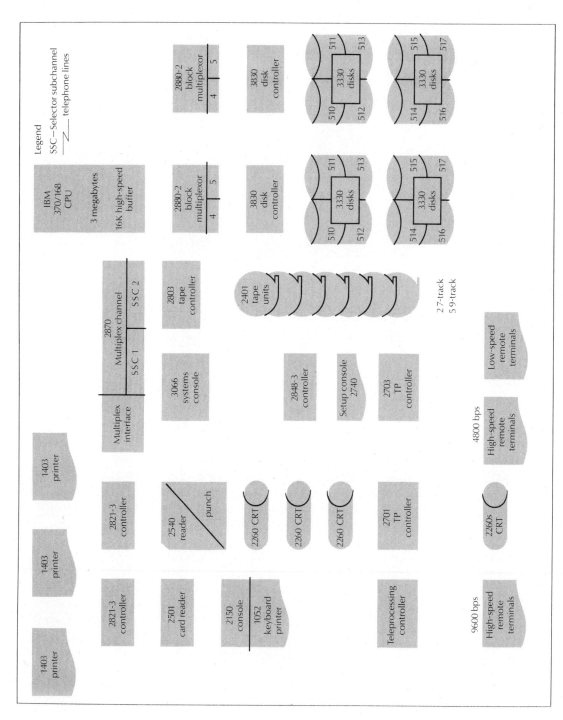

Figure 14–10. Hardware configuration of the COLLEGE computing network

TABLE 14.5   A TYPICAL MONTH FOR THE **COLLEGE** COMPUTING NETWORK

Job Class	Number of Jobs	Percentage of Total	Average CPU Time (sec.)	Average Chan Time (sec.)	Average Cards Read	Average Lines Printed
A	2368	4.2	13	11	344	853
B	1039	1.8	39	62	276	4343
C	7730	13.6	9	15	232	672
D	2010	3.5	24	54	296	2517
E	827	1.5	36	42	620	4061
F	222	0.4	57	38	512	5209
G	582	1.1	34	45	311	2029
H	2318	4.1	17	12	536	1240
I	762	1.3	42	57	381	2260
J	2428	4.3	16	10	441	1037
K	0	0.0	0	0	0	0
L	33	0.1	117	265	6	559
M	195	0.3	62	28	1372	3657
N	85	0.1	70	45	54	1995
O	65	0.1	97	202	14	387
P	0	0.0	0	0	0	0
S	1049	1.8	7	36	166	608
T	0	0.0	0	0	0	0
V	832	1.5	16	27	342	1924
W	23,888	42.0	1	0	76	111
X	6581	11.6	6	7	203	472
Z	3863	6.3	6	1	405	335
Total	56,877	100.0	9	11	217	700

This center runs whatever applications the users request. Access requires an approved account number, such as a course account or the general student account (class W). Each class has defined budget and job limits. One major advantage of the large center is the availability of in-memory compilers for FORTRAN, COBOL, and PL/1. These save time otherwise needed for reading the appropriate compiler in and out for each short source program.

Jobs are read in from any of several locations. They are then transferred to disk and enter an input queue of jobs waiting for processing. Depending on their job class and sequence within class, they are transferred to main storage as it becomes available. Jobs sufficient for nearly three shifts are read in each weekday, mostly during daytime hours. Thus, a backlog of unprocessed jobs builds up on the disks. Short jobs, such as class W, are given high priority so that their turnaround time is only a matter of minutes. Weekends are used for large jobs, system testing, scheduled maintenance, and installation changes.

The operating system manages and schedules this input queue of jobs as well as a similar output queue waiting for printers or other output devices. It also manages the multiprogramming allocation of main memory using virtual storage. Thus, memory is allocated on the dynamic needs of the programs currently being run.

SUMMARY Five representative information systems were described in this chapter, including mini, medium, and large business systems; database; and university computer centers. Hardware configurations, their evolution over time, and each organization's applications were discussed, as well as staffing and budgets. This chapter concludes Part 4.

CONCEPTS

service bureau	scratch pad	job
unit record	decision support system	job class
equipment	run book	

QUESTIONS
1. Which applications do you think are most important for a particular small business to computerize (you choose the company)?
2. Estimate the number of transactions that a $1,000 per month computer might typically process on a representative day. State your assumptions about the amount of time such a computer would be in use, its CPU utilization, and the processing it would perform on a typical transaction.
3. What types of applications might a large nationwide manufacturing company prefer to handle locally and why? What types of applications might it prefer to run centrally?
4. Regional or national computing networks are increasingly practical. Design and diagram a hardware configuration that you believe is suitable for a nationwide off-track betting system. Assume an average of 1 million bets on each of 6 days per week and a total of 500 offices in 100 cities that can enter these bets on any of 100 horse races per day.
5. Trace the evolution of computing at your university or firm. How has cost per unit of storage or processing trended?

Chapter 15 **Managing Information Systems**

Management commitment is a key ingredient in application specification, development and funding, plus it tends to assure use and payoff.

Chapter 16 **Computer Impact—Present and Future**

The computer industry has become a major economic factor and will continue to influence our lives more in the future.

Part Five

Management Issues

Chapter Fifteen

Managing
Information
Systems

Computers have profoundly affected management methods. Other types of organizations—from city police forces to space exploration agencies to high school curriculum committees—have also had to consider the impact of computers. Most organizations still seek traditional goals, but they now use much more computer-produced information in the process of striving for those goals. Within most organizations the computer group itself has become a major functional activity, requiring management.

In this chapter, we will discuss management's role in information systems and managing computer-related activities. We will review several key studies that provide historical perspective. We will then be concerned with managing the computer group, including organizing and staffing its activities and scheduling and budgeting them. We will summarize managing systems development and computer operations and discuss hardware selection and financing. We begin this management overview with a survey of management's role.

MANAGEMENT'S ROLE

Managing information systems involves three levels:

- top management
- user management
- computer group management

Top management can ill afford to shirk management responsibility for the usefulness and efficiency of the computer effort. Yet, historically, some technically uninformed managers have given free rein to the computer staff. Alternately, a too skeptical top management may withhold investment in this area, cutting progress and incentive. The involvement, leadership, and support of top management aids success and is often vital to it.

User management has a direct interest in successful systems development and ongoing applications. Users may be members of top management, but, generally, they are lower in the organization. The best assurance of a system's usefulness and acceptance is for users to participate in its design. Otherwise they may have a scapegoat—the computer or systems staff can be blamed for the system's failure. Indeed, assigning ultimate responsibility and allocating costs to the users gives them an active interest in system success.

Computer group management is charged with the direct supervision of information systems activities. This involves the usual management tasks: plan, organize, staff, direct, and control. The **EDP master plan** is key to all this (EDP stands for electronic data processing). In particular, it calls for setting priorities on which systems to develop and how to schedule, fund, and control both development and operations.

Historical Perspective

Over the years, several studies have asked: How effectively do organizations use computers? What factors appear to promote MIS success? What applications do they use them for? How much do they spend?

One early study concluded that only one-third of the companies had achieved measurable success with computer systems. Such a conclusion, of course, depends on one's definition of EDP success. This study required that the firm's computer effort show a tangible return on investment. Computer applications development, like investments in plant, equipment, or inventory, should show a satisfactory return on the necessary investment. Many firms even today fail to measure this adequately.

Also, the success rating was given only if a firm achieved further intangible benefits by applying the computer broadly throughout its organization. That is, in addition to systemizing routine procedures, the organization might then derive benefits from quick information and decision support. Hopefully, these gains exceeded the costs involved.

This measure of success penalizes firms that emphasize computers in only one or a few areas, typically accounting. It implies that, after these bread-and-butter accounting applications have been computerized, the most fertile areas for subsequent applications probably lie in other functions. Yet, many organizations tend to "fine tune" existing systems, thus constricting the breadth of their computer effort.

Certain organizational factors tend to contribute to effective computer use. The study concluded that *success is not a technical problem, but a managerial one*, requiring:

- involvement of top management
- active participation of user management
- broad outlook of computer group management

In the successful companies, top management tended to:

1. Approve projects only after careful feasibility studies had realistically weighed costs against expected benefits
2. Establish interim goals
3. Measure progress against interim goals
4. Appraise carefully the completed projects to ensure that anticipations had been realized.

In any organization, the day-to-day decisions are within the province of operating management—the computer users. Clearly, top management cannot specify the details of user needs any more than the computer personnel could do it alone. Thus, active participation by user management was found to be correlated with success. This means:

- participation in project selection
- membership in project development staff
- responsibility for results

Computer group managers in the unsuccessful firms tended to have backgrounds in narrow fields. Computer managers in the successful firms tended to possess a broader background and range of skills. The study revealed the danger signal that EDP managers may tend to overemphasize applications in their own area of expertise. A cross-functional tool such as MIS requires management with a broad-based outlook.

Throughout the 1960s, computer technology expanded faster than user's ability to absorb and apply it effectively. The gap between capability and achievement actually widened during that decade. Until about 1970, many studies concluded that organizations were investing more in computer hardware, software, and conversion than they were getting back in operational benefits. Yet organizations were also paying a penalty through computerization opportunities that they overlooked or hadn't yet implemented.

Budget Guidelines   A typical data processing department's budget as of 1970 appeared as follows:

equipment—35 percent
operations—30 percent
new programs—20 percent
program maintenance—15 percent

Equipment expense is for its rental, lease, or amortization. Operations costs include the computer operations staff and supplies and data preparation activities. The categories of new programs and program maintenance also need some explanation. The costs for new programs include systems analysis, design, and programming. The meaning of program maintenance can vary, but it can be defined as any programming activity that does not seek a new application program as its end result. Thus, program maintenance would include modifying the operating system, reprogramming an old application into a language such as PL/1, and modifying existing programs.

It is interesting to view this budget as it might be seen by someone charged with budget cutting. Three of the categories—equipment, operations, and program maintenance—are relatively impervious to short-run cost cutting. The most vulnerable area, for which costs are most easily postponed, is the new programs category. It should be remembered, however, that long-run "success" is enhanced by just such new applications development, provided that today's costs are more than returned by high future benefits.

EDP budget size is often measured as a percentage of company sales. Although this is useful for comparing similar organizations, it does not always provide a reliable comparison between firms in different industries. A graphic example is provided by analyzing a supermarket's sales. This sales figure is large relative to the supermarket's own activity because nearly 80 cents of each sales dollar goes for purchased goods. In contrast, a hospital spends most of its revenue dollar on staff salaries—only about 20 cents goes for supplies purchased from others. In economic terms, the remaining 20 cents that the supermarket contributes to its sales dollar is called its **value added**. The hospital's value added is 80 cents of each revenue dollar. This is a valid index of the actual activity of the supermarket or hospital (or other organization). The EDP budget is thus best compared to the firm's value added, because using sales as an index of an organization's internal activity can give a false impression of its true size.

For example, suppose that both a supermarket and a hospital were equally dependent on computers at the rate of 2 percent of each organization's internal activity, or value added. They would then exhibit drastically different EDP-budget-to-sales percentages. The supermarket's EDP-budget-to-sales index would be 2 percent times the 20 percent of sales that represents its value added, or 0.4 percent of sales. In contrast, the hospital's EDP-budget-to-sales index would be 2 percent times the 80 percent of revenues that represents value added, or 1.6 percent of sales. In this case, both organizations devote 2 percent of internal resources to computer activities. Yet they show lower and widely differing EDP-budget-to-sales figures.

Table 15.1 shows survey data reflecting the 1970 EDP budgets of 245 major firms in several different industries. The various manufacturing industries are relatively uniform in their dependence on computers—at a level ranging around 1.5 percent of value added. Other surveys indicate that certain service industries have higher computer dependencies—typically, 3 percent for financial firms, government, higher education, and computerized medical institutions. Overall, computer expenditures averaged about 2 percent of the gross national product (GNP), the economy-wide value added.

The data listed in the Table 15.1 show not only the EDP-budget-to-sales percentage, but also the hardware expenditure per dollar of EDP salary, and the percentage of "computer people" to total employment.

This survey provided a useful comparison of computer utilization in

TABLE 15.1   1970 EDP BUDGETS FROM 245 MAJOR FIRMS

Industry	EDP-Budget-to-Sales, %	Hardware Outlay per EDP Salary, $	EDP Staff, % of Total
Aerospace and defense	2.23	.76	2.39
Airlines	2.04	1.33	1.58
Apparel	.76	.58	.96
Automotive products	.78	.78	1.35
Banking	.22[a]	.67	6.43
Building materials	.69	.45	.92
Chemicals	.86	.69	1.27
Department and variety stores	.30	.73	.49
Electronics and electrical products	1.41	.74	1.41
Energy	.70	.62	2.37
Food and beverage	.44	.63	1.04
Forest products and packaging	.62	.62	.78
Household and personal products	.62	.64	1.27
Industrial equipment	.82	.65	1.14
Information processing	1.43	.76	1.41
Leisure and education	1.29	.64	1.68
Life insurance	1.20[b]	.56	3.50
Manufacturing, average	.90	.66	1.34
Metals	.61	.68	.88
Motor freight	.66	.52	1.07
Multicompanies	1.14	.63	1.15
Railroads	.86	.92	.73
Specialty stores	.63	.63	1.52
Supermarkets	.26	.75	.73
Utilities	.63	.72	2.24

[a]Data processing budget as a percent of deposits.
[b]Data processing budget as a percent of premium and annuity income.

various industries. Most of a firm's value added is spent for employee salaries. Therefore, the percentage of EDP employees out of the total is a good index of the firm's internal dependence on computers. With three exceptions, this figure ranged from .73 percent of employment to 2.39 percent. This is a significantly more uniform degree of computer utilization than implied by the EDP-budget-to-sales data. The three exceptional industries are banking and life insurance—both financial services with much paperwork and transactions processing—and department/variety stores—which had not yet begun their heavy computerization with point-of-sale terminals.

Another interesting deviant was the airlines industry. It was the only one spending more than a dollar on hardware per dollar spent on EDP staff salaries. This comparatively heavy use of hardware reflects the then existing online reservations systems. These use massive disk, terminal, and communications resources. In addition, these very large systems are highly automated, requiring few computer operators despite their size. And the user, acting through a remote keyboard, usually provides the data entry. All this made the hardware cost larger than the cost of the airlines' direct EDP staff.

During the 1970s additional studies resulted in further publicized guidelines. One survey positively linked EDP expenditure levels with better profitability. Although no causal relationship can be concluded, the more profitable companies spent a significantly larger portion of their resources on EDP than did the less profitable ones.

Another study, published in 1971 and updated in 1973, surveyed 89 representative companies and 155 installed computers. It measured the utilization rates of these machines. **Utilization rate** is a measure of operating intensity, but it does not necessarily measure either the effectiveness or the efficiency of an information system. Nonetheless, the results were revealing. Most users strive for multiple-shift computer operations. The average computer was in use, actually running programs, 48 percent of a 7-day week and 24-hour day. For large computer systems, the productive utilization time was even higher—62 percent. Compare this with a personal auto, used perhaps 1 hour per day on average. And even high-priced equipment, such as a Boeing 747, is hard to utilize more than 12 hours a day, or 50 percent of the time.

ORGANIZING FOR INFORMATION SYSTEMS

Today, most firms' computer-related activities have grown severalfold and may have existed for 15 to 20 years. They usually began as tabulating and accounting groups or as a systems and procedures staff.

Since then, the EDP organization has become more important and has affected broader functions and higher levels. As a result, EDP organizational structures have changed.

As computer applications crossed functions and the EDP budget increased, a trend began toward elevating and removing it from the direct control of the accounting function. The publicized studies cited above encouraged this trend. However, nearly half of all EDP groups still report to a senior financial officer. This is particularly true in small firms and among relatively new users. However, as discussed in Chapter 10, computers are increasingly found distributed throughout the organization. In the sections that follow, we will discuss two related EDP issues: staffing and the most common ways of organizing this group.

Staffing   Historically, there have been two approaches to the staffing problem—train people from within the organization or hire people trained or experienced from without. The first approach requires selecting those with aptitudes and interests that justify the training investment. One must also hope that they do not leave the organization soon thereafter. Computer staffs have had a high rate of personnel turnover, although this has moderated in the last decade as the field matured. When the costs of recruitment must be borne, each firm's gain usually represents another firm's loss.

Entry-level jobs include those of programmer, computer operator, and keypuncher (or equivalent). It should be recognized that each specialty requires different backgrounds, skills, and aspirations, and that there are several proficiency levels within each. Programmers, for example, range from coders to programmer/analysts. Computer operators may be trained for one or many machines. They may have other skills, such as diagnosing and correcting operating problems.

The key role of systems analyst has typically been filled from within the organization often by elevating a super programmer or by training a middle manager from a user department. Alternately, an experienced analyst may be recruited from a similar firm. Formally trained but less experienced specialists are increasingly being hired. However, since a firm usually has about twice as many programmers as systems analysts, fewer analyst jobs are available at the entry level.

The management of data processing is an especially difficult task. Most such managers have technical backgrounds. But the problems they deal with are largely managerial. Clearly, achieving the dual goals of system effectiveness and efficiency requires that managers know both the user's and the technician's points of view and have organizational strengths.

Organization Structures   The computer-related staff can be organized in several ways. The "director of information systems" probably reports to the firm's vice-presidential level or is a vice-president. Evidence suggests that this position should report to either the chief operating officer, chief staff officer, or vice-president for finance and administration. It is often desirable to form a **steering committee** composed of high-level management and charged with overall project selection, priority, and control.

Many possibilities exist for organizing the staff under this top computer executive, particularly if divisional computer operations are maintained. There are four general approaches:

- by data processing function
- by user function
- by project
- by liaison with divisions

Organization Data Processing Function.   In this organizational structure, the EDP function is treated as a business in itself. It is separated into its major activities: systems analysis, programming, operations, and data preparation. In addition, large staffs may have experts who concentrate on such specialties as minicomputers, telecommunications, operating systems software, database management systems, management science methods, data processing training, and so forth. Thus, the EDP effort may be organized as depicted in Figure 15-1.

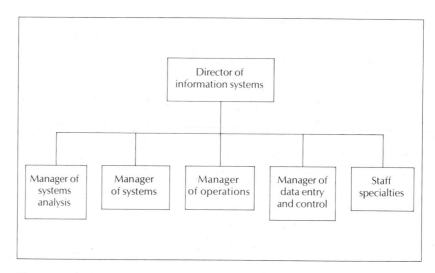

Figure 15-1.   EDP organization by data processing function

The systems analysis effort might be organized as individuals or groups, depending on the number of systems analysts. Similarly, the programming effort may be partitioned into new and maintenance programming. Managerial roles would involve motivating, supervising, and controlling creative professionals.

In contrast, operations management is more akin to production or factory supervision. Operations requires scheduled tasks to be completed by defined deadlines. Efficient equipment utilization is a key goal. The details of loading programs and mounting tapes and disks require relatively constant attention. Hardware or program **crashes**, or malfunctions, need to be diagnosed quickly and productive work resumed. Frequently, a shift manager heads each team of a multiple-shift operation.

Data entry sometimes reports to the operations function rather than as shown in Figure 15–1. In any case, it is the most routine and lowest salaried task. A senior operator may supervise 10 or even 20 operators and also administer their assignments and monitor their performance. This group may also handle the library functions of maintaining programs and data, as well as the administration of input procedures and report distribution.

Staff specialists are usually justified in larger EDP organizations. These should include technical experts and also a training specialist, who should acclimate users to computer capability as well as keep the data processing staff expert. A key means of reducing staff turnover and increasing effectivenesses is to upgrade skills systematically and develop career paths for advancement.

Organization by User Function.   This structure tailors EDP functions to user requirements. It establishes groups and charges them with meeting users' functional needs. Performance evaluation and promotion still resides within EDP lines in addition to these obligations to users. In essence, such an EDP staff mirrors the rest of the organization, as shown in Figure 15–2.

Organization by Project.   Alternately, the EDP analysts and programmers can be combined by project assignment. These teams change from time to time as projects move through the system development cycle. Project teams help when tasks are too large and urgent for assignment to one individual or when projects are cross-functional in nature. Frequently, these teams include user representatives on a full or partial assignment. This scheme is illustrated in Figure 15–3.

Organization by Liaison with Divisions.   Decentralized computer operations result in multiple computing centers and staffs. Their organiza-

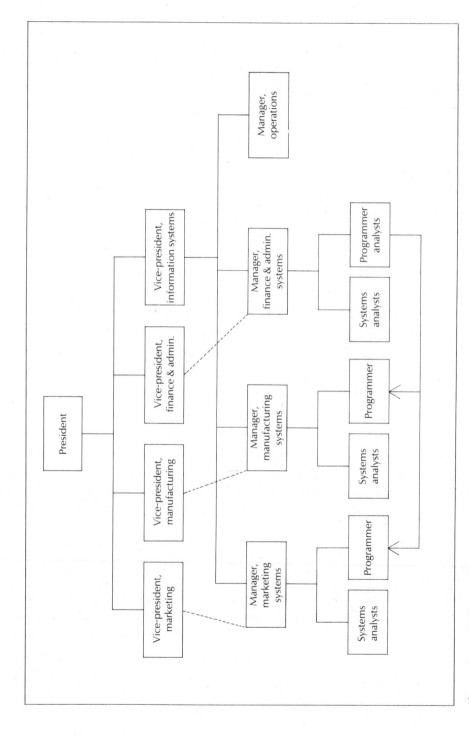

Figure 15-2. EDP organization by user function

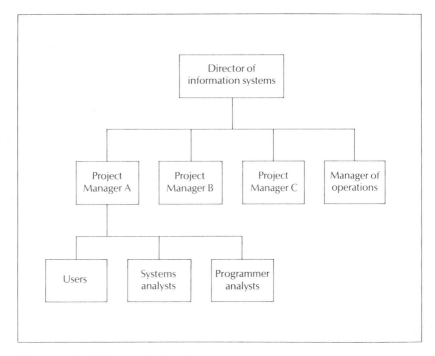

Figure 15-3. EDP organization by project

tional relationships are more complex. Although large autonomous divisions can operate separately, they usually adopt some centralized guidance and controls. Typically, operations management is decentralized in each computing center. Thus, the degree of liaison between central and divisional staff varies. This concept is shown in Figure 15-4.

MANAGING SYSTEMS DEVELOPMENT

Systems development was discussed at length in Chapter 13. Meeting user specifications requires the proper management of this activity. A new project always breaks some new ground and thus is not amenable to precise prediction. Systems development nonetheless requires systematic controls. A sample systems development plan and schedule are shown in Figure 15-5. Periodic formal reviews can pinpoint problems and allow resources to be shifted to prevent delays. A similar development plan and schedule should be prepared for each major application undertaken.

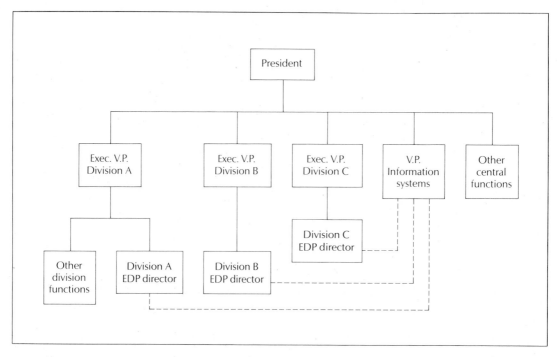

Figure 15-4. Liaison between central and divisional staff

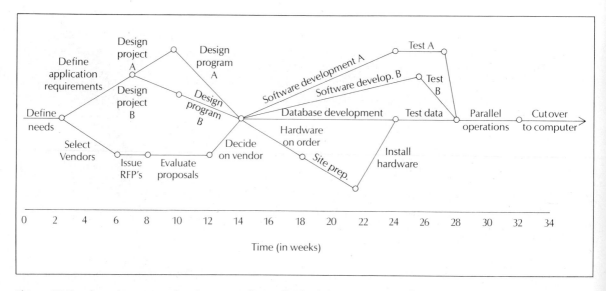

Figure 15-5. Sample systems development plan and schedule

MANAGING COMPUTER OPERATIONS

Efficient computer operations are a must for effective information systems. Today's large-scale, interacting, online, real-time, multiprogrammed computers are under operating system control to help reach the goals of efficiency and effectiveness. But achieving component balance and high throughput requires knowledgeable job scheduling and matching of hardware capacities. A **monitor** is a device that helps diagnose a system's dynamic operating characteristics. For example, a hardware monitor might show that a CPU is busy 30 percent of the time but channels are 60 percent active for some applications. Another job might be more processor-bound. Such data can lead to scheduling and hardware adjustments.

In addition to moment-to-moment utilization, it is usually economical to use computers, particularly large ones, on multiple-shift operations. The incremental costs are largely for salary differentials and other late-opening costs and for any added rental and maintenance. Also, hardware must be periodically maintained and repaired if it malfunctions. Maintenance costs about 8 to 12 percent of hardware rental, if it is not included in the rental agreement. CPU maintenance is generally lower than this but maintenance for peripherals runs higher.

SYSTEMS SELECTION

The choice of a computer system should reflect both the applications it is to handle and the full range of available equipment. The present or proposed job mix should be defined. Then, potential hardware vendors should be identified. They should be notified of the system's requirements and invited to bid on fulfilling them.

Equipment Evaluation

A letter of **request for proposal (RFP)** should be sent to each vendor offering suitable equipment. A sample outline for this bid request is shown in Table 15.2. This document should give the bidder sufficient information to determine which equipment best suits the user. The manufacturer's sales staff will probably also wish to discuss requirements with the buyer. This is generally useful for the education of both parties.

The responding hardware manufacturers may suggest additional applications. They may also provide alternative designs adapted to their hardware. Any benefits of such recommendations can be considered as valid additions to that supplier's proposal. The specific proposals of different vendors must then be evaluated and compared.

Judging performance in relation to price is the general objective of proposal comparison. Prices are usually readily determined or are quoted for specific proposals. Performance comparison is much more

TABLE 15.2 SAMPLE OUTLINE OF REQUEST FOR PROPOSAL
FROM EQUIPMENT VENDORS

A. Summary of System Requirements

    1. Overview of organization requesting bids
    2. Summary description of applications
    3. Overview of current equipment
    4. Procedure and schedule for submitting bid proposals

B. Present and Future EDP Applications

    1. List of present applications to be run on the new hardware including file size, storage media, programming language, I/O procedures, and present run times and frequency
    2. List of proposed applications for the new hardware, including estimates of the above application characteristics

C. Existing Equipment and Operations

    1. Manufacturer and model of all relevant equipment
    2. Price, lease terms, and other conditions
    3. Existing operating staff
    4. Current operations load and schedule

D. Detailed System Specifications

    1. Hardware performance requirements such as speed, storage capacity, reliability, I/O rates, communications capability, inquiry response, and so forth
    2. Systems software requirements such as job and task management, virtual storage, high-level languages, utility programs for sorting, merging, card-to-disk, database management, and so forth
    3. Support services requirements such as applications software availability, maintenance, training, systems design, delivery and installation assistance, and so forth
    4. Installation schedule requirements and recommended testing or parallel operations

involved. Not only must hardware characteristics such as speed, capacity, compatibility, and reliability be measured, but also service factors like systems analysis, maintenance, training, and financing must be considered. Hardware performance can often be determined by **benchmark testing**. However, care should be exercised that such sample runs are both representative of the user's applications mix and are suitably adapted to the hardware being tested.

The availability, costs, and performance of software are also very important. Manufacturers usually charge for some system software, such as high-level language compilers, and most applications packages. But their availability may tremendously cut the cost and time of getting applications running. Finally, the vendor's breadth of products, reliability, proximity, reputation, and financial strength are also considerations when one embarks on a long-term business relationship.

Buy-Rent-Lease Decision   A part of the hardware selection decision is determining how to finance its acquisition. There are many alternatives. Rental from the hardware manufacturer has been the traditional method. This involves only a short-term obligation; it typically allows cancellation with only 90-days notice. Rental simplifies the user's decision and preserves maximum flexibility. Rental or lease also eliminates a large purchase outlay by the user, and the risks of ownership remain with the hardware supplier.

Many users decide to lease computers for several years. By doing so they can contract for lower monthly charges. **Third-party leasing** firms often arrange such long-term leases with users and purchase the necessary equipment from manufacturers. By pricing lower, the discount lessors obtain business and still profit by the long contracts financed by debt capital. Such loans are available because of the long-term nature of their contracts, much like mortgages are available on buildings with good tenants and leases. (The computer leasing business will be discussed further in Chapter 16.)

Long-term leasing really represents a financial alternative to buying the hardware outright. The pattern of cash outflow is different although the obligation is much the same. Frequently, in fact, long-term leases include an option to purchase the leased item after several years. (Recent accounting rule changes now call for an ownership presentation for long-term leases.) Also, there are often no extra usage charges for second- and third-shift operations, as there are with most short-term rental contracts.

Both long-term leasing and purchase involve the user in a somewhat inflexible arrangement. This is acceptable when the user has long-term plans and the equipment's usefulness can be forecast with confidence. However, the user will suffer from any decline in the hardware's economic worth due to the introduction of improved equipment. The choice between purchase and such long-term leasing hinges on traditional capital budgeting factors, such as the availability and cost of capital. Further specifics of the lease or purchase contract are important, including maintenance, other ongoing services, investment tax credits, extra-shift charges, purchase or sale options, lease cancellation fees, and the like.

Thus, the buy-rent-lease decision involves technology issues (utilization rate, expected obsolescence, EDP planning horizon, user self-sufficiency) and financial issues (capital availability, capital cost, tax aspects, options). A typical decision is illustrated by Figures 15–6 and 15–7. These graphs illustrate the monthly cost and cumulative outlay for different ways of acquiring computer hardware. It is assumed that the rental period is 4 years, at which point new hardware that halves the price for the same performance will be introduced. The lease

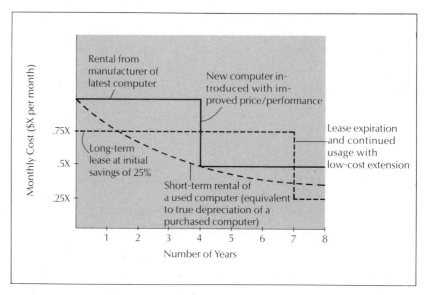

Figure 15-6. Monthly cost for acquiring constant computer power

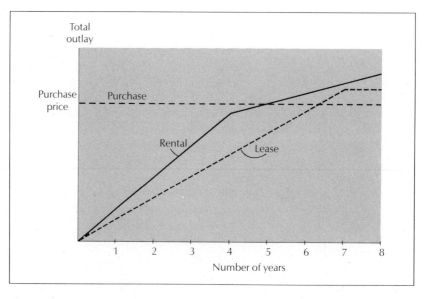

Figure 15-7. Total outlay for acquiring constant computer power

alternative is assumed to be for 7 years at 75 percent of the manufacturer's rental rate. Short-term rental of a used computer reflects its historically eroding value of approximately 15 percent of the prior year's value per year.

In conclusion, this buy-rent-lease analysis almost always shows that it is cheaper to lease and eventually cheaper still to purchase. However, long-term leasing and purchase have the hidden cost of lost flexibility. Purchase also ties up capital sooner than rental or lease payment plans. In general, however, the longer the user can comfortably plan, the more he or she can save by avoiding short-term rental.

SUMMARY   The computer has had a significant impact on organizations, if not on their overall purpose. Technological advances have often outpaced users' ability to implement new information systems. However, in the 1970s organizations have applied this maturing technology more effectively. They have more consistently required and got economic benefits from computer expenditures.

The involvement of top management and the active participation of user management are especially important. An ideal top computer executive should be broad in his or her outlook and report relatively high in the organization. The computer staff and hardware are frequently centralized or are evolving into a network or matrix of linked and coordinated operations. Staff positions may be grouped by systems functions, by user activities, by project, or by liaison among decentralized computing centers.

One index of an organization's internal utilization of computers is to compute its EDP staff as a percentage of total employees. In general, manufacutring firms have about 1.5 percent of employees in EDP while service organizations average around 3 or 4 percent. The expenditure for this staff typically averages one and a half times the outlay for computer-related hardware. The systems analysis and programming budget, including software maintenance and outside services, approximates hardware costs.

Managing computer operations is a production-type activity. High machine utilization is sought; most larger computers are run for two or three shifts per day. Managing skilled and creative analysts and programmers is more difficult but also requires both incentives and controls. Selecting hardware should involve a detailed comparison of alternate vendor proposals made in response to specific user requirements. The buy-rent-lease decision is an integral part of this hardware decision.

Chapter Sixteen

**Computer
Impact—
Present and
Future**

The information explosion—fueled by computers and communications—has spawned the fastest growing industry of modern times. In terms of its benefits, its rapid progress, and its declining costs per unit, the computer industry rivals any other recent technology. Worldwide computer-related expenditures now approximate $80+ billion annually for hardware and staff. This outlay equals nearly 2 percent of the gross national product of developed countries. As we will see in this chapter, this industry has several sectors and its impact is—and will be—felt in many ways.

In today's "postindustrial" society, most income earners are in white-collar jobs where information is a key ingredient. Thus, we can forecast with confidence an increasing role for computers in society. Some organizations, such as banks, insurance, and brokerage firms, are already vitally dependent on computers for high-volume paperwork and transactions processing. Service industries, such as education, health care, communications, and travel, use electronic information processing extensively. Similarly, the government is a major user of computer capabilities—spanning from tax collection to "war game" simulations to a national crime control database. Even manufacturing firms, which must spend for raw materials, plant, and labor, also depend significantly on computers. Meanwhile, retailers are rapidly adopting point-of-sale and supermarket checkout terminals to support computerized transactions processing and managerial planning and control.

In this chapter we will discuss several sectors of the computer marketplace (both in the United States and international); hardware; and services. We will then speculate on the future technology and the applications that users will find for it. It is likely that frequent consumer access to computers may become routine in the 1980s. Computers may stand by awaiting their owner's personal bidding, much as a car stands by today. Ultimately—and society must assure this—computers should serve and improve human welfare.

MARKET STRUCTURE   The computer industry consists of several leading hardware vendors, although IBM is by far the largest. The leading computer users are national governments and large manufacturers and financial service firms. The capabilities of suppliers and the demands of users have resulted in rapidly rising hardware shipments. As of 1978, about $80 billion worth of computers (at cost) were in use throughout the world. In addition, each hardware dollar produces more computational capacity as technology improves over time. Combining these two trends, the world's capacity to compute has doubled every 2 years or less during the past 30 years.

The international market for computer hardware has for several years experienced a faster growth rate from a smaller base than the United States market. Four major European manufacturers, some resulting from governmental merger and consolidation efforts, serve their domestic market and other countries. Only ICL (*International Computers Limited*) of the United Kingdom has a domestic market share comparable to IBM's share of that market. The remaining companies are CII (Compagnie *I*nternationale pour l'*I*nformatique of France), Siemens (Germany), and Philips (Benelux countries). Various cooperative research and marketing arrangements are being pursued to strengthen these companies further in the worldwide competition for computer customers.

The Japanese market is the third largest after the United States and Europe. Again, government support in research and consolidations among smaller firms have been important factors. Currently, Japan's computer manufacturers have most of the local market. IBM-Japan supplies about one-fourth of the overall demand.

The Soviet Union's computer industry and number of installations lag behind those of the United States, Europe, and Japan. During the 1970s, the United States had installed more than 10 times the number of computers as the Soviet Union. East-West trade in large-scale computer hardware has begun, although it is still limited. A comparison of the computer's penetration into these different international markets is presented in Table 16.1.

HARDWARE SECTOR   Computer hardware and services are the two major sectors of each of these geographic markets. We will discuss the industry and its worldwide hardware sector in terms of:

- computer mainframes
- peripheral devices
- mini- and microcomputers

TABLE 16.1   COMPUTER PENETRATION IN INTERNATIONAL
MARKETS—1978

Market	Mainframe Computers Installed	Computers per Hundred Thousand Population	Computers per Billion $ of GNP
United States	200,000	100	100
West Europe	150,000	50	65
Japan	100,000	80	60
Soviet Union	20,000	10	20

Computer Mainframes

Computer **mainframes** include the CPU and main memory, and in some usages of the term even the secondary storage and I/O devices such as disks, terminals, printers, and so forth. However, the equipment for storage and I/O are usually called **peripheral devices**. Computer mainframes are usually thought of as medium to large scale, rather than minicomputers or small personal computers. The mainframe market is dominated by IBM's products, which account for about half of this sector, worldwide.

Enormous capital resources are required to compete in the mainframe market. For example, all major U.S. suppliers are multi-billion-dollar corporations; most international competitors are, too. There are large economies of scale, such as in research, hardware design, systems software, applications software, and general marketing support. The larger firms can spread these necessary costs over more units; thus they have an efficiency advantage. In addition, the rental/lease tradition of financing computers imposes a large capital barrier to potential manufacturers without the "blue chips" to play the game.

Peripheral Devices

Sales of peripheral devices have grown greatly, prompted by the standardization of computer components. In particular, a **plug-to-plug compatible** interface between computers and peripherals has lead to interchageability and easy installation of printers, plotters, disks, tapes, terminals, readers, scanners, microfilmers, and so forth. Such peripheral devices now account for more than half the cost of computer systems. As shown in Table 16.2, disks and terminals have become especially popular for storage and I/O. Communications-oriented and online systems, the trend of the future, typically have a more than normal need for peripheral devices.

Peripheral devices are often sold as well as leased. Software support, such as providing operating systems or applications programs, is not a critical part of the product. Also, each item has a lesser dollar cost than mainframes. This enables many small- to medium-sized companies to

TABLE 16.2 INFORMATION SYSTEMS BUDGETS FOR 1978 (CATEGORIZED BY FUNCTION AND HARDWARE VERSUS BUDGET SIZE)

	to $25K	to $100K	to $250K	to $500K	to $1M	over 1M
Personnel	63.7	53.7	47.7	49	48.1	45.3
Hardware and Maintenance	21.6	32.9	41.2	37.9	39.5	37.7
Supplies and Accessories	10.7	7.7	5.5	7.3	4.8	6.1
Communications	.3	1.8	1.2	1.4	2.9	6.3
Packaged Software	2.2	2.1	1.8	2.5	1.9	2.0
Outside Services	1.5	1.8	2.6	1.9	2.8	2.6
Total for Functions	100%	100%	100%	100%	100%	100%
Central Site Hardware						
Data Entry		5.9	6.0	6.4	3.4	1.6
Computers and Memory		46.6	45.0	41.6	47.4	54.0
Peripherals		37.8	30.3	34.7	30.0	21.7
Communication Equipment		4.0	5.0	2.3	7.6	2.3
Terminals		2.8	5.1	3.7	2.4	6.9
Other		1.0	2.9	2.1	2.2	13.0
Remote Site Hardware		1.9	5.7	9.2	7.0	11.3
Total for Hardware		100%	100%	100%	100%	100%

compete successfully in this business. Price discounting and innovative designs by the makers of plug-to-plug compatible equipment have been their main marketing strategy against mainframe manufacturers. Many firms specialize in a particular device which is marketed to **OEMs** (original equipment *m*anufactures) for assembly or inclusion in their products and systems.

Mini- and Microcomputers

Minicomputer systems have grown up to applications in business and time-sharing as well as their traditional uses in process control and scientific/engineering calculations. Their benefit is in being effective without being gigantic—in size or cost. A CPU and memory, plus peripherals, can be bought for prices ranging from $1000 to $100,000. Larger systems have typically rented for that much money *per month*.

The strong cost reduction trend for **microcomputers**, or "computers on a chip," has allowed their application in such single-purpose environments as TV games, machine controls, detector systems, electronic cash registers, and so forth. Microcomputers are currently only one-tenth of the $4 billion annual minicomputer market. However, a growing wave of computer hobbyists and computer-knowledgeable design engineers assures rapid growth of their sales volume and useful applications.

SERVICES SECTOR   The computer services sector is as large, measured in expenditures, as the hardware sector. However, computer users typically supply most such services with their internal staff, as Part 4 discussed. Nonetheless, a large (currently over $5 billion per year) and rapidly growing market exists for externally supplied software, processing, management, and financing. We will discuss this services sector in the following categories:

- software
- processing
- facilities management
- computer leasing

Software   In facing the make or buy software decision, many computer users feel that "our problem is unique." Increasingly, however, existing software is becoming helpful in avoiding "reinventing the wheel." A **proprietary software package** is a program developed by a supplier to be sold or leased to many users. When such a package exists and fits the user's needs (or can be easily adapted), its price is almost certainly less than that of in-house program development. Furthermore, such packages are usually well debugged and documented. Any ongoing maintenance or support is usually guaranteed with such costs spread among many users.

Alternately, when a suitable package cannot be found, outside software expertise and experience may still be utilized via **contract programming**. In contract programming, an outside supplier creates specified software for a particular buyer, usually on a fixed-fee basis or for time-and-materials costs. Complex programs, one-time staffing problems, or processing requirements similar to existing packages are often justifications for contracting with a firm specializing in such work.

It is relatively easy to enter the software industry. At the minimum, a pencil, paper, and a programmer are required. Consequently, many small firms have been formed. Furthermore, during the 1970s, most mainframe suppliers **unbundled** (began to charge separately for) most software. Thus, independent suppliers no longer had to compete with software that the user had perceived as "free," since it was supplied with the hardware.

However, many of these new entrants, who often had inadequate marketing and business experience, fared poorly. This situation was aggravated by the reduced demand for outside computer services accompanying the 1970–71 and 1974–75 economic recessions. Many users were not satisfied with outside programming and cost overruns were all too frequent.

Since then, proprietary packages, in particular, have become much more acceptable to users, and major competent suppliers have emerged. Increasingly, user managements are willing to go outside for software, particularly for existing, tested packages. In-house analysts/programmers are now asked to justify development rather than purchase, lease, or subcontracting of software. Consequently, there is now a broad market for commonly used applications programs, such as in accounting and financial analysis, and for systems programs such as programming aids and database management systems.

Other software-related services have also been developed. Many companies offer programmer training: personnel recruitment, consulting in specialties such as online systems, minicomputers, or applications about software. Another large service field, discussed below, provides access to external software and hardware.

Processing

When computer processing is performed outside the organization, the supplier is usually referred to as a **service bureau**. It may provide data entry service, and pick up and delivery, if not an online operation. Alternately, the users may enter data and make inquiries and modifications from their own locations, via communication to the processing firm's hardware/software complex, such as that illustrated in Figure 16–1.

To attract customers, service bureaus usually offer larger equipment, more fully utilized, that their customers could otherwise afford. But, with the advent of economical minicomputers and in-house time sharing, external processing vendors have increasingly marketed their applications software, often tailored to an industry group such as hospitals or auto dealers, or to a particular application such as payroll or credit card verification. A communications network for toll-free nationwide access, proprietary database, and redundant systems for reliability are additional appeals.

Facilities Management

Facilities management (FM) consists of a specialist firm running the computer installations of a user-client. Usually, the computers are at the client's location, but sometimes the physical processing takes place elsewhere. This allows the facility manager to consolidate hardware and perhaps serve several customers at less cost. The business concept recognizes that data processing is not the objective of the basic business, but rather is separable, like cafeteria management or advertising, and can safely be delegated to an outside specialist.

Facilities management permits some sizable savings or better service. Centralizing hardware or using it more productively can produce savings. Standardized software or in-depth industry experience may

Figure 16-1. Service bureau, showing computer mainframe, peripheral devices, and operating staff.

permit the specialist firm to develop more economical software. Also, computer personnel are more easily attracted to professional firms where competence in their specialty is recognized and advancement within the organization is possible on that basis. Furthermore, highly skilled systems people are generally more cost/effective than less-experienced ones, despite their different salary levels.

The facilities manager is able to achieve relatively low marketing expenses by contracting over long periods of time. In contrast, software and service bureau vendors usually experience higher selling costs. For example, they must often perform a modestly thorough systems analysis just to submit an intelligent bid. Since the low bidder among competitors often wins, the profitability of such contracts is often low while the bid losers incur selling costs without any offsetting revenues. In FM, this problem is preempted, since the FM firm acts as the sole source of computer expertise.

In some instances, the FM firms may also provide a package that includes the hardware and software to be used by the client. This practice is referred to as providing a **turnkey system:** The client's problems are met and she or he need only "turn on the key." Usually, the supplier of turnkey systems has purchased hardware at wholesale from the original equipment manufacturer and packaged it with the appropriate proprietary software. Ongoing hardware operations and maintenance may also be provided.

There is a potential problem in the FM concept. As "data processing" evolves further into "information systems," including management-reporting, database, and decision support systems, this function becomes drastically less separable from the organization. A management information system is in effect the organization's central nervous system. A critical dependence is established when such computer activities are delegated to an outside supplier, however specialized and professional she or he may be.

Computer Leasing Computer leasing is a financial service; it is not especially related to computer technology itself. Any user of computer hardware faces a decision about its financing. IBM fostered computer rental, including short-term termination rights. This encourages customers by easing the "install or not" decision. Also, the computer manufacturer then has better control over the equipment and can make higher long-run profits. As a competitive tool it preempts the entry of firms that lack the huge financial resources needed to build computers and collect their revenues over several years.

As we noted earlier, some computer users are willing to commit to particular hardware for periods of from 2 to 8 years. By giving up short-term flexibility, they can get a price discount. Thus, computer leasing has become popular. A lease spanning a period long enough to pay for the equipment fully is called a **financial lease**. Shorter contracts are called **operating leases**.

The economics of computer leasing were extremely favorable in the latter 1960s and many firms were founded. First, the product was in growing demand. It was typically the IBM product line (then System/ 360) that was purchased by the lessors; this system was experiencing a 25 percent per year growth in demand. Furthermore, the submarket of those willing to sacrifice the flexibility of 30-day notice in return for price discounts was largely unpenetrated.

Computer lessors signed long-term contracts, allowing them to arrange sizable loans from lending institutions. Also, securities were easily sold to the public on favorable terms to augment both debt and equity capital. This allowed lessors to generate attractive returns from discounted lease prices, typically 10 to 30 percent lower than direct rental, depending on the lease's length. Further profitability was reported based on low depreciation assumptions, investment tax credits, deferral of marketing costs, and similar accounting treatments.

By the early 1970s, the bright economics of the computer leasing industry were tarnished. New hardware was announced that cast doubt on assumed depreciable lifetimes—often as long as 10 years. Tight money prevailed for both debt and equity. The investment tax credit on purchased equipment had been suspended, restored, cancelled, and reinstituted. Discounting among lessors had become very competitive and the submarket of lease signers was saturated. IBM increased the selling prices of the System/370 models relative to their rental prices. This thwarted those who buy computers to lease them since their prices were now competitive with the manufacturer's rental rate. IBM also began to offer some price reductions for those wishing intermediate-term leases of from 1 to 4 years. Thus, computer leasing is now carried out by larger financial firms and the independent companies have seen their best days.

FUTURE TECHNOLOGY

Progress in reducing the cost of computing will continue. Ongoing technological improvements can be foreseen for processors, main memories, disk and tape secondary storage, terminals, other I/O devices, communications, and software. For example, semiconductor circuitry will decline further in cost as manufacturing productivity and yield improve. This will lower processor and memory costs per unit of performance.

New techniques for storing data have also become feasible, such as **bubble memory**. It relies on creating and manipulating tiny magnetic fields in a crystalline or semiconductor material. Since "magnetic domains" as tiny as a few hundred molecules in diameter can be controlled, the density of data storage is astounding. It has been said that such storage density would permit just one barrel full of such devices to equal the capacity of all the world's main memory installations. In the meantime, semiconductor memory is expected to continue on a faster price decline curve than core memory, making it obsolete, as shown in Figure 16-2.

Recent tape drives that use high storage densities have maximum data transfer rates of over 1 million characters per second. That is fast enough to read (or write!) this entire book in under 1 second. Disk and

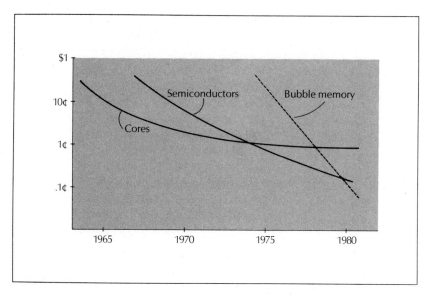

Figure 16-2.   Comparative main memory technologies

tape drives should become even faster and less expensive. The prices of disk packs and tapes may decrease further. New techniques of mass storage include automatic tape libraries and laser holography, for example. This technique records optical patterns that are created and read by the action of monochromatic light waves. It permits an extremely high density of data storage.

Terminals will become smaller, cheaper, more versatile, and far more numerous. By 1980, over 2 million computer-connected terminals will be installed at retail checkout counters, investment firms, banks, sales offices, computer departments, homes, and so forth.

Terminals depend on data communications with some, usually remote, computer. Thus, data communications outlays will climb nearly tenfold from 1975 to 1985, despite falling prices. A system of microwave data transmission links now connects the major cities throughout the country. And satellite data communication is an everyday reality, especially for multinational operations. The data-carrying ability of modulated laser light carried by optic fibers is enormous and will likely become commercially feasible soon.

Software advances are a pressing need. Simplified languages with fewer arbitrary conventions and syntax constraints are being researched. Handprinted and voice inputs and outputs already simplify commucation with the machine in some applications. However, the standardization and widespread adoption of new languages is a time-consuming process that tends to require industry or governmental leadership. However, someday a "FORTRAN 14" may allow computer programming by donning a suitable helmet and merely thinking about the problem!

The most dramatic near-term benefit may come from the accelerating acceptance of **canned software**, or programs prepared and packaged for sale or lease to others. Standardization of procedures, as has occurred in banking or among small business users, will lead to development of broadly applicable and certified software. Organizations may adopt programs and databases that already exist, rather than insisting that customized systems be developed. The universal product code adopted by grocers and food manufacturers is an example. Hardware and software have followed in its wake.

FUTURE APPLICATIONS

As computer power becomes cheaper and people power more expensive, the trade-off will continue to shift toward automated information processing. Indeed, in a service-oriented, white-collar society, the computer's productivity potential may have arrived just in time to maintain our accustomed annual increase in productivity and real growth. Computers will be used more to wait on people, rather than vice versa as has often been the case. This means that computer applications will be feasible, despite lower hardware utilization, if this provides better service. Also, extra hardware will be employed for redundancy and backup to guarantee accuracy, availability, reliability, and security.

Applications will rely heavily on online data storage and interactive access. Decision support systems, including ones dependent on more comprehensive databases, will become prominent. Management information systems applications will probe higher into organizational ranks, but will probably have less impact on top management where strategic decisions tend to be long-range, unstructured, personal, and qualitative, and where the decision requirements are often unknown in advance and therefore difficult to model.

Training using computers will grow. **Computer-assisted instruction (CAI)** may become economically feasible via inexpensive terminals and interactive software. Training about computers themselves may become commonplace.

Databases will aid many everyday decisions. Job opportunities, product listings, available charter flights, current phone numbers of friends, regional weather conditions and forecasts, securities trading, and other routine information may be made available, almost ubiquitously. Sensitive information, such as political standing, credit rating, and health records, may also be maintained (hopefully, authorized access and security will be controlled). However, computer technology, in addition to lowering costs, can also provide *better* access controls than the typical manual procedures used, or not used, today. But the opportunities for computer fraud and unauthorized access will increase. Society must assure that individual rights and privacy are respected.

Computers will not only assist data retrieval and processing on the job, but will also affect one's off-hours transactions and decisions. For example, they may make purchasing at home possible when coupled with telephones or community antenna television systems (CATV) for two-way audio or audiovisual communication. They will also entertain—providing a chess or backgammon opponent when desired.

During the 1980s, we may develop electronic mail, reduce check flow, and decrease cash usage. For this to happen, an identification technique will be required to authorize activity on one's account, allowing the instant processing and payment of transactions. Over 70 billion transactions of more than $2 in amount (including nearly 30 billion checks) now occur each year between consumers and banking, commercial, and retail establishments. With automated instantaneous handling of these events, one's periodic statements would literally write a transactional diary and biography.

IMPACT ON SOCIETY Computer impact on society is enormous and growing. Some claim computers are the engine of a "second industrial revolution" or of a "postindustrial society." Combined with communications, computers are making it possible that any data, processed in any stated matter, be available anywhere, and *now*. Will this make us more efficient or merely more nosy? Will computers make us more productive and add to our material and intellectual welfare or will we become mired in an overabundance of printouts?

Federal legislation, and that of states, has been enacted to protect rights of individual privacy and to assure that certain government files are made known to the public. Access to information, correction privileges, and security against unauthorized access, tampering, or fraud are continuing public concerns.

The next generation of people, not computers, will regard the latter with much less awe than those reared in an earlier era. TV games, personal computers, credit cards, calculators, high school programming courses, computer addressed magazines, punched-card registration forms, and the like have made EDP mundane, just as cost reduction has made it ever present. Growing understanding will make more of our society aware of the computer's proper role.

SUMMARY   The computer industry is maturing. Its hardware sector includes the mainframes, peripheral devices, and mini- and macrocomputers, both in the United States and around the world. The computer services sector includes canned and custom software, processing via batch or online operations, facilities management, and leasing. Overall, computer technology will continue to decline in price and its uses will broaden.

Applications will use this increasingly cheaper technology with less concern for hardware efficiency and utilization whenever a trade-off exists with increasingly costly personnel resources. Thus, reliability, convenience, and standby capability will be supplied via hardware resources. Many more decision support and database applications will be implemented in addition to the nearly complete automation of transaction processing. Instructing computers will be simplified, and standardized programs will be more widely adopted. With proper social controls, computers can stimulate new improvements in our worldwide standard of living.

CONCEPTS

mainframe	proprietary software	turnkey system
peripheral device	package	financial lease
plug-to-plug	contract programming	operating lease
compatible	unbundled	bubble memory
OEM	service bureau	canned software
minicomputer system	facilities management	computer-assisted
microcomputer	(FM)	instruction (CAI)

QUESTIONS

1. Cite those parts of the computer market that you believe will grow the fastest. Which do you expect to grow least?
2. Why is IBM's size an important factor in the computer marketplace?
3. Why have Europe and other parts of the world tended to lag behind the United States in applying computers?
4. Discuss the evolution of the market for software services.
5. What future do you forecast for in-company networks and distributed processing?
6. How can a facilities management firm achieve data processing economies?
7. Do you believe that computers will continue to improve in price and performance? At which annual rate of improvement?
8. Describe an application that you foresee becoming worthwhile because of computers.
9. What legislative controls do you believe are desirable in our computer-using society?

Index